CRITICAL INSIGHTS

Gustave Flaubert

CRITICAL
INSIGHTS

Gustave Flaubert

Editor
Tom Hubbard
Novelist and poet from Scotland

SALEM PRESS
A Division of EBSCO Information Services, Inc.
Ipswich, Massachusetts

GREY HOUSE PUBLISHING

Publisher's Cataloging-In-Publication Data
(Prepared by The Donohue Group, Inc.)

Gustave Flaubert / editor, Tom Hubbard, novelist and poet from Scotland. -- [First edition].

   pages ; cm. -- (Critical insights)

Edition statement supplied by publisher.
Includes bibliographical references and index.
ISBN: 978-1-61925-824-2 (hardcover)

1. Flaubert, Gustave, 1821-1880--Criticism and interpretation. 2. French fiction--19th century--History and criticism. I. Hubbard, Tom, Dr. II. Series: Critical insights.

PQ2249 .G87 2015
843/.8

11/17

Contents _____

Acknowledgments

A number of chapters in this volume have appeared earlier in longer versions and/or in different contexts, and we wish to credit all previous editors and publishers of such material.

Priscilla Meyer's chapter appeared in previous versions in *The Russian Review* 54 (April 1995) © The Ohio State University Press and in her book *How the Russians Read the French: Lermontov, Dostoevsky, Tolstoy* (University of Wisconsin Press, 2008). Germaine Greer's "Memoirs of a Madman" originally appeared as the foreword to Gustave Flaubert's *Memoirs of a Madman* (Hesperus Press, 2002). Leah Anderst's chapter has previously appeared in *Orbis Litterarum* 67.4 (2012). Mark Conroy's chapter is a shortened version of his essay in *L'Époque conradienne* 37 (2011), published by the Presses Universitaires de Limoges (PULIM), and also derives from his book *Modernism and Authority: Strategies of Legitimation in Flaubert and Conrad* (John Hopkins Press, 1985). Elizabeth Rottenberg's chapter is a shortened version of material in her book *Inheriting the Future: Legacies of Kant, Freud, and Flaubert* (Stanford University Press, 2005).

Thank you also to Leah Middleton of Aitken Alexander Associates Ltd., Dr. Jamie Reid-Baxter, Professor Rosemary Lloyd, the staff of Edinburgh University Library, and the National Library of Scotland.

About This Volume

Tom Hubbard

"[J]e crois reconnaître des signes littéraires nouveaux," wrote the critic Charles Augustin Sainte-Beuve in the course of one of the most quoted contemporary reviews of Gustave Flaubert's *Madame Bovary* (1857): "science, esprit d'observation, maturité, force, un peu de dureté. Ce sont les caractères que semblent affecter les chefs de file des générations nouvelles." (Sainte-Beuve 1857). So, from its first appearance in book form, Flaubert's novel was seen as a turning-point in the history of literature in general and of the novel in particular.

However, Flaubert was not a one-book author, and he continued to innovate and astonish—not that his upsetting of expectations, often bizarrely, would necessarily go down well with his contemporaries. Indeed, in the wake of modernism—of which Flaubert was acknowledged to be a major precursor—it is twentieth-century readers, rather than their nineteenth-century counterparts, who have enabled him to come into his own. That said, Flaubert was not without his admirers (and even disciples) in his later years: to them he was the "cher Maître."

Today, Flaubert's works—in particular *Madame Bovary* and the *Trois contes* (1877)—are studied in schools and universities and not always in the French and Modern Languages departments. As a major figure in Western literature and culture, he is also studied, in translation, as part of survey courses in literature and the humanities.

The main chapters of the present volume consist of four studies of Flaubert in context, followed by a series of more detailed critical and often close readings. Our contributors include both well-known figures in Flaubert studies, as well as younger scholars who have begun to make their mark. It is an honor to have worked with such distinguished colleagues in the compilation of this book.

I open the collection of "Critical Contexts" chapters with an account of our author in relation to the social and historical matrix of his mid-nineteenth century. Such an emphasis inevitably foregrounds his *L'Éducation sentimentale* (1869). A group of English novels from the 1840s to the 1860s, by writers as various as Charles Dickens, Benjamin Disraeli, George Eliot, Elizabeth Gaskell, and Charles Kingsley, is concerned with the economic, political, and social forces of these times: these books have been described collectively as "Condition-of-England" novels. *L'Éducation sentimentale* is Flaubert's Condition-of-France novel.

My chapter attempts to demonstrate the fascinating contradiction of a man who was notoriously "monkish" in the lonely, ascetic pursuit of his art and yet who enjoyed a social life as and when that was possible for him, who hobnobbed with members of the literary and politico-imperial establishment. For Flaubert, as for the American-born novelist Henry James (they met in Paris during the early 1870s), art was superior to life, but still depended on life for its raw material. How to handle this was, according to James, the artist's "perpetual predicament": the attitude to life had to be "at once intensely to consult and intensely ignore it" (James 5). Flaubert would have agreed.

Today Flaubert is acknowledged as one of the "greats," and it can come as a shock to discover how his work was the target of so much negative criticism in his own day. Even critics such as Sainte-Beuve and Henry James, who were prepared to write at length on his work, were at best ambivalent and at worst severe. Since 1857, the year of *Madame Bovary*, the corpus of writings on Flaubert has grown exponentially, and to attempt manageability for a chapter in the present volume, I felt it necessary to concentrate on criticism up to around 1921, the centenary of Flaubert's birth: in any case, the body of work over the sixty-odd years up to that date pretty well lays the foundations for the critical studies thereafter, in terms of the development of, and dissent from, what had gone before.

Priscilla Meyer follows with a shrewd, compellingly detailed comparison of the Russian novelist Lev Tolstoy's *Anna Karenina* (1877) and Flaubert's *Madame Bovary*. The two novels are often discussed together in view of their common theme of adultery, but beyond that there are the subtle artistries that mark them as two of the greatest works of fiction from the latter half of the nineteenth century. The American novelist Edith Wharton challenged her friend Henry James for having cooled in "his early admiration" for Flaubert: "James objected that Flaubert's subjects were not worth the labor spent on them; to which I returned: 'But why isn't Madame Bovary as good a subject as Anna Karenina? Both novels turn upon a woman's love-affairs.' 'Ah,' he said, 'but one paints the fierce passions of a luxurious aristocracy, the other deals with the petty miseries of a little *bourgeoise* in a provincial town" (qtd. in Edel 32). Henry James could be a sharp critic of social inequalities, but he could also be a terrible snob, as that remark would suggest. However, there is more to it than that. Another critic from the English-speaking world, Matthew Arnold, also preferred *Anna Karenina* to *Madame Bovary*, and in both these responses, there is a sense that Anna possesses a certain dignity and nobility (in the moral-spiritual rather than the social-class meaning of that word) lacking in Emma. There developed a consensus that Russian realism in fiction was distinguished from its French counterpart by a tendency to expansiveness in spirit and subject-matter, by greater seriousness and depth. A certain puritanism isn't absent from that judgment: there was a perception that the Russians, compared with the French, weren't so preoccupied with sexual content.

That said, Tolstoy himself admired Flaubert's novel, and Professor Meyer demonstrates how he entered into a dialogue with it. As a distinguished specialist in Russian literature, Professor Meyer is well placed to introduce us to the convergences and divergences of these two novels and their authors and thus implicitly to encourage us to consider the convergences and divergences of Russian and French cultures.

Beryl F. Schlossman addresses herself to Flaubert's second novel, *Salammbô* (1862), which has as its setting ancient Carthage, though some critics (as Professor Schlossman remarks) have seen it is a kind of Condition-of-France novel in disguise. Professor Schlossman's chapter is more wide-ranging than that, however, both culturally and geopolitically, not least by also taking into account Flaubert's travel writings. She offers a multiplicity of perspectives, which include postcolonial theory, anthropology, gender, race, textual interpretation, and verbal art. She draws on an impressive array of theorists including—above all—Edward Said, whose response to Flaubert occupies several pages of his book *Orientalism* (1978) and which Professor Schlossman subjects to forensic probing. With her model of what a "critical lens" chapter should be, Professor Schlossman closes our collection of contextual studies and, at the same time, develops her abiding interest in "the orient of style." She stresses, in *Salammbô*, Flaubert's *modernism*, a necessarily recurrent motif in the present volume.

With her characteristic pungency, Germaine Greer opens our series of "critical insights" as our volume moves from literary and cultural history towards close readings of specific texts. Professor Greer's very readable account of an early work by Flaubert—*Mémoires d'un fou* in the original—was originally written for an English translation. Professor Greer introduces us to a piece of writing that is part autobiography and part fiction—that appropriate *mélange* for an adolescent author—written long before he developed his notion of "impersonality" and his mature aim to keep himself out of his work.

Vaheed Ramazani leads us through a labyrinth of ironies in *Madame Bovary*, ironies emanating from aspects of narrative voice, perspective, and style. Along the way, he points out Flaubert's coinage of "l'indisable," and he is especially illuminating on Emma's subjection to commodity fetishism (which alone, we might add, would become one of modernism's darker concerns, via Karl Marx). Professor Ramazani demonstrates how irony in this novel can be partly a response to changing material circumstances of artistic production and reception during the nineteenth century.

Élodie Laügt considers *Madame Bovary* as mediated into other languages and cultural forms and draws on the work of such theorists as Jacques Rancière. I was glad here to be introduced to adaptation studies, as I have, in recent years, encountered a *bande dessinée* (graphic novel) version of the *Trois contes*, a French TV dramatization of *Bouvard et Pécuchet*, and Ernest Reyer's 1890 opera based on *Salammbô*. Claude Chabrol's movie of *Madame*

Bovary is well-known and receives most welcome attention from Professor Laügt.

There follow three chapters on *L'Éducation sentimentale*. In my native Scotland, the word "rare" has two meanings—uncommon; impressive. The chapter by Professor Leah Anderst, one of the younger generation of Flaubert scholars, is indeed rare. There are few opportunities for readers to benefit from an analysis of the 1845 novel bearing the title *L'Éducation sentimentale*. Dr. Anderst rightly stresses that this is not an early version of the canonical novel of 1869, but a very different work, though her discussion demonstrates the value of considering the two texts together. Dr. Anderst is particularly good on point of view and how this distinguishes the narrative technique of the 1869 novel from that of its 1845 namesake.

One of the most prolific of Flaubert scholars, Éric Le Calvez addresses himself to *L'Éducation sentimentale*, on which he is a leading authority. Professor Le Calvez is concerned with how time is represented in this novel, with flashbacks, memory, repetition, and parallelism. Flaubert has a "plan" (such as he found wanting in Dickens's *Pickwick Papers*) that was at odds with conventional linear narrative. *L'Éducation sentimentale* was much admired by Proust, and what Professor Le Calvez traces is, in effect, akin to Tolstoy's claim (against accusations of his lack of a "plan") that *Anna Karenina* was structurally robust in view of its "labyrinth of linkages" that went deeper than what we'd call its storyline.

Of English-language writers, Joseph Conrad matches Flaubert in terms of structural and thematic subtlety, as well as in deployment of irony. The degree of Flaubert's influence on Conrad—who, as a native Pole, learned French before he settled for English—has been much argued. As a professor of English, Mark Conroy is well placed to consider the two writers together, and he offers us penetrating comparisons of *Madame Bovary* and *L'Éducation sentimentale* with Conrad's *Lord Jim* and *Nostromo*. A reviewer of Professor Conroy's book on the two novelists remarked that it was "written against any simple idea of a pure and innocent expressiveness which would exist outside the circulation of conventional language and political conditions which govern this circulation" (Roussel 246). Professor

Conroy is concerned with ways in which a collective story, or myth, can be adapted by an individual to provide a personal myth.

For many students, their first introduction to Flaubert will be not *Madame Bovary*, but one of the *Trois contes*, most likely "Un Cœur simple": the tale of Félicité and her fetishized parrot is the staple of many a course in short fiction. Kathryn Oliver Mills explores phenomena of verbal and non-verbal/visual communication in each of the three pieces, which in turn can be seen as evidence of Flaubert's artistic agenda for his work as a whole. Together with Baudelaire, Flaubert ushered in a "formal revolution" which aimed to challenge conventional assumptions about the relationships of poetry and prose to each other: here were two nineteenth-century French writers who were, in effect, setting out their manifestos for modernity. Equally original in his approach, Michael Sayeau focuses on "Un Cœur simple" and again demonstrates Flaubert's modernity, by means of his analysis of eventfulness—more specifically, *un*eventfulness—and the everyday. Flaubert yearned to write a book "sur rien" in the belief that the most beautiful works were those with "le moins de matière"; Professor Sayeau's chapter is invaluable for its discussion of the challenge which nothingness presents to somethingness.

"Visual communication" as a motif in the present volume reappears in Michael Tilby's innovative and amusing account of Flaubert's response to nineteenth-century French visual caricature, of which (to put it mildly) there is no shortage. Professor Tilby examines Flaubert's application of this irreverent tradition to his own art, culminating in his last and unfinished novel *Bouvard et Pécuchet*. That work is explored by Elizabeth Rottenberg in our penultimate chapter, where she homes in on the significance of grammar—notably the various forms, in French, of past tense—and syntax in the novel, and she explores related implications of the "*trottoir roulant*" familiar from Proust's essay on *L'Éducation sentimentale*. Professor Rottenberg practices formidably diverse skills as a scholar of language and literature, professor of philosophy, and practicing psychoanalyst. Tellingly, she quotes Guy de Maupassant's 1881 article on *Bouvard et Pécuchet*. It is there that Flaubert's sometime-protégé reads the novel as a modern, bourgeois version of the myth of Sisyphus, who was doomed forever to push a large boulder to a high summit only for it to roll down again. Sisyphus would become Albert Camus's point of reference for his theory of the absurd. Michael Tilby makes a not dissimilar connection when he refers to *Bouvard et Pécuchet* as anticipating Samuel Beckett's *En attendant Godot/Waiting for Godot*. (I might add that while I have seen *Bouvard et Pécuchet* as a parody of the Faust legend, it might also be read—albeit implicitly and retrospectively—as a comic turn on Friedrich Nietzsche's "Eternal Recurrence:" B. and P. leave their jobs as copyists to experience the eternal recurrence of failure in all their subsequent endeavors, only to return to their copying.)

Anthony Cascardi rounds off the volume with a chapter ranging across Flaubert's longer fiction, a chapter that casts a retrospective glow over the complex of ideas with which the book as a whole has been concerned. Professor Cascardi is the author of *The Bounds of Reason: Cervantes, Dostoevsky, Flaubert* (1986) and is well equipped to offer us such an intellectually and culturally expansive chapter: if Flaubert resisted being contextualized by nineteenth-century bourgeoisdom, there is no shortage of considerably less mediocre contexts in which he can be situated. Moreover, though Flaubert may not have shown an interest in the visual arts such as that displayed by his friend Charles Baudelaire, his desire to write a book "sur rien" inevitably raises questions of comparative aesthetics, and Professor Cascardi's chapter includes illuminating discussion of relationships between the various arts. Flaubert's notorious "monkish cell" breaches its walls: his work, like Shakespeare's, is "not [only] of an age, but for all time."

Works Cited

Edel, Leon, ed. *Henry James: A Collection of Critical Essays*. Englewood Cliffs, NJ: Prentice-Hall, 1963.

James, Henry. *The Art of the Novel*. New York: Scribner's, 1934.

Roussel, Roy. Reviewed Work: *Modernism and Authority: Strategies of Legitimation in Flaubert and Conrad* by Mark Conroy. *Nineteenth-Century Literature* 41.2 (September 1986): 246–8.

Sainte-Beuve, Charles. "Causeries du lundi: *Madame Bovary* par Gustave Flaubert." *Le Moniteur universel* (4 mai 1857).

CAREER,
LIFE AND
INFLUENCE

"L'Homme n'est rien: l'œuvre est tout": On Gustave Flaubert

Tom Hubbard

> *Quand un artiste a le malheur d'être plein de la passion qu'il veut exprimer, il ne saurait la peindre, car il est la chose même au lieu d'en être l'image. L'art procède du cerveau et non du cœur. Quand votre sujet vous domine, vous en êtes l'esclave et non le maître.*
>
> (Honoré de Balzac, *Massimilla Doni*, 1839)

In a letter of December 20, 1875 to his dear friend and fellow writer, George Sand—and written some four months before her death—Flaubert took up her accusation that he lacked "une vue bien arrêtée et bien étendue sur la vie." His reply was at once assenting and ironic— "Vous avez mille fois raison!"—as he explained that, yes, he wanted no metaphysics, no big words like "Progrès," "Fraternité," "Démocratie," "Égalité," and so on. No, he told Sand, it wasn't possible today to establish any new principles, or to respect the old ones. There was, however, one thing needful, though elusive. "Donc je cherche, sans la trouver, cette Idée d'où doit dépendre tout le reste" (Flaubert, *Correspondance* 4: 1000).

He was echoing his notable utterance of twenty-two years earlier: "je crois même qu'un penseur (et qu'est-ce que l'artiste si ce n'est un triple penseur ?) ne doit avoir ni religion, ni patrie, ni même aucune conviction sociale" (Flaubert, *Correspondance* 2: 316). His friend, the poet Charles Baudelaire, shared the disdain of the artist for the popular mind-set, but definitely adhered to a "religion": an idiosyncratic Catholicism that held God to be the creator of an indivisible totality, and thus each of our human senses possessed a relationship to all the others: a sound, a color, a taste, mutually "corresponded." Therefore, a painter could be discussed as if he were a melodist, and a composer could be discussed as if his music suggested that which was pictorial. This theory of "correspondances" pervaded Baudelaire's poetry and prose.

Flaubert rejected any such system, any integrated vision of life. In his *The Hedgehog and the Fox: An Essay on Tolstoy's View of History* (1953), Isaiah Berlin attempted a flexible classification of writers into two camps, along the lines of an utterance by the Greek poet Artilochus: "The fox knows many things but the hedgehog knows one big thing." The hedgehog possesses an integrative vision, a clear system of thought and feeling: everything is related to such a unitary way of looking at the world, everything is interrelated. The fox, however, follows no single set of principles and prefers to pursue a plethora of "often unrelated and even contradictory" phenomena; his "thought is scattered or diffused, moving on many levels, seizing upon the essence of a vast variety of experiences and objects, for what they are in themselves." While warning against oversimplifying categorizations, Berlin suggests that writers such as Dante, Dostoevsky, Nietzsche, and Proust are (broadly speaking) hedgehogs; Shakespeare, Goethe, Balzac, and Joyce are foxes. We could, I suggest, add Baudelaire to the list of hedgehogs; Flaubert tends towards the fox.

Yet in coming to Tolstoy, who is the focus of his book, Berlin suggests that the great Russian novelist "was by nature a fox, but believed in being a hedgehog" (Berlin 7–11 and *passim*). Tolstoy wanted "the one big thing." In his own, very different way, Flaubert also agonized about dealing with the multifariousness of things and people (and which so often excited his disgust) and yearned for his one thing needful, his "one big thing," his "Idée." In essence, that would be Art, Art with a capital A, which he would pursue with almost a religious fervor, with a notoriously monkish asceticism in the way he practised that Art to the exclusion of so much else in life. "Le mariage pour moi," he wrote to his mother in December 1850, "serait une apostasie qui m'épouvante. [...] Tu [i.e., himself!] peindras le vin, l'amour, les femmes, la gloire, à condition, mon bonhomme, que tu ne seras ni ivrogne, ni amant, ni mari, ni tourlourou. Mêlé à la vie, on la voit mal; on en souffre ou [on] en jouit trop. L'artiste, selon moi, est une monstruosité, – quelque chose de hors nature" (Flaubert, *Correspondance* 1: 720).

To summarize: a fox's obsession with his art makes him hedgehoggy, and Flaubert knew how to be both crafty and prickly.

Such complexity raises the question: could Flaubert see patterning, principle, only in the practice of Art? Wasn't there something more to his hedgehog's vision of ultimate-essence as distinct from the fox's recognition of actual existence? Flaubert was, after all, a reader as well as a writer and possessed of a culture wider than that of many a narrowly focused practitioner of arts and crafts. He ruminated much on the hedgehog-essence of such great fox writers as Shakespeare and Goethe, especially their respective *Hamlet* and *Faust*. (The latter may well have influenced his own *La Tentation de saint Antoine*, whose protagonist is tempted by the devil, and *Bouvard et Pécuchet* whose eponymous pursuers of knowledge are, in effect, a double-act parody of the legendary German scholar.) There is a revealing but little-noticed passage in an 1853 letter in which Flaubert reflects on two of the greatest literary archetypes of all time: here he seems to transcend his obsession with his own artistry: "Hamlet ne réfléchit pas sur des subtilités d'école, mais sur des pensers humains. C'est, au contraire, ce perpétuel état de fluctuation d'Hamlet, ce vague où il se tient, ce manque de décision dans la volonté et de solution dans la pensée qui en fait tout le sublime. Mais *les gens d'esprit* veulent des caractères tout d'une pièce et *conséquents* (comme il y en a seulement dans les livres). Il n'y a pas au contraire un bout de l'âme humaine qui ne se retrouve dans cette conception. Ulysse est peut-être le plus fort type de toute la littérature ancienne, et Hamlet de toute la moderne" (Flaubert, *Correspondance* 2: 368).

Hedgehog and fox, it would seem, are constantly aspiring to become each other. The Russian novelist Ivan Turgenev, one of Flaubert's closest friends, gave a lecture on "Hamlet and Don Quixote," in which he suggested that the Danish prince was the great ironist and the Spanish knight was the great enthusiast: for that and much more they represented two contradictory principles in human life, "for ever uniting and for ever parting with one another"

(Turgenev 200). Turgenev's lecture has served as a key to his fiction: we might here invite readers to consider Flaubert's remarks on Hamlet and Ulysses as similarly illuminating on his work as a whole. Flaubert was, after all, both a Hamlet-like skeptic/ironist and a *voyageur* in a modern counterpart to the Ulyssean tradition. (He wrote that austere letter of December 1850, as quoted above, from Constantinople: in spite of its "ni amant" claims, his behavior with indigenous women during his Oriental travels was hardly consistent with monkish chastity...)

Moreover, as regards literary archetypes, Flaubert could be said to have created one of his own, worthy (or, arguably, unworthy) enough to stand alongside Hamlet, Faust, Quixote, and others. In 1902, Jules de Gaultier brought out his book *Le Bovarysme*, the title of which is his own term that he defines as "as a basic human faculty, the power to conceive of oneself as other than what one is" (qtd. in Porter 43). Though the term immediately and obviously refers to Emma Bovary, "Gaultier sees variants of bovarysme in other works of Flaubert: in *La Tentation de saint Antoine*, it is the attempt to surpass human limitations; in *Bouvard et Pécuchet*, it is the disproportion between human knowledge and the individual's illusory attempt to appropriate it" (Porter 43).

Before focusing on Flaubert's art *per se*, it is worth continuing to situate him in wider literary and cultural contexts. One striking example of such is a very French context: he shares with his contemporaries and compatriots a fascination with relationships between the sublime and the grotesque, and the extent to which these polarities actually approach and even blend with each other. In his capacity as an art critic, Baudelaire suggested that a meeting-place of the two could be discovered in the monstrous visions of the Spanish artist Francisco Goya; Victor Hugo, who praised a mingling of the sublime and the grotesque in the plays of Shakespeare, followed that example in his own work, as witnessed by the personally-admirable though physically-deformed Quasimodo and Gwynplaine in, respectively, his novels *Notre Dame de Paris* (1831) and *L'Homme qui rit* (1869). For his part, Flaubert referred to "le grotesque triste" (Flaubert, *Correspondance* 1: 307), and the darkly comic was for him more than just a laughing matter. In the course of writing *Madame Bovary*, he maintained that "L'ironie n'enlève rien au pathétique. Elle l'outre au contraire.—Dans ma 3e partie, qui sera pleine de choses farces, je veux qu'on pleure" (Flaubert, *Correspondance* 2: 172). How far this would apply to the ever-exploited, parrot-worshipping Félicité in his later tale "Un cœur simple" is at least debatable: many if not most would feel that here (as well as elsewhere in his fiction) the grotesque holds sway over the sublime. For more detailed consideration of this story, the reader is referred to the chapters by Kathryn Oliver Mills and Michael Sayeau in the present volume.

At the core of Flaubert's aesthetic is his doctrine of impersonality: this is the expression, in his writing practice, of his detached, ironic, and even disgusted attitude to life. In one of the much quoted items in his correspondence, he writes: "L'artiste doit être dans son œuvre comme Dieu dans la création, invisible et tout-puissant; qu'on le sente partout, mais qu'on ne le voie pas" (Flaubert, *Correspondance* 2: 691). James Joyce, who was considerably influenced by Flaubert, echoes this passage in the course of a conversation between the self-conscious, posing student-aesthetes of his novel *A Portrait of the Artist as a Young Man* (1916): "The artist, like the God of the creation, remains within or behind or beyond or above his handiwork, invisible, refined out of existence, indifferent, paring his fingernails" (Joyce 221). Joyce is part-mocking, part-according with this utterance by the sophomoric Stephen Dedalus, his novel's main character and not altogether unmodelled on himself.

However, Flaubert wanted to keep himself, the man Gustave Flaubert, out of his work altogether; indeed, in reading his books, one often has the sense that they created themselves, without external human (or, for that matter, divine) intervention. His most succinct statement on his "impersonality" came in the course of that 1875 letter to George Sand cited at the beginning of this chapter: "L'homme n'est rien, l'œuvre est tout" (Flaubert, *Correspondance* 4: 1000). This has the quirky distinction of being quoted by Sherlock Holmes, no less, at the conclusion of Conan Doyle's 1891 story "The Red-Headed League."

For Flaubert, then, the art of fiction was just that, an art, to be sharply distinguished from messy "life," even if it drew its subject-matter from "life." It was no wonder that Flaubert resented being labelled a "realist," as that would imply that he was relying too heavily on "life," that he was leaving his raw material pretty well unprocessed—leaving it, as it were, raw. "La Réalité, selon moi," he wrote to Turgenev in 1877, "ne doit être qu'un *tremplin*" (Flaubert, *Correspondance* 5: 337).

The most "impersonal" of all the arts is music: it is the least autobiographical, and for the most part, we are unaware, as we listen, of the composer himself as an actual human being. (There are exceptions—for example, Tchaikovsky). Flaubert led the way in what would become a tendency, in the late nineteenth and early twentieth centuries, to distance literature from too-obvious reference to "life." The challenge here was that words *mean* something. Ideally, Flaubert wanted to drain them of meaning, of any connection with the banal bourgeois reality that he so loathed:

> Ce qui me semble beau, ce que je voudrais faire, c'est un livre sur rien, un livre sans attache extérieure, qui se tiendrait de lui-même par la force interne de son style, comme la terre sans être soutenue se tient en l'air, un livre qui n'aurait presque pas de sujet ou du moins où le sujet serait presque invisible, si cela se peut. Les œuvres les plus belles sont celles où il y a le moins de matière […] (Flaubert, *Correspondance* 2: 31).

Accordingly, he stressed the necessity for prose, no less than poetry, to *sound* well, whatever the *sense*, if any, might be. As the poet Verlaine would later proclaim: "De la musique avant toute chose" (Verlaine 23). Musicality is a recurrent theme in Flaubert's correspondence, and this goes a long way towards explaining why he would labor for the maximum of hours and days for even the minimum of sentences that would be easy on the ear: "Quand je découvre une mauvaise assonance," he told George Sand, "ou une répétition dans une de mes phrases, je suis sûr que je patauge dans le Faux; à force de chercher, je trouve l'expression juste, qui était la seule—et qui est, en même temps, l'harmonieuse" (Flaubert,

Correspondance 5: 26). He would make passionate claims for the verbal music that was possible to the writer who wished to rise above the general mediocrity: "Nous avons un orchestre nombreux, une palette riche, des ressources variées" (Flaubert, *Correspondance* 1: 627); he aspired to a style "avec des ondolations, des ronflements de violoncelle" (Flaubert, *Correspondance* 2: 79). François Coppée's praise for Flaubert as the Beethoven of prose may be taken as no little recognition of his success in that regard.

It wasn't only literature that was moving in such a direction; indeed the critic Walter Pater—a leading English admirer of Flaubert—famously declared that "All art constantly aspires towards the condition of music." (Pater 140). "All" art included painting, and the American James Whistler took that art a long way towards the abstract; he disdained the primacy of subject-matter and would call his pictures "symphonies" or "nocturnes" (that later term a favorite of Chopin's), irrespective of their apparent depictions of Battersea Bridge, the River Thames, or a lone figure approaching a well-lit tavern on a misty night.

The English novelist E. M. Forster seems almost to echo Flaubert when he ruefully observes "Yes—oh dear yes—the novel tells a story [...] and I wish that it was not so, that it could be something different—melody, or perception of the truth, not this low atavistic form" (Forster 34). The French were very much ahead of the English in seeking to overcome this malady, if malady it was; style, composition, shape, structure—these qualities mattered more to Flaubert and his "disciples" more than telling a rattling good yarn. He had a certain regard for Charles Dickens's *Pickwick Papers* (1837), "mais quelle composition défectueuse! Tous les écrivains anglais en sont là, W. Scott excepté. Ils manquent de plan! cela est insupportable pour nous autres Latins" (Flaubert, *Correspondance* 4: 547).

The most celebrated aspect of Flaubert's art, however, is his deployment of *style indirect libre*, the nature of which is well summarized by the critical theorist Gérard Genette: "le narrateur assume le discours du personage, ou si l'on préfère, le personage parle par la voix du narrateur, et les instances sont alors confondues" (Genette 194). This device both intensified Flaubert's irony and looked forward to the interior monologue and stream of consciousness techniques that would be taken up by Proust and Joyce. Here is one of the many examples of *style indirect libre* in *Madame Bovary* and indeed throughout his œuvre: Emma Bovary is attending a performance of Donizetti's opera *Lucia di Lammermoor* with her decent, but dull, husband Charles: her sometime toyboy, Léon, is also in the audience. Emma, all too prone to romantic fantasizing, compares the opera's female protagonist, the unhappily married Lucia, to herself:

> Lucie s'avançait, à demi soutenue par ses femmes, une couronne d'oranger dans les cheveux, et plus pâle que le satin blanc de sa robe. Emma rêvait au jour de son mariage; et elle se revoyait là-bas, au milieu des blés, sur le petit sentier, quand on marchait vers l'église. Pourquoi donc n'avait-elle pas, comme celle-là, résisté, supplié? Elle était joyeuse, au contraire, sans s'apercevoir de l'abîme où elle se précipitait ... Ah! si, dans la fraîcheur de sa beauté, avant les souillures du mariage et la désillusion de l'adultère, elle avait pu placer sa vie sur quelque grand cœur solide, alors la vertu, la tendresse, les voluptés et le devoir se confondant, jamais elle ne serait descendue d'une félicité si haute. (Flaubert, *Œuvres complètes* 349)

The charismatic, if hammy, tenor Lagardy appears on stage:

> [...] entraînée vers l'homme par l'illusion du personnage, elle tâcha de se figurer sa vie, cette vie retentissante, extraordinaire, splendide, et qu'elle aurait pu mener cependant, si le hasard l'avait voulu. Ils se seraient connus, ils se seraient aimés! Avec lui, par tous les royaumes de l'Europe, elle aurait voyagé de capitale en capitale, partageant ses fatigues et son orgueil, ramassant les fleurs qu'on lui jetait, brodant elle-même ses costumes; puis, chaque soir, au fond d'une loge, derrière la grille à treillis d'or, elle eût recueilli, béante, les expansions de cette âme qui n'aurait chanté que pour elle seule; de la scène, tout en jouant, il l'aurait regardée. Mais une folie la saisit: il la regardait, c'est sûr! Elle eut envie de courir dans ses bras pour se réfugier en sa force, comme dans l'incarnation de l'amour même, et de lui dire, de s'écrier : « Enlève-moi, emmène-

moi, partons! À toi, à toi! toutes mes ardeurs et tous mes rêves!
Le rideau se baissa. (Flaubert, *Œuvres complètes* 350)

Pathos ends in bathos. Emma has been seduced by layers of illusion: the singers are performing, not actually feeling, the emotions represented in a French translation of the libretto of an Italian opera, which in turn derives from a novel by a Scotsman, Walter Scott (as pointed out in Porter 243).

Style indirect libre can create a sense of both detachment on the part of the author (and/or narrator), but as it is merging a character's subjective point of view with omniscient narration, such ambivalence can also create the opposite mode, i.e., a closeness, even an identification, of the author with the character. Flaubert may have resisted the label of realist, but he had an awareness that he was a frustrated romantic—not altogether unlike Emma Bovary; his well-known utterance "Madame Bovary, c'est moi" is not as enigmatic as it first appears. When he composed the scene in which Emma poisons herself, he could taste the arsenic in his own mouth, and this caused him to vomit. He was compelled to confess that he wasn't as aloof as his artistic credo would suggest.

"Je ne me reconnais pas le droit d'accuser personne," he wrote to George Sand in 1868. "Je ne crois même pas que le romancier doive exprimer *son* opinion sur les choses de ce monde. Il peut la communiquer, mais je n'aime pas à ce qu'il la dise" (Flaubert, *Correspondance* 3: 786). That indeed echoes the familiar claim of standing apart from the world and from his own creations. However, the ambivalence is subtly there. It doesn't mean that he *lacks* opinions: it's a question of how they're conveyed. In other words, if we apply this to the representation of his characters, of their thoughts, feelings and actions, Flaubert the novelist may *imply* his judgment of them, though he's certainly not going to *pronounce* such judgment.

Moreover, there's an inevitability about the implying. We come back to the inescapable fact that words have meaning, are referential, and cannot entertain the *neutrality*, as it were, of musical expression. Words are loaded, biased: we know this at the crudest levels from the practice of politicians and advertisers, when they choose language that is meant to bamboozle us with its seemingly innocent, pseudo-objectivity of tone. That's the nature of ideology, and we may well feel no little sympathy with Flaubert for his mistrust of the big words, such as "Progrès" and so on.

The artist, according to Flaubert, is "invisible" in relation to his work, "comme Dieu," but he is also "tout puissant," and as a god, he both directs and judges, his judgments being both artistic and, yes, moral. The moral dimension is, however, conveyed by techniques that are as "indirect" as *style indirect libre*, which itself, as we've observed in Emma Bovary's musings at the opera, can brilliantly suggest (rather than state outright) a character's sadly self-indulgent and deluded attitudes. Another much celebrated device in *Madame Bovary* is the ironic juxtaposition of two different and seemingly contrasted discourses occurring at the same time and almost in the same space: the instance here is the agricultural show in Part 2, Chapter 8, where the councillor's pompous speech is intercut with the mocking comments of Rodolphe in the course of a tête-à-tête with Emma.

We can take it that Flaubert himself would go some way with Rodolphe's sentiments regarding the smug pronouncements of a pillar of the provincial community. Indeed the author's implicit sympathy with an old peasant woman, as she awkwardly mounts the platform to receive her silver medal (valued at a mere twenty-five francs) from the excruciatingly patronizing bigwigs, is pretty clear: "Ainsi se tenait, devant ces bourgeois épanouis, ce demi-siècle de servitude" (Flaubert, *Œuvres complètes* 283). However, Flaubert's satirical purpose, for such it is, includes Rodolphe as much as the smug dignitaries droning on and on, as Emma's beau drops from his silver tongue the kind of romantic (or rather sentimental) clichés that are the stock-in-trade of an equally smug seducer; Rodolphe's utterances are just as shallow and insincere as those of the self-important Monsieur Lieuvain on his petty pedestal. One kind of bullshit is countered by another.

Following his novel about Emma Bovary the frustrated romantic, Flaubert wrote another novel, which was the expression of

Gustave Flaubert the frustrated romantic: *Salammbô*, a lurid tale of extreme passions, of lust and cruelty conducted in the exotic setting of ancient Carthage. It couldn't be further, surely, from the humdrum quotidian life of provincial, bourgeois France; it was grand-operatic in tone, all high (if bloody) heroics. Certain twentieth-century writers shared something of Flaubert's mood. The poet T. S. Eliot, also a keen satirist of the mediocrity (as he saw it) of his own times, invoked ancient splendors that had been long lost: "Where are the eagles and the trumpets?" (Eliot 45). James Joyce's *Ulysses* (1922) takes Homer's epic as a template for a mock-heroic exploration of the dingy Dublin of 1904.

Flaubert's attraction to the distant past can be viewed in the context of a widespread devotion, among nineteenth-century French writers, to the novels of Sir Walter Scott. Stendhal, Balzac, Hugo, Dumas the elder, and Flaubert himself were, in their various ways, indebted to him. Scott has been regarded as a major influence on that romanticism which came late to France, and, more universally, as the father of the historical novel. For all its reconstructions of ancient Carthage, however, could *Salammbô* really be considered a historical novel? Scott's *Waverley* (1814) was set "sixty years hence," in relative terms, not all that long before its date of publication. Such was the gist of the judgment of the critic Charles Sainte-Beuve: for him, *Salammbô* was a work whose splendors were ultimately sterile. A similar position was argued, and with greater sophistication, by the Hungarian Marxist Georg Lukács in his book *The Historical Novel*: Flaubert may have aimed to write a "modern" novel set in ancient times, but the result was oddly disjointed. "When Scott describes a medieval town or the habitat of a Scottish clan, these material things are part and parcel of the lives and fortunes of people whose whole psychology belongs to the same level of historical development and is a product of the same social-historical ensemble as these material things. This is how the older epic writers produced their 'totality of objects.' In Flaubert, there is no such connection between the outside world and the psychology of the principal characters. And the effect of this lack of connection is to degrade the archaeological exactness of the outer world: it becomes a world of historically exact *costumes* and *decorations*, no more than a pictorial frame within which a purely modern story is unfolded" (Lukács 224–5).

L'Éducation sentimentale, set during the period of the 1848 Revolution and thus within Flaubert's own lifetime, would appear to come closer to the genre of the historical novel, though Lukács does not discuss it at length and indeed finds Flaubert's choice of historical subject-matter to be quite "arbitrary" (Lukács 265). However, what unfolds in *L'Éducation sentimentale* is not *history*, with its organic relationships between private individuals and the public events that affect them (or are affected by them), but *time*. No wonder Marcel Proust was such an admirer of the novel.

Time: and so we have the poignancy of Frédéric's last meeting with his ideal woman, his "Madonna" figure Madame Arnoux, when as a parting gift she hands him a lock of her hair, which has turned white. *Time*: when Frédéric and his down-to-earth "whore" figure, Rosanette, visit the once royal palace of Fontainebleau, there is the sense that all of us, high or low, have our little lives that will pass. Even this mellow mood can't escape Flaubert's wicked desire to undercut it: he has Rosanette make a characteristically crass response:

> Les résidences royales ont en elles une mélancolie particulière, qui tient sans doute à leurs dimensions trop considérables pour le petit nombre de leurs hôtes, au silence qu'on est surpris d'y trouver après tant de fanfares, à leur luxe immobile prouvant par sa vieillesse la fugacité dès dynasties, l'éternelle misère, l'éternelle misère de tout;— et cette exhalaison des siècles, engourdissante et funèbre comme un parfum de momie, se fait sentir même aux têtes naïves. Rosanette bâillait démesurément. Ils s'en retournèrent à l'hôtel. (Flaubert, *Œuvres* 353–4)

It's a moment comparable to the theatre curtain falling abruptly on Emma Bovary's *Lucia di Lammermoor*-induced fantasies. However, Flaubert's poetic insight survives even Rosanette's yawns and is, moreover, intensified a little later in the couple's expedition: here, the point is that, for all the transience of human life, there is much in our universe and our planet, which endures. Frédéric is Flaubert's

---

ineffectual anti-hero, yet he is affected by the scene much as Flaubert himself would be: reality is bigger than Frédéric Moreau; bigger also than Gustave Flaubert. Rosanette, of course, has to say the wrong thing; yet she's attracted to the pretty purple flowers that, for all their own transience of being, are part of that which is in nature and is perpetual:

> Un bruit de fer, des coups drus et nombreux sonnaient; c'était, au flanc d'une colline, une compagnie de carriers battant les roches. Elles se multipliaient de plus en plus, et finissaient par emplir tout le paysage, cubiques comme des maisons, plates comme des dalles, s'étayant, se surplombant, se confondant telles que les ruines méconnaissables et monstrueuses de quelque cité disparue. Mais la furie même de leur chaos fait plutôt rêver à des volcans, à des déluges, aux grands cataclysmes ignorés. Frédéric disait qu'ils étaient là depuis le commencement du monde et resteraient ainsi jusqu'à la fin; Rosanette détournait la tête, en affirmant que « ça la rendrait folle », et s'en allait cueillir des bruyères. Leurs petites fleurs violettes, tassées les unes près des autres, formaient des plaques inégales, et la terre qui s'écroulait de dessous mettait comme des franges noires au bord des sables pailletés de mica. (Flaubert, *Œuvres* 357)

Opinion has always been divided on *L'Éducation sentimentale*. The very title of his essay on the novel, "The Politics of Flaubert," indicates that the critic Edmund Wilson found it solidly sociohistorical in content and treatment. "There are no hero, no villain, to arouse us, no clowns to entertain us, no scenes to wring our hearts," writes Wilson. "Yet the effect is deeply moving" (Wilson 95). The chapter just quoted has surely much to do with that. An equally respected critic, Martin Turnell, disputes Wilson's enthusiasm for a novel, which he, for his part, finds diffuse and artificial, though not without its merits (Turnell 292–311, *passim*). Readers are advised to weigh up Wilson's and Turnell's assessments: over fifty years on, both critics have much to teach us about *L'Éducation sentimentale*.

The *Trois contes* of 1877 are a distillation of Flaubert's art: their relative brevity brings home to us the precision and shapeliness of his work as a whole. The put-upon servant woman Félicité in "Un cœur simple" is a reincarnation of the old woman receiving her cheap prize in *Madame Bovary*'s agricultural show; "La Légende de saint Julien l'Hospitalier" displays the craftsmanly care of the stained-glass window that inspired the story; "Hérodias" sums up the exotic-erotic in Flaubert.

In *L'Éducation sentimentale*, Frédéric Moreau is one of those "Young Men from the Provinces" whom the critic Lionel Trilling perceived as an archetype of nineteenth-century fiction: such youthful fellows were new arrivals in the big city, ambitious if not opportunistic in their pursuit of social, political, artistic, and/ or sexual success. True, Frédéric is passive and half-hearted when compared to Stendhal's Julien Sorel in *Le Rouge et le noir* (1830) and Balzac's Rastignac in *Le Père Goriot* (1834), but Trilling still includes him alongside these more ruthless souls (Trilling 72–5). When we come to Flaubert's last novel, the unfinished *Bouvard et Pécuchet,* we might be forgiven for feeling that Flaubert is having a retrospective joke at the expense of the Young Man from the Provinces pattern. For here, we have a couple of old-timers who make a reverse journey from Paris to the sticks, where they aspire to become walking encyclopedias. Yet even here Flaubert can blend the grotesque with the sublime: our two ageing idiots are not without an awareness (like Frédéric Moreau) that the universe is bigger than they are. *Bouvard et Pécuchet* is tragedy disguised as farce.

La Tentation de saint Antoine (1874), one might think, does not seem to be by the same man who left *Bouvard et Pécuchet* behind him. It's the exotic-erotic again, surely, and indeed together with *Salammbô* and "Hérodias" this strange novel was plundered by the symbolists and decadents working in both literary and nonliterary media during the decades following Flaubert's death in 1880. *La Tentation de saint Antoine*'s legacy to the *fin-de-siècle* sensibility was a parade of *femmes fatales*, like the novel's Queen of Sheba and, towards its end, personifications of "La Mort" and "La Luxure" and the vision of a skull with a crown of roses, atop the white torso of a woman whose body forms a tail that undulates like a giant worm. A Glasgow School of Art colleague once summed up French symbolism/decadence for me as "sexy Death" and not something to

---

be taken over-solemnly. If we, no doubt unfairly, blamed all this on Flaubert, we might consider that *La Tentation de saint Antoine* was farce disguised as tragedy.

Yet the most abiding, and most disturbing, scene to be found in *La Tentation de saint Antoine*, in its concluding pages, is that between the Sphinx and the Chimera (Chimère). These are symbols (though not intentionally proto-Symbolist) and are, therefore, extremely complex and subtle, not reducible to a few glib or easily-abstracted concepts. However, it's the nature of symbols to be suggestive, and the appearance of these contrasting figures has occasioned much discussion of their possible significance. The Sphinx and the Chimera could even be two sides of Flaubert himself, in conflict with each other, respectively as the coolly scientific observer versus the passionate romantic, the sceptical rationalist versus the idealistic pursuer of pure "Art." Such speculations may not, after all, be all that far-fetched. One early critic remarked that "On peut dire de Flaubert que l'imagination était sa muse et la réalité sa conscience" (Faguet 66)—with, we might add, the Chimera as the first and the Sphinx as the second. This was Flaubert's ultimate challenge as an artist: to reconcile the Sphinx with the Chimera, as the Hedgehog with the Fox. If he failed in that, or if he believed he had failed, it would be his tragedy, his farce, or both.

Works Cited

Berlin, Isaiah. *The Hedgehog and the Fox: An Essay on Tolstoy's View of History*. New York: New American Library, 1957.

Eliot, T. S. *The Complete Poems and Plays of T.S. Eliot*. London: Faber, 1969.

Faguet, Émile. *Flaubert*. Paris: Hachette, 1899.

Flaubert, Gustave. *Correspondance*. Ed. Jean Bruneau. 5 vols. Paris: Gallimard, 1973–2007.

_____. *Œuvres*. Vol. 2. Paris: Gallimard, 1963.

_____. *Œuvres complètes*. Vol. 3, 1851–1862. Paris: Gallimard, 2013.

Forster, E.M. *Aspects of the Novel*. Harmondsworth, UK: Penguin, 1962.

Genette, Gérard. *Figures III*. Paris: Le Seuil, 1972.

Joyce, James. *The Essential James Joyce*. Harmondsworth, UK: Penguin, 1969.

Lukács, Georg. *The Historical Novel*. Harmondsworth, UK: Penguin, 1969.

Pater, Walter. *The Renaissance*. Revised & enlarged ed. London: Macmillan, 1888.

Porter, Laurence M., ed. *A Gustave Flaubert Encyclopedia*. Westport, CT: Greenwood Press, 2001.

Trilling, Lionel. *The Liberal Imagination*. Harmondsworth, UK: Penguin, 1970.

Turgenev, Ivan. "Hamlet and Don Quixote." *The Fortnightly Review* 56 (1894): 191–205.

Turnell, Martin. *The Novel in France*. Harmondsworth, UK: Penguin, 1962.

Verlaine, Paul. *Jadis et Naguère*. Paris: Léon Vanier, 1884.

Wilson, Edmund. *The Triple Thinkers*. Harmondsworth, UK: Penguin, 1962.

The Kindly Misanthrope: A Biographical Sketch of Gustave Flaubert

Tom Hubbard

As the son and the brother of medical men, Gustave Flaubert seemed almost destined to be routinely described as coldly surgical in his attitude to his writing in general, and to his fictional characters in particular. As far as his personal circumstances are concerned, the more important point is that Achille-Cléophas Flaubert, our man's father, was a surgeon of eminence and wealth: he bought land and property, including a house at Croisset, near Rouen. This would become Gustave's workplace, and with no need to earn a living other than as a writer, he could afford to be unrelentingly scrupulous about his art. He would pursue "le mot juste," or, as he himself put it, "l'expression juste"; in the course of writing *Madame Bovary*, he confessed that it had taken him five days to write one page (Flaubert, *Correspondance* 2: 238). The legend of Flaubert as an ascetic monk in his cell took hold and with a persistence to match that of the image of the cruel dissector.

Given the Scandinavian origins of the people of Normandy, together with his physical presence (including, doubtless, the long droopy moustaches), Gustave Flaubert attracted another image: the imposing Viking. This might suggest a certain belligerence in his character, but it actually attracted a mixture of awe and affection. The American novelist Henry James—who would match Flaubert in his own fastidious attitude to his art—met him in Paris during 1876 and pictured him as having been "the tall and splendid youth, green-eyed and sonorous" and still "distinguished" in "stature and aspect" (James, *Selected* 175). James found Flaubert to be "simple, honest, kindly, and touchingly inarticulate" (James, *Letters* 38). This will astonish many who are familiar with Flaubert the savage misanthrope (as well as with the obsessive stylist), but a person's private persona can often be less formidable, and more attractive, than his or her public one.

Moreover, for a figure who has commanded the attention of countless intellectuals noted for their sophistication and cosmopolitanism, Flaubert set much of his best fiction, such as *Madame Bovary* and "Un cœur simple" not in Paris, but in his own corner of France, there in the northwest, in the sticks. Even a tale so apparently rarefied as "La Légende de saint Julien l'Hospitalier" owes its existence to Flaubert's memory of a stained-glass window, depicting the saint, in the cathedral of his home town of Rouen. If Flaubert could mock the provincial bourgeoisie with such authority, it was because—objectively rather than subjectively—he was one of them.

Flaubert's "bourgeoisophobie" is a leading motif in his work; of his critics, it is Vladimir Nabokov who has been especially enlightening on this point, as in his posthumously published lecture on *Madame Bovary* and elsewhere: "Flaubert never uses the word *bourgeois* with any politico-economic Marxist connotation. Flaubert's bourgeois is a state of mind, not a state of pocket [...] Let me add for double clarity that Marx would have called Flaubert a bourgeois in the politico-economic sense and Flaubert would have called Marx a bourgeois in the spiritual sense; and both would have been right, since Flaubert was a well-to-do gentleman in physical life and Marx was a philistine in his attitude towards the arts" (Nabokov, *Lectures on Literature* 127). "A bourgeois is a smug philistine, a dignified vulgarian" (Nabokov, *Lectures on Russian* 309). There's much there with which to take issue, not least its gross misrepresentation of Marx's literary and cultural interests; nonetheless, we learn (and relish) much from Nabokov when he's at his most provocative.

Flaubert had periods of residence in Paris, as when he studied law during the early 1840s (he never practiced), as well as later that decade and subsequently; however, it was never "his" city as it was in the life and work of his predecessors and successors in the French novel, such as Honoré de Balzac and Émile Zola. Even so, *L'Éducation sentimentale* is very much his Paris novel, with its detailed descriptions of domestic interiors and the vivid account of the 1848 Revolution, which he personally witnessed. From his provincial retreat he mourned the devastation of the city in the wake of the war and siege of 1870–71.

Flaubert's famous doctrine of "impersonality" led him to claim that his art was greater than himself. Nevertheless, his correspondence reveals much about both the artist and the man. The major recipient of his earlier letters, up to their rupture in 1854, was his "Muse" and most long-term sexual partner, Louise Colet; thereafter, close friends, such as George Sand and Ivan Turgenev, engaged with him in some of the most probing and moving literary correspondence that has ever been made public.

Flaubert could be careful about what he wrote to whom, up to a point. Towards the end of his travels in the Near-and Mid-East, in December 1850, he wrote from Constantinople to his mother, telling her that, as an artist, he must have no commitments, such as a lover or a wife: "Je me fous du monde," he continued, "de l'avenir, du qu'en dira-t-on, d'un établissement quelconque, et même de la renommée littéraire, qui m'a jadis fait passer tant de nuits blanches à la rêver. Voilà comme je suis; tel est mon caractère, mon caractère est tel" (Flaubert, *Correspondance* 1: 720). No reports of sexual excess there, then, to reveal himself as other than Gustave the good boy, though such an austere attitude as he expresses here might— one would have thought—be somewhat alarming to his parent.

Nine months earlier, and to one of his male friends, the writer Louis Bouilhet, he had made a very different confession. In Egypt, he had been enjoying the delights on offer from the courtesan Kuchuk Hanem and her colleagues:

Il y avait 4 femmes danseuses et chanteuses [...] Quand il a fallu partir, je ne suis pas parti. [...] Je suis descendu au rez-de-chaussée dans la chambre de Kuchuk. [...] Je l'ai sucée avec rage; son corps était en sueur, elle était fatiguée d'avoir dansé, elle avait froid [...] En contemplant dormir cette belle créature qui ronflait la tête appuyée sur mon bras, je pensais à mes nuits au bordel à Paris, à un tas de vieux souvenirs [...] Quant aux coups, ils ont été bons. Le troisième, surtout, a été féroce, et le dernier, sentimental. Nous nous sommes dit là beaucoup de choses tendres, nous nous serrâmes vers la fin d'une façon triste et amoureuse. [...] Si le cerveau baisse, la pine se relève" (Flaubert, *Correspondance* 1: 606–9).

Note that "féroce" followed by "sentimental" and "choses tendres:" that is typical of the man.

So: Gustave Flaubert the ascetic; Gustave Flaubert the sensualist. He was both. Indeed, in his letters he refers to his antithetical nature—"Il y a en moi, littérairement parlant, deux bonshommes distincts" (Flaubert, *Correspondance* 2: 30)—and so much the better for his art. The man's contradictions released energies that fuelled his art, for art thrives on contradictions. In Flaubert's work, opposites animate each other: the sublime and the grotesque, tragedy and farce. Such creative tensions are discussed further in the present volume.

It was as well that the letter on the night with Kuchuk Hanem was not available to the would-be censors of *Madame Bovary*. Cuts had already been made for the novel's serialization in *La Revue de Paris*, much to Flaubert's fury. In the novel *Our Mutual Friend* (1865) by Charles Dickens—a writer for whom Flaubert had a certain limited admiration—there is a strong portrayal of an English example of the smug bourgeois philistine, a Mr. Podsnap, who characteristically deplores all influences from the European continent, especially France. Such a mentality—a common one—held that France was the main source of all that was immoral and unclean in literature and art. At a dinner party, Podsnap patronizes one of the guests, a visiting Frenchman who responds graciously, if confusedly, to the Englishman's crass utterances.

Podsnap holds "that there is in the Englishman [...] an absence of everything calculated to call a blush into the cheek of a young person" (Dickens 1: 170). The 1857 trial of *Madame Bovary* demonstrated that the likes of Podsnap would, after all, have found no shortage of allies—at least as regards a hypocritical prudery— in that supposedly free-and-easy country on the wrong side of the English Channel. The trial ended in an acquittal; still, for Flaubert the damage had been done—not in terms of his novel's fortunes: bad publicity is still pretty good publicity—but as contributing still further to his disgust with his fellow-countrymen and with mankind as a whole.

In the course of composing *Madame Bovary*, Flaubert wrote to Louise Colet of how he was attempting to achieve just that—*composing*: aiming for an effect that was "symphonique" (Flaubert, *Correspondance* 2: 426, 449). To treat the novel as an art form, based on criteria of abstract beauty more obviously belonging to music, was to distance himself from philistine obsessions with subject matter, from all manner of bourgeois obtuseness and literal-mindedness. Flaubert's uncompromising insistence on the symphonic and the lapidary carried him through his subsequent works: *Salammbô* (1862), set in Carthage, which he had visited in 1858; *L'Éducation sentimentale* (1869); *La Tentation de saint Antoine* (1874), drawing on memories of his time in Egypt (not least as regards its sexier pages); *Trois contes* (1877), collectively a kind of miniaturization of the leading motifs of the novels; the unfinished *Bouvard et Pécuchet*, with its unwittingly pioneering Odd Couple of the That's-another-fine-mess-we've-got-ourselves-into genre, but also with its author's characteristic blend of irony and pathos.

As the 1870s advanced, age didn't mellow Flaubert; in the aftermath of the Franco-Prussian War, if anything, he felt increasingly isolated and bitter. Despite his vaunted doctrine of "impersonality," of his insistence that he'd keep himself out of his work, he couldn't resist using some of his fictional characters as his mouthpieces. In *La Tentation de saint Antoine*, the pagan god Jupiter thunders against humankind: "Que la Terre les garde, et qu'ils s'agitent au niveau de sa bassesse! Ils ont maintenant des cœurs d'esclaves, oublient les injures, les ancêtres, le serment; et partout triomphe la sottise des foules, la médiocrité de l'individu, la hideur des races" (Flaubert, *La Tentation* 222).

Yet that other, gentler, side was never far away. The lonely bachelor was also a devoted family man: childless himself, he lavished a paternal love on his niece Caroline. Uncle and niece faced financial ruin as a result of her husband's business debts. On May 8, 1880, the death of Gustave Flaubert was sudden. Its cause has been disputed: Apoplexy? Epilepsy? He had certainly suffered from the latter.

A fellow epileptic was the great Russian novelist Fyodor Dostoevsky, whom he never met, but who refers to Saint Julien l'Hospitalier—the subject of the second of the *Trois contes*—in the course of his novel *The Brothers Karamazov* (1880). Dostoevsky would have known Turgenev's Russian translation of Flaubert's tale. Flaubert and Turgenev had felt a deep brotherly love for each other: their relationship helped to sustain Flaubert through difficult times. Turgenev was in Russia at the time of his friend's passing: he learned of it from the newspapers. "The death of Flaubert has affected me deeply," he wrote; "The last time I saw him (at Croisset), he had no presentiment of his approaching end—neither did I—and yet he spoke quite freely about death" (Flaubert & Turgenev 13). There can be few more moving personal utterances by one great novelist on another.

Works Cited

Dickens, Charles. *Our Mutual Friend.* 2 vols. Philadelphia: T.B. Peterson, 1865.

Flaubert, Gustave. *Correspondance.* Ed. Jean Bruneau. 5 vols. Paris: Gallimard, 1973–2007.

_____. *La Tentation de saint Antoine.* 2d ed. Paris: Charpentier, 1874.

Flaubert, Gustave & Ivan Turgenev. *Flaubert & Turgenev: A Friendship in Letters: The Complete Correspondence.* Ed. Barbara Beaumont. New York: Fromm International, 1987.

James, Henry. *Letters*, vol. 2, 1875–1883. Ed. Leon Edel. Cambridge, MA: Harvard UP, 1975.

_____. *Selected Literary Criticism.* Ed. Morris Shapira. Harmondsworth: Penguin Books, 1968.

Nabokov, Vladimir. *Lectures on Literature.* San Diego: Harcourt, Brace, 1980.

_____. *Lectures on Russian Literature.* London: Pan Books, 1983.

CRITICAL
CONTEXTS

"J'ai toujours tâché de vivre dans une tour d'ivoire:" Gustave Flaubert's Life and Times___

Tom Hubbard

Unconsciously, prophetically, Flaubert recorded memories of his adolescence in terms that link them to his contemporary Charles Baudelaire and to his successor Marcel Proust. "Tous mes souvenirs de ma jeunesse," he wrote to his lover Louise Colet in 1853, "crient sous mes pas, comme les coquilles de la plage. Chaque lame de la mer que je regarde tomber éveille en moi des retentissements lointains. J'entends gronder les jours passés et se presser comme des flots toute l'interminable série des passions disparues" (Flaubert, *Correspondance* 2: 404). Flaubert would fondly—and erotically—recall family vacations in the coastal resort of Trouville, where in 1836, aged fourteen, he encountered the beautiful twenty-five-year-old Madame Elisa Schlésinger.

The seashore tends to prompt, in the souls of the sensitive, deep spiritual yearnings, accompanied or not by those more carnal. "Pourqoi le spectacle de la mer," pondered Baudelaire, "est-il si infiniment et si éternellement agréable?" He proceeded to answer his own rhetorical question. "Parce que la mer offre à la fois l'idée de l'immensité et de mouvement. Six ou sept lieues représentent pour l'homme le rayon de l'infini [...] Douze ou quatorze lieues [...] de liquide en mouvement suffisent pour donner la plus haute idée de beauté qui soit offerte à l'homme sur son habitacle transitoire" (Baudelaire 696). Baudelaire reveals the source of the creativity of many artists, and for Flaubert, the earliest reworkings of his coastal experiences are the semi-autobiographical fictions *Mémoires d'un fou* and *Novembre*. It is at the (fictional) resort of Balbec—like Trouville on La Manche (the English Channel)—that Proust's (fictional) Marcel encounters a "somewhat rowdy band of young girls with bicycles, and then one of them in particular, Albertine, apparently their leader. Her free behavior carries a hint of license and even of vice" (Shattuck 53). Albertine becomes woven into the complex web of Marcel's experiences and subsequent memory: she appears and reappears according to the subtle, intricate promptings of his (un)conscious mind. Proust, in his great *roman fleuve*, *À la recherche du temps perdu* (1913–27), learned not a little from the technical innovations of the mature Flaubert, who in his unique way was a pioneer of the psychological novel.

A fashionable resort, Trouville was represented in the paintings of Eugène Boudin (1824–98), and in one of them, there walks by the sea, accompanied by her entourage, the Empress Eugénie, who would feature in Flaubert's life when he had gained a measure of "official" recognition. Claude Monet (1840–1926) was the impressionist master who produced many works depicting Trouville as well as the wilder and lonelier stretches of the coast, with their dramatically-shaped cliff-faces. Moreover, French and Belgian symbolist poets and painters, toward the end of the century, would add an even more mystical dimension to their meetings of land and sea: images of seashells, seahorses and all manner of marine and submarine phenomena would become objective correlatives of the deeper reaches of human psychology.

All this, if related somewhat retrospectively to Flaubert, would suggest that he lived a largely interior life, recoiling from the crudities of everyday socioeconomic and political realities, and devoted to his own ruminations on and for his art. That would not be far wrong.

The exploration of his interior world would, in due course, find a counterpart in the exterior world when he visited Egypt and points east. Again, there is a striking similarity with his friend Baudelaire, in poems such as "La Vie antérieure," "À une Malabaraise," and, above all, "L'Invitation au voyage," with its search for "luxe, calme et volupté." Flaubert's pursuit of the exotic-erotic was undertaken in temporary flight from the tedium of bourgeois France and provided material for such fictions as *Salammbô*, *La Tentation de saint Antoine*, and "Hérodias;" in the present volume, Beryl F. Schlossman recounts how Edward Said had something to say about this in his book *Orientalism*. There is an extraordinary passage in one of Flaubert's earlier letters to Louise Colet, dated October 7,

1846, where images of colonization and the Baudelairean "voyage" mesh with a primitive attempt at (as it were) autopsychoanalysis:

> Parmi les marins, il y [en] a qui découvrent des mondes, qui ajoutent des terres à la terre et des étoiles aux étoiles. Ceux-là ce sont les maîtres, les grands, les éternellement beaux. D'autres lancent la terreur par les sabords de leurs navires, capturent, s'enrichissent et s'engraissent. Il y en a qui s'en vont chercher de l'or et de la soie sous d'autres cieux. D'autres seulement tâchent d'attraper dans leurs filets des saumons pour les gourmets et de la morue pour les pauvres. Moi, je suis l'obscur et patient pêcheur de perles qui plonge dans les bas-fonds et qui revient les mains vides et la face bleuie. Une attraction fatale m'attire dans les abîmes de la pensée, au fond de ces gouffres intérieurs qui ne tarissent jamais pour les forts. Je passerai ma vie à regarder l'Océan de l'Art où les autres naviguent ou combattent, et je m'amuserai parfois à aller chercher au fond de l'eau des coquilles vertes ou jaunes dont personne ne voudra; aussi je les garderai pour moi seul et j'en tapisserai ma cabane. (Flaubert, *Correspondance* 1: 378)

Two years later, in 1848, Flaubert witnessed the latest of France's uprisings, and his disgust with politics would pervade much of his correspondence and at least one of his novels, *L'Éducation sentimentale* (1869). This book, among much else, offers a mordant survey of the French public scene through the reign of "Le Roi citoyen," Louis-Philippe, his overthrow in 1848 and the consequent rise of Louis-Napoléon Bonaparte, later known as Napoléon III. All sections of society, through these decades, were to Flaubert involved in a project of narrowly materialistic aspiration: as one helpful cliché sums it up, all snouts were in the trough. Flaubert draws on his memories of '48 to damn the lot of them: "On se redit, pendant un mois, la phrase de Lamartine sur le drapeau rouge, « qui n'avait fait que le tour du Champ de Mars, tandis que le drapeau tricolore », etc ; et tous se rangèrent sous son ombre, chaque parti ne voyant des trois couleurs que la sienne et se promettant bien, dès qu'il serait le plus fort, d'arracher les deux autres" (Flaubert, *Œuvres* 325).

During the twentieth century, there was a strong tendency for French writers to be politically committed—*engagé(e)s*; not so

Flaubert. He had an aversion to novels with a political, even a moral-political agenda and made this clear in his assessment of Harriet Beecher Stowe's *Uncle Tom's Cabin* (1852):

> [...] l'*Oncle Tom* me paraît un livre étroit. [...] Les qualités de sentiment, et il y [en] a de grandes dans ce livre, eussent été mieux employées si le but eût été moins restreint. Quand il n'y aura plus d'esclaves en Amérique, ce roman ne sera pas plus vrai que toutes les anciennes histoires où l'on représentait invariablement les mahométans comme des monstres. [...] Les réflexions de l'auteur m'ont irrité tout le temps. Est-ce qu'on a besoin de faire des réflexions sur l'esclavage? Montrez-le, voilà tout. [...] Mme Stowe a exploité la manie-égalitaire. (Flaubert, *Correspondance* 2: 203–4, 599)

(It should be added that Flaubert's stance has nothing to do with Napoléon III's future support for the South in the American Civil War.)

Moreover, and despite his generally strong respect for Victor Hugo—the great exile from Napoléon III's régime—Flaubert felt that the elder author's *Les Misérables* (1862) was a farrago of well-meaning, but sentimental, improbabilities: "Ce livre est fait pour la crapule catholico-socialiste, pour toute la vermine philosophico-évangélique. [...] Décidément ce livre, malgré de beaux morceaux, et ils sont rares, est enfantin. [...] C'était un bien beau sujet pourtant, mais quel calme il aurait fallu et quelle envergure scientifique" (Flaubert, *Correspondance* 3: 236). Perhaps these missing qualities could be supplied by himself, in such an alternative Condition-of-France novel as *L'Éducation sentimentale*. Flaubert's career coincided with the régime, and after its demise (in the wake of the Franco-Prussian War of 1870) with the early years of the Third Republic. Napoléon III's period was known as the Second Empire and was regarded by skeptical souls as a frivolous parody of the First: the nephew simply couldn't reprise the glories of the uncle. As Karl Marx put it: "Hegel remarks somewhere that all the great events and characters of world history occur, so to speak, twice. He forgot to add: the first time as tragedy, the second as farce" (Marx 146). From his exile in the Channel Islands, Victor Hugo issued his condemnation of a régime that was possibly farcical and certainly sinister in its authoritarianism: the title of his pamphlet was *Napoléon le petit* (1851). For his part, Flaubert maintained his customary aloofness from it all: "Laissons l'Empire marcher, fermons notre porte, montons au plus haut de notre tour d'ivoire, sur la dernière marche, le plus près du ciel" (Flaubert, *Correspondance* 2: 180). That "tour d'ivoire" would find a more melancholy echo in a later item of his correspondence.

Then came the first great test of his relationship with the France beyond his desk at Croisset's "tour d'ivoire": the prosecution of *Madame Bovary*. There were times when Flaubert felt that he had done rather well out of it. "La police s'est méprise," he wrote to his brother Achille shortly before the acquittal of February 1857, "elle croyait s'en prendre au premier roman venu et à un petit grimaud littéraire; or, il se trouve que mon roman passe maintenant (et en partie grâce à la persécution) pour un chef-d'œuvre" (Flaubert, *Correspondance* 2: 670). Flaubert's fellow-persecutee Baudelaire was less fortunate. A sense of solidarity grew between the two writers, and indeed Baudelaire provides a touchstone for subtler aspects of Flaubert's alienation from his times. The poet's "Une Charogne," where the rotting corpse of a dog can be taken partly as an image of the general corruption, finds more than a hint of itself in the later pages of Flaubert's last, unfinished novel, *Bouvard et Pécuchet*. Flaubert praised Baudelaire for qualities to which he aspired in his own work: "J'aime votre âpreté, avec ses délicatesses de langage, qui la font valoir comme des damasquinures sur une lame fine" (Flaubert, *Correspondance* 2: 744).

Napoléon III's Prefect of the Seine *département*, Baron Haussmann, ruthlessly pulled down the old city of Paris to make way for brash new boulevards. Baudelaire's "Le Cygne" laments the changes: "La forme d'une ville/Change plus vite, hélas! Que le cœur d'un mortel" (Baudelaire 85).

However, even if Flaubert got off lightly by comparison with Baudelaire, the attempts at censorship still rankled. That young writer about whom Flaubert was often ambivalent, Émile Zola, wrote a novel, *Son Excellence Eugène Rougon* (1876), which retrospectively captures the authoritarian nature of the Second Empire. The careerist politician Rougon confronts a newspaper editor who has been publishing instalments of a realist novel:

> "[…] Votre feuilleton est odieux… Cette femme bien élevée qui trompe son mari, est un argument détestable contre la bonne éducation. On ne doit pas laisser dire qu'une femme comme il faut puisse commettre une faute.
> — Le feuilleton a beaucoup de succès, murmura le directeur, inquiet de nouveau. Je l'ai lu, je l'ai trouvé très-intéressant.
> — Ah ! vous l'avez lu… Eh bien ! cette malheureuse a-t-elle des remords à la fin?
> Le directeur porta la main à son front, ahuri, cherchant à se souvenir.
> — Des remords? non, je ne crois pas.
> Rougon avait ouvert la porte. Il la referma sur lui, en criant:
> — Il faut absolument qu'elle ait des remords !… Exigez de l'auteur qu'il lui donne des remords! " (Zola 287)

It's not too difficult, here, to catch an echo of the heavy-handedness directed at *Madame Bovary* in the early weeks of 1857. The historian Alistair Horne gives us a flavor of the pruderies of a period otherwise tolerant of vice in high places; as well as Flaubert's prosecution, Horne writes, "Manet was subjected to most virulent Press attacks for the 'immorality' of his *Olympia* and the *Déjeuner sur l'herbe*; and women smoking in the Tuileries were as liable to arrest as were young men bathing without a top at Trouville" (Horne 37). Flaubert himself nailed the prevailing hypocrisies in his satirical collection of typical fatuities, the *Dictionnaire des idées reçues*: "COURTISANNE *(sic)*. Est un mal nécessaire. - Sauvegarde de nos filles et de nos sœurs. Devraient être chassées impitoyablement. Sont toujours des filles du peuples débauchées par des bourgeois" (Flaubert, *Œuvres* 1005). (Post-Napoléon and during the Third Republic, which he despised, Flaubert took great delight in the fall of the Comte de Germiny, a proclaimer of conservative Catholic values, who was caught with a young proletarian male in a *pissoir*.)

Flaubert's attitude to the man at the top of the Second Empire was more nuanced. In 1864, Flaubert was actually the guest of the emperor and, in due course, was awarded the Légion d'Honneur. He was, therefore, able to observe His Imperial Majesty at close quarters and act out the results for the amusement of his irreverent young friend Zola: "Dressed as usual in his lounging robe, [Flaubert] imitated the Emperor's dragging gait, one hand behind his bowed back, another twisting his mustache, while emitting characteristically inane remarks" (Walker 121).

Flaubert could play a double game. He was also a member of the salon of the Princess Mathilde Bonaparte: the man who railed at the bourgeois establishment had a yearning to be part of it, and who could be more bourgeois than the *arrivistes* of the Bonaparte family, there on the summit of the dung-heap? From his Marxist-existentialist perspective Jean-Paul Sartre denounced Flaubert for bad faith—and indeed from a broadly Sartrean point of view, Flaubert was guilty of making a clear choice to inveigle himself with a society that he professed so loftily to deplore, guilty of having his moral cake and eating it (Sartre 1971–72, *passim*). Of his former friend Gustave Moreau (a painter whom Flaubert admired), Edgar Degas remarked caustically that he was a hermit who knew the times of the trains; much the same could be said of Flaubert.

In 1863, Flaubert met both George Sand and Ivan Turgenev, with whom he entered into the two greatest literary (and personal) friendships of his later years. Flaubert did not share Sand's democratic socialist leanings, but that did not stand in the way of deep mutual affection and respect. Flaubert regarded Sand as almost a big sister or even mother-figure (she consoled him movingly on the death of his mother in April 1872). Flaubert's correspondence with Sand is a major source of his reactions to events in the public sphere, and particularly revealing is this discovery, in 1867, of a group of people whom he regarded as fellow-aliens:

> Je me suis pâmé, il y a huit jours, devant un campement de Bohémiens qui s'étaient établis à Rouen.—Voilà la troisième fois que j'en vois.—Et toujours avec un nouveau plaisir. L'admirable, c'est qu'ils excitaient la *Haine* des bourgeois, bien qu'inoffensifs comme des moutons. Je me suis fait très mal voir de la foule en leur donnant quelques sols.—Et j'ai entendu de jolis mots à la Prudhomme. Cette

haine-là tient à quelque chose de très profond et de complexe. On la retrouve chez tous les *gens d'ordre*. C'est la haine que l'on porte au Bédouin, à l'Hérétique, au Philosophe, au solitaire, au poète, et il y a de la peur dans cette haine. Moi qui suis toujours pour les minorités, elle m'exaspère.—Il est vrai que beaucoup de choses m'exaspèrent. Du jour où je ne serai plus indigné, je tomberai à plat, comme une poupée à qui on retire son bâton.

(Flaubert, Correspondance 3: 653–4)

This is very much Flaubert the romantic rebel from a privileged class rather than the serious political activist. It's a syndrome that Raymond Williams has called "negative identification," whereby the outcasts who are the object of the identification are not really considered in their own right, but are a screen on which the rebel can project his frustrations in an essentially superficial and callow sense of pseudo-solidarity. Negative identification, writes Williams, "has been responsible for a great deal of adolescent socialism and radicalism, in particular in the adolescent who is breaking away from [...] the social standards of his own class." Williams takes an example from the novel *The Unclassed* (1884) by the English realist George Gissing, where a disillusioned intellectual smiles at the radical posturings of his youth: "I identified myself with the poor and ignorant; I did not make their cause my own, but my own cause theirs" (Williams 178). George Sand possessed patience as well as wisdom in her willingness to be a sounding-board for Flaubert's effusions.

By 1869, Flaubert was entering the final and darkest phases of his life, his art and his responses to the outside world. This was the year in which *L'Éducation sentimentale* appeared; it is considered by many—including the present writer—to be his greatest novel. Five years earlier, he had heralded the project in a letter to his friend Mademoiselle Leroyer de Chantepie: "Je veux faire l'histoire morale des hommes de ma génération; «sentimentale» serait plus vrai. C'est un livre d'amour, de passion; mais de passion telle qu'elle peut exister maintenant, c'est-à-dire inactive" (Flaubert, *Correspondance* 3: 409). Insofar as it offers a sampling of social, economic, and political types as distinct from its main character,

---

the ineffectual Frédéric Moreau with his unsatisfactory love affairs, *L'Éducation sentimentale* fulfils the wider implications of "l'histoire […] de ma génération." Jacques Arnoux the art-dealer and husband of Frédéric's ideal woman, is the archetype of the conniving businessman with a crassly genial front to the world (and not unlike Napoléon III in that respect): in Scotland we'd call him a chancer. Monsieur Dambreuse, husband of another object of Frédéric's skirt-chasing, is an aristocratic banker utterly dedicated to the pursuit of money: "l'oreille dans tous les bureaux, la main dans toutes les entreprises, à l'affût des bonnes occasions, subtil comme un Grec et laborieux comme un Auvergnat, il avait amassé une fortune que l'on disait considérable […] Une énergie impitoyable reposait dans ses yeux glauques, plus froids que des yeux de verre" (Flaubert, *Œuvres* 50–51). Then there is Sénécal, the doctrinaire socialist who is supposed to be the defender of the working class, and in diametric opposition to the foregoing, but who turns out to be merely the unsmiling authoritarian who will uphold whichever status quo best serves his personal interests. To Flaubert—and in this he was more prophetic than Marx—the proletariat were as narrow and grasping in their aspirations as the class above them: "Moi, je comprends dans ce mot de «bourgeois» les bourgeois en blouse comme les bourgeois en redingote" (Flaubert, *Correspondance* 3: 642).

When Henri Céard, one of a new generation of writers, visited Flaubert to tell him how much he admired *L'Éducation sentimentale*, the master countered: "—N'empêche, […] c'est un livre condamné, mon bon ami, parce qu'il ne fait pas ça." Céard described how Flaubert then joined his hands together in the form of a pyramid, and explained to his young friend: "—Le public veut des œuvres qui exaltent ses illusions, tandis que l'*Éducation sentimentale*…" Céard continues: "Il renversa ses grandes mains, fit le geste que tous les rêves renversés tombaient dans un trou sans espoir" (Deffoux & Zavie 125).

Ten years earlier, as if in desolate anticipation of that gesture, he had written to Mlle Leroyer de Chantepie:

Je suis sûr que le public va rester indifférent à cette collection de chefs-d'œuvre! Son niveau moral est tellement bas, maintenant! On pense au caoutchouc durci, aux chemins de fer, aux expositions, etc., à toutes les choses du pot-au-feu et du bien-être; mais la poésie, l'idéal, l'Art, les grands élans et les nobles discours, allons donc! (Flaubert, *Correspondance* 3: 46)

The year 1869, when *L'Éducation sentimentale* was published, was also the year of the death of an artist whom Flaubert admired for his integrity and disdain for the philistines: Hector Berlioz, who had so admired *Salammbô* (whose setting, Carthage, was also that of Berlioz's grandest of grand operas, *Les Troyens*). Berlioz had been cold-shouldered by Second Empire Paris and had made his reputation elsewhere in Europe: a notable example of the prophet without honor in his own country. By contrast, Jacques Offenbach, the prolific composer of light operas, such as *Orphée aux enfers* (1858) and *La Belle Hélène* (1866), excited only Flaubert's contempt, and was still very much alive and popular. As regards the visual arts, while Flaubert did not set himself up as an art critic in the manner of his colleagues Baudelaire and Zola (the latter of whom vigorously championed the impressionists against an obtuse art establishment), he defended the early-symbolist Gustave Moreau, whose *Salomé dansant devant Hérode* (1876) would have an obvious appeal to the future author of "Hérodias." Here was an artist, he wrote, whom "beaucoup de nos amis n'ont pas, selon moi, suffisament admiré" (Flaubert, *Correspondance* 3: 807).

The year 1870 saw the outbreak of the Franco-Prussian War. To George Sand, Flaubert expressed his disgust and despair: "C'est l'envie de se battre pour se battre. Je pleure les ponts coupés, les tunnels défoncés, tout ce travail humain perdu, enfin une négation si radicale!" (Flaubert, *Correspondance* 4: 211). Yet though he deplored the war-fever of his fellow French, he decided to act in the country's defense by becoming a lieutenant of his local militia and drilling his men (there is perhaps more than a hint of self-mockery in *Bouvard et Pécuchet*, where a rag-tag platoon of village worthies are put through their paces).

Paris was under siege. Flaubert lamented the fate of the city that, in his fashion, he had come to love: "je le trouve héroïque. Mais, si nous le retrouvons, ce ne sera plus notre Paris. Tous les amis que j'y avais sont morts ou disparus. Je n'ai plus de centre" (Flaubert, *Correspondance* 4: 265). Given his low opinion of the working class as no better than the bourgeoisie (if not actually worse), he fulminated against the further depredations, as he saw them, of the Commune. His friend Maxime du Camp records how he accompanied Flaubert, in June 1871, through the center of the ruined city. Flaubert turned to him and said, "Si l'on avait compris *L'Éducation sentimentale*, rien tout cela ne serait arrivé" (Du Camp 474).

It was in April of 1871 that Flaubert made one of the most quoted statements of his extreme misanthropy: "Au Paganisme a succédé le Christianisme. Nous entrons maintenant dans le *Muflisme*" (Flaubert, *Correspondance* 4: 313). There could be no more devastating rejection of the nineteenth century's complacent belief in Progress with a capital P. To his few remaining intimates, it seemed, he could combine the warmth of his personal affection with his vomit-inducing detestation of most of humanity: the effect is—oddly—both disturbing and pitiable. Writing in November 1872 to Ivan Turgenev, the Russian novelist for whom he felt an intense brotherly love, he returned to an image that he had earlier deployed in less melancholy fashion; from the topmost stair, there was no more opportunity to view the stars: "J'ai toujours tâché de vivre dans une tour d'ivoire. Mais une marée de merde en bat les murs, à la faire crouler" (Flaubert, *Correspondance* 4: 605).

George Sand died in June 1876. Flaubert himself was running out of time as he wrestled with *Bouvard et Pécuchet*, which would appear posthumously five years later. To take a break from that "espèce d'encyclopédie critique en farce" (Flaubert, *Correspondance* 4: 559), he wrote his *Trois contes*, containing the (relatively) gentle "Un Cœur simple," the haunting "La Légende de saint Julien l'Hospitalier," and the sexily bloody "Hérodias." His remaining literary friend of the two from 1863, Turgenev, set to work on a Russian translation of the second of the tales.

If Flaubert felt increasingly isolated, that did not stop him from keeping himself up to date on the works of his contemporaries, including those of generations beyond his own. He continued to be mixed in his views on Zola: of *L'Assommoir* he expressed his dislike and felt that its author was adhering too strictly to his doctrine of naturalism: "Le *Système* l'égare. Il a des Principes qui lui rétrécissent la cervelle. [....] Quant à la poésie et au style, qui sont les deux éléments éternels, jamais il n'en parle!" (Flaubert, *Correspondance* 5: 142–3). That statement of December 1876, in a letter to Turgenev, sums up the essential differences between Flaubert and Zola and warns against lazy reductions of the two to something called "French realism." Just weeks before his death on May 8, 1880, however, Flaubert offered ample praise—if with reservations—to Zola's most recent novel: "Je trouve que *Nana* contient des choses merveilleuses: [...] et la fin qui est *épique*. C'est un colosse qui a les pieds malpropres, mais c'est un colosse" (Flaubert, *Correspondance* 5: 886). He was also impressed by the story "Boule de Suif" by his young friend Guy de Maupassant, and told him so (Flaubert, *Correspondance* 5: 807).

Turgenev introduced Flaubert to a masterpiece from his own country, Tolstoy's *War and Peace*, and it is fitting that the life of one great writer should close as he absorbs the work of another. "Quel peintre et quel psychologue!" Flaubert enthuses to Turgenev in a letter of January 1880. "Il me semble qu'il a parfois des choses à la Shakespeare?" (Flaubert, *Correspondance* 5: 790). That latter comment takes on a retrospective irony, given Tolstoy's low opinion of Shakespeare; it was as well, perhaps, that Tolstoy wasn't around to answer Flaubert's rhetorical question.

With that other of the two Russian giants, Dostoevsky, Turgenev did not get on. Flaubert would not have known of Dostoevsky's *Notes from the Underground* of 1864, but in many respects, it anticipates the savage satire of *Bouvard et Pécuchet*, which is predicated on the futility of human endeavor. Dostoevsky's Underground Man wants to stick out his tongue at the nineteenth century's Crystal Palace of "Progress" and perversely suggests that it would be charming if two multiplied by two could equal five. Flaubert departed from the scene with a grim smile at his two autodidactic clerks and their bungling attempts to attain scientific certitude in a world where nothing was of value—nothing, that is, except as material for art.

Works Cited

Baudelaire, Charles. *Œuvres completes*. Vol. 1. Paris: Gallimard, 1975.

Deffoux, Léon & Émile Zavie. *Le Groupe de Médan*. Paris: Payot, 1920.

Du Camp, Maxime. *Souvenirs littéraires*. Vol. 2. Paris: Hachette, 1883.

Flaubert, Gustave. *Correspondance*. Ed. Jean Bruneau. 5 vols. Paris: Gallimard, 1973–2007.

_____. *Œuvres*. Vol. 2. Paris: Gallimard, 1952.

Horne, Alistair. *The Fall of Paris: The Siege and the Commune 1870–71*. Harmondsworth, UK: Penguin, 1981.

Marx, Karl. *Surveys from Exile*. Harmondsworth, UK: Penguin, 1973.

Sartre, Jean-Paul. *L'Idiot de la famille*. 2 vols. Paris: Gallimard, 1971–72.

Shattuck, Roger. *Proust*. [London:] Fontana/Collins, 1974.

Walker, Philip. *Zola*. London: Routledge & Kegan Paul, 1985.

Williams, Raymond. *Culture and Society 1780–1950*. Harmondsworth, UK: Penguin, 1961.

Zola, Émile. *Son Excellence Eugène Rougon*. Paris: Gallimard, 1982.

"Ce grand *Trottoir roulant*:" The Critical Reception of Gustave Flaubert

Tom Hubbard

The first arena for discussion of Flaubert was a court of law. In January 1857, *Madame Bovary* was on trial for its perceived offense to public morality and religion. In due course, the novel would be judged on a wider—and more sophisticated—range of criteria, but the implications of the trial have no little relevance nearer (and in) our own times.

"Qui est-ce qui lit le roman de M. Flaubert? Sont-ce des hommes qui s'occupent d'économie politique ou sociale?" asked the prosecutor, Ernest Pinard, before going on to provide the answer to his own question. "Non! les pages légères de *Madame Bovary* tombent en des mains plus légères, dans les mains de jeunes filles, quelquefois de femmes mariées" (Flaubert, *Œuvres completes* 479). A little over a hundred years later, in 1960, D.H. Lawrence's novel *Lady Chatterley's Lover* was receiving similar attention in an English court. Almost echoing Pinard, the English prosecutor Mervyn Griffith-Jones revealed that certain patronizing, patriarchal assumptions had not altogether disappeared: "[…] would you approve of your young sons, young daughters—because girls can read as well as boys—reading this book. Is it a book that you would even wish your wife or your servants to read?" (Rolph 17). In the event, both books survived their respective ordeals: there are times when enlightened attitudes prevail. Nevertheless, prosecutor Pinard sought to reduce Flaubert's novel to "la poésie de l'adultère" (Flaubert, *Œuvres completes* 471). That seemed odd to other readers then and since: had not Flaubert demonstrated how little "poésie" could be discovered in the affairs of Emma Bovary? One of the most quotable lines in Flaubert's novel is this: "Emma retrouvait dans l'adultère toutes les platitudes du mariage" (Flaubert, *Œuvres completes* 406). Poetry yields memorable lines: they're rarer in prose fiction. At the time, the defense counsel, Maître Jules Sénard

---

argued that *Madame Bovary* was in fact an extremely moral book; a not dissimilar defense was made on behalf of *Lady Chatterley's Lover*. The tables could be successfully turned.

Beyond the trial, there were eminent critics and writers who were happy to advance the counter-intuitive view that *Madame Bovary* was far from being a book that would corrupt and deprave the vulnerable. Henry James remarked that "It is a book adapted for the reverse of what is called family reading, and yet we remember thinking, the first time we read it, in the heat of our admiration for its power, that it would make the most useful of Sunday-school tracts." James went on to cite a French source, a satire by Hippolyte Taine, in which there takes place "a conversation at a dinner party between an English spinster of didactic habits and a decidedly audacious Frenchman. He begs to recommend to her a work that he has lately been reading and that cannot fail to win the approval of all persons interested in the propagation of virtue. The lady lends a sympathetic ear, and he gives a rapid sketch of the tale—the history of a wicked woman who goes from one abomination to another, until at last the judgment of Heaven descends upon her, and, blighted and blasted, she perishes miserably. The lady grasps her pencil and notebook and begs for the name of the edifying volume, and the gentleman leans across the dinner table and answers with a smile—'*Madame Bovary*, or, The Consequences of Misconduct.'" (James, *French Poets* 255). James's Scottish colleague and close friend, Robert Louis Stevenson, concurred, if with a self-consciously over-the-top manner of expressing his view: "When Flaubert wrote *Madame Bovary*, I believe he thought chiefly of a somewhat morbid realism; and behold! the book turned in his hands into a masterpiece of appalling morality" (Stevenson 59).

The first major professional literary critic—as distinct from a lawyer—to respond at length to *Madame Bovary* was Charles Sainte-Beuve. His method could best be described as reptilian: he seemed to praise and blame simultaneously. For Sainte-Beuve, *Madame Bovary* was a pioneering novel, but a cruel one:

[…] je crois reconnaître des signes littéraires nouveaux: science, esprit d'observation, maturité, force, un peu de dureté. Ce sont les caractères que semblent affecter les chefs de file des générations nouvelles. Fils et frère de médecins distingués, M. Gustave Flaubert tient la plume comme d'autres le scalpel. Anatomistes et physiologistes, je vous retrouve partout! (Sainte-Beuve 1857)

Such an assessment would also be taken up by a caricaturist who depicted Flaubert as a scientifically-aloof dissector, cutting open the corpse of Emma Bovary and brandishing her blood-dripping heart impaled on a surgical instrument.

Remarks on Flaubert's impersonal method could easily mesh with moralistic disapproval—as if Flaubert could be both indifferent and sadistic at the same time. In a reprise, as it were, of prosecutor Pinard's patriarchal stance, critics deplored the novel's lack of sympathetic characters and, in particular, considered that the mediocrity of Charles Bovary meant that his wife was deprived of a guide and protector. English commentators had a strong tendency to regard themselves as more reliable guardians of morality than the French who, according to prevalent clichés, were hopelessly and frivolously degenerate—against all the evidence that the French, when they had a mind to it, could be just as puritanical and prudish as the English.

Even Matthew Arnold, the most urbane of English critics, is harsh on Flaubert's novel, on the grounds that it is "a work of *petrified feeling*" (Arnold's italics). Arnold is too worldly and unhysterical to labor any objection to the book for sexual offensiveness, but he is nevertheless morally-driven in his argument that Flaubert is cold-hearted, even cruel, towards his Emma: "he pursues her without pity or pause, as with malignity; he is harder upon her himself than any reader even, I think, will be inclined to be." Arnold prefers Tolstoy's *Anna Karenina* to Flaubert's *Madame Bovary*—indeed, his essay chiefly concerns Tolstoy's novel—as a more expansive, generous, more genuinely tragic book, as indeed a more charming book than Flaubert's: "Much in *Anna Karénine* is painful, much is unpleasant, but nothing is of a nature to trouble the senses, or to please those who wish their senses troubled" (Arnold 275–6). In the present volume, Priscilla Meyer compares Tolstoy's and Flaubert's novels at greater length and depth.

For a novelist generally regarded as a father-figure of realism in fiction, Flaubert received one of the early negative assessments of *Madame Bovary* from a perhaps surprising quarter, in the journal *Réalisme*. In his review here, Louis-Edmond Duranty complained that Flaubert had reduced everything to a dead level: no detail was rendered as more important than another (a phenomenon that would for many become a virtue in the twentieth-century *nouveau roman*).

> Il n'y a ni émotion, ni sentiment, ni vie dans ce roman, mais une grande force d'arithméticien qui a supputé et rassemblé tout ce qu'il peut y avoir de gestes, de pas ou d'accidents de terrain, dans des personnages, des événements et des pays *donnés*. […] toujours *description* matérielle et jamais *impression*. (Duranty 1857)

This pretty well accorded with the consensus of Flaubert as the cold dissector, but who was moreover something of a desiccated calculating machine. Flaubert might well have felt that if Duranty's preferences amounted to the aesthetic philosophy of this journal called *Réalisme*, then such was not for him; in any case, Flaubert maintained that he served not realism, but art. It was fitting, then, that some months later in 1857, Flaubert found his most ardent champion in the poet Charles Baudelaire. Both men held to a lofty conception of art and a concomitant disdain for the philistine crowd. The poet's own *Les Fleurs du mal* was hauled before the courts, but the verdict was an unhappier one than that for *Madame Bovary*. If anyone was going to challenge the repetitiously negative critics of Flaubert's novel, it had to be Baudelaire. One bold spirit recognized another: for Baudelaire, *Madame Bovary* was "une gageure, une vraie gageure, un pari, comme toutes les œuvres d'art." Baudelaire scorned the moralizers: "Une veritable œuvre d'art n'a pas besoin de réquisitoire. La logique de l'œuvre suffit à toutes les postulations de la morale, et c'est au lecteur a tirer les conclusions de la conclusion." Far from being merely the pathetic, deluded woman-from-the-sticks who goes to the bad, Emma Bovary is for Baudelaire "vraiment grande"; yes, "son imagination" runs away with her, but "elle se donne magnifiquement, généreusement, d'une manière toute masculine, à des drôles qui ne sont pas égaux, exactement comes les poètes se livrent à des drôlesses" (Baudelaire, *Œuvres* 1958: 1008–10). "Imagination," for Baudelaire, was the queen of the faculties, it was the source of all poetry and art: he clearly felt that Emma, in some sense, was a kindred spirit, an exile in her/his own land. If Flaubert could confess that "Madame Bovary, c'est moi," Baudelaire might have added, "c'est moi, aussi." Baudelaire yearned for "le voyage" to a land blessed with "calme, luxe et volupté"; as Victor Brombert has observed, "*Anywhere out of the World*—the title of Baudelaire's prose-poem—could sum up Emma's chronic yearning for the exotic" (Brombert 59). Baudelaire goes on to liken Emma to "une petite lady Macbeth accouplée a un capitaine insuffisant" (Baudelaire, *Œuvres* 1958: 1009). This is telling: Baudelaire is attracted to the "Idéal," even if this contravenes conventional bourgeois morality, even if this means admiring Shakespeare's "fiend-like" Scottish queen: "Ce qu'il faut à ce cœur profond comme un abîme,/ C'est vous, Lady Macbeth, âme puissante au crime" (Baudelaire, *Œuvres* 1975: 22).

It was to another strong, sexy woman—and like Lady Macbeth from the distant, heroic past—that Flaubert turned for his next novel, *Salammbô*. Its most sustained critique came from the ubiquitous Sainte-Beuve, who regretted that Flaubert had not given his new work a contemporary setting, instead of ancient Carthage: "Comment voulez-vous que j'aille m'intéresser â cette guerre perdue, enterée dans les défilés ou les sables de l'Afrique […]?" The whole thing, according to Sainte-Beuve, was too laboriously and artificially put together: "tout ce livre est pavé non seulement de belles intentions, mais de cailloux de toute couleur et de pierres précieuses." (Sainte-Beuve, "*Salammbô*")

In other words, exquisite stuff, but hardly engaging. Flaubert was, as it were, ransacking the distant past to no justifiable purpose. If *Salammbô* was aspiring to be a historical novel, it was failing: the master and founder of the historical novel, Walter Scott, "vivait dans son Écosse" and was able to bring to life the events and the personalities of a past that belonged to his people's collective memory over several generations. By contrast, Flaubert was a mere antiquarian, poring over books in search of his material: such erudition, as deployed in *Salammbô*, could only leave us cold. Too much pastiche, too much pedantry.

Moreover, Sainte-Beuve reprised his earlier assessment of *Madame Bovary* and "un peu de dureté," which he found there. This time, however, Flaubert was evidencing more than "un peu de dureté" in *Salammbô*. Sainte-Beuve objected to the gratuitous cruelty that pervaded the new novel: "La peur de la sensiblerie, de la pleurnicherie bourgeoise l'a jeté, de parti pris, dans l'excès contraire; il cultive l'atrocité" (Sainte-Beuve, "*Salammbô*").

One could conclude that, despite Sainte-Beuve's negativity (for the most part), he was actually paying the novel a compliment by devoting three long articles to it over successive weeks in the journal *Le Constitutionnel* of December 1862! However, Flaubert could barely contain his fury, and in his letter of self-defense to Sainte-Beuve, one senses the strain of maintaining a certain dignity. (There was a preparedness to concede that *Salammbô* had its faults—"Le piédestal est trop grand pour la statue.") Flaubert protested that "j'ai voulu fixer un mirage en appliquant à l'Antiquité les procèdes du roman modern, et j'ai tâché d'être simple." He repudiated the charge of digging up dead things and leaving them dead:

> Je me moque de l'archéologie! Si la couleur n'est pas une, si les détails détonnent, si les mœurs ne dérivent pas de la religion et les faits des passions, si les caractères ne sont pas suivis, si les costumes ne sont pas appropriés aux usages et les architectures au climat, s'il n'y a pas, en un mot, harmonie, je suis dans le faux. Sinon, non. Tout se tient. (Flaubert, *Correspondance* 3: 284, 276, 282–3)

In spite of Sainte-Beuve, *Salammbô* had its early champions, not least the poet Théophile Gautier: "Ce n'est pas un livre d'histoire, ce n'est pas un roman, c'est un *poème èpique*" (Gautier 1862). Comparisons with Walter Scott, then, would seem to be superfluous. There was an even more dramatic (quite literally, dramatic) expression of enthusiasm for *Salammbô*, with (in effect) a redefinition of its genre. Initially, this was not intended favorably: Sainte-Beuve suggested (in his slyly indirect manner) that *Salammbô* possessed an operatic quality; in their journal, the brothers Jules and Edmond Goncourt had said as much when they described one of the principal characters in Flaubert's novel: "son Mathô n'est, au fond, qu'un tenor d'opéra dans un poème barbare" (Goncourt 373). But it was a composer of operas, Hector Berlioz, who paid passionate tribute to the book: "ce style calme dans sa force immense et si coloré, qu'il donne au lecteur des éblouissements" (Berlioz 1862). Berlioz composed one of the greatest operas of all time, *Les Troyens*, set—like *Salammbô*—in ancient Carthage: he knew what he was talking about. There was much discussion, during Flaubert's lifetime and not without his approval, of a possible opera based on his book; eventually, in 1890—ten years after Flaubert's death— Ernest Reyer's *Salammbô*, "opèra en 5 actes, d'après le roman de Gustave Flaubert" was premièred at the Théâtre de la Monnaie in Brussels. It's a strong, sensuous work, eminently worthy of the original, and for good measure, the ear picks up hints of Berlioz's own Carthaginian masterpiece.

With *L'Éducation sentimentale*, Flaubert returned to the contemporary scene, but that did not necessarily win over the critics. The novel was attacked for its perceived vulgarity; for its unheroic hero (the conclusion—where Frédéric and Deslauriers consider their finest hour to have been their failed visit, as adolescents, to a brothel—was particularly deplored); there were too many descriptive passages; the book had no clear plot. Moreover, Flaubert had satirized all ideological standpoints, so their partisans were quick to condemn him. For example, Amélie Bosquet—a feminist herself—was offended by the portrayal of La Vatnaz, the novel's feminist participant in the 1848 Revolution.

The most thoughtful of the detractors was Edmond Scherer, who questioned the relevance of the book's title; he would have preferred it to have been called *Les Bonnes fortunes du M. Frédéric*. He tacitly accorded with the conventional view that the book was all over the place, even if he expressed that opinion more intelligently and memorably than most:

> L'ouvrage n'est pas composé. Nous voyons passer devant nous des personnages, des scènes, mais comme au hasard. On dirait une suite de médaillons, une collection de photographies, admirables épreuves, il est vrai, découpées dans la réalité à l'emporte-pièce d'une pleine lumière, mais dont chacune est là pour son compte. C'est une collection, une série, ce n'est pas un tableau. (Scherer 1869)

Scherer does, however, pay strong homage to Flaubert's style.

The most downbeat critic in the English-speaking world was Henry James, who found *L'Éducation sentimentale* to be "mechanical and inanimate" and the reading experience "like masticating ashes and sawdust" (James, *French Poets* 258, 267). Some decades later, James is still far from won over by the novel, which he now (1902) describes as "an epic without air, without wings to lift it; [it] reminds us in fact more than anything else of a huge balloon, all of silk pieces strongly sewn together and patiently blown up, but that absolutely refuses to leave the ground" (James, *Selected* 265). In contrast, the Irish-born novelist and critic George Moore made dramatically large claims for *L'Éducation sentimentale*. It was one of these books that increased a reader's perceptions of life, as distinct "from those which have merely enabled him to pass the time"; not only that, it was "a new force, a new influence that was not there before, and will be there for ever—the time when it should be forgotten is unthinkable [...] The mechanical critics have not perceived that the impact of this book is like that of a religion; that it forms the souls of at least thirty or forty readers in every generation." Moore's choice of the word "mechanical" takes on no little irony when it's compared to James's use of the same word.

George Moore was an ardent admirer of the music of Richard Wagner, and he praises *L'Éducation sentimentale*—in terms its author would have welcomed—for a structural complexity that animates the book at a level deeper than its unfolding narrative and the interaction of its characters. That is to say, for Moore, the novel can be appreciated as an abstract composition, like a piece of music, irrespective of its more obviously verbal (and therefore referential) qualities: "The texture is woven as closely as [... Wagner's music-drama] 'Tristan'—echoes, transformations, modulations, never a

---

Ce grand *Trottoir roulant*   47

full close, always a suspended cadence" (Moore 38–59, *passim*). Wagner challenged conventional notions of music, and Moore constructs a subtle argument to demonstrate that Flaubert is doing likewise as regards the novel: the listener/reader is him/herself challenged not to expect neat resolutions. The nineteenth century's certainties are giving way to the fluidities of modernity, and all the arts are undergoing radical transformations.

Back in France, *L'Éducation sentimentale* had its no less eloquent and forward-looking champions. Émile Zola belonged to that generation of novelists who would succeed Flaubert. An artist who is also a critic will be prone to justify his own aesthetic in the course of commenting on another artist, and Zola's own practice was to emphasize heredity and environment as determinants of his characters' actions. The school of naturalists, of which Zola was the leading exponent, held that we could, on no account, abstract characters from their genes or their surroundings. Accordingly, Zola stoutly defends the descriptive passages of *L'Éducation sentimentale*: "c'est par le dehors qu'il nous fait connaître le dedans. [...] les paysages proprement dits, dans Gustave Flaubert, ne sont-ils pas nécessaires aux personnages? Si l'on veut faire connaître un homme, il faut le montrer dans l'air qu'il respire" (Zola). Anticipating George Moore somewhat, the poet Théodore de Banville read *L'Éducation sentimentale* not so much in Zola's proto-naturalist terms but rather as a work of protomodernism—not that Banville, in 1880, would have used such terminology, but there's more than a hint here of how fiction would change in the twentieth century: "[Flaubert] devait, dans l'*Education sentimentale*, montrer par avance ce qui n'existera que dans bien longtemps: je veux dire le roman *non romancé*, triste, indécis, mystérieux comme la vie elle-même, et se contentant, comme elle, de dénouements d'autant plus terribles qu'ils ne sont pas *matériellement* dramatiques" (Banville 160). This is amply confirmed by the practice of Marcel Proust in his masterpiece *Á la recherché du temps perdu* (1913–27) with its innovative techniques, with its representations of time and consciousness, producing effects that are at once psychologically penetrating and deeply moving. A half-century earlier, Flaubert had pointed the way, as

---

48

Proust acknowledged in his essay on *L'Éducation sentimentale*: "ce grand *Trottoir roulant*, que sont les pages de Flaubert, un defilement continu, monotone, morne, indéfini" (Proust 587).

The 1847 version of *La Tentation de saint Antoine* was dimly received by Flaubert's friends Louis Bouilhet and Maxime du Camp; the final version did not appear until 1874. The tale of a saint living a hermit-like existence in the desert, but subject to the attractions of worldly pleasures, drew many strong comparisons with Goethe's *Faust*, itself based on the tradition of an introverted scholar, Doctor Faust, who finds himself making a pact with the demon Mephistopheles. The German-speaking world, to which the legend belonged, was bound to have its opinions on Flaubert's new work.

The Faustian comparisons didn't escape the French critics, who variously preferred the presentation of Flaubert's St. Antony to that of Goethe's Faust, or who contrasted Antony's piety to Faust's amorality and materialism. The German critics, for their part, resented such claims of St. Antony's superiority over their man, as if the frivolous French were attempting, via literary criticism, to obtain revenge for their defeat by Germany in the Franco-Prussian War of 1870. (Freienmuth von Helms, *passim*).

There was even a claim by a German Protestant critic that *La Tentation de saint Antoine* was pervaded by Roman Catholic fanaticism. Aren't we getting a strong sense of culture clash— the German Protestant work ethic, its drive, its practicality, its discipline, as against French Catholic decadence in the form of self-indulgent mysticism? One French critic, Émile Faguet, seems almost tacitly to admit as much:

> Faust se promène par le monde. Donc il est actif, il est un coureur d'aventures, il est curieux, il va de l'avant, il finira par l'activité proprement dite, celle qui crée quelque chose, et, en elfet, c'est bicn par la qu'il finit. Saint Anloine est immobile. Les motifs d'agir ou les motifs de penser vicnnent le chercher. Il ne les suit pas. Il est tout passif et il a une résistance toute d'inertie. C'est ce qu'il doit être. (Faguet 57)

However, the German-speaking world, as well as the Western world more generally, would soon be faced with fresh insights that delved deep below the traditional cultural fault-lines, or at least promised to interpret them anew. These explorations could be summed up as the new science—if science it was—of psychology and something called the unconscious mind. If there were varying degrees of human consciousness (or sub- or un-consciousness), literary criticism would have to take note. Literature itself was already doing just that, as a young Viennese medical doctor called Sigmund Freud discovered in 1883. The future "father of psychology" read *La Tentation de saint Antoine* while traveling by train to the Austrian Alps:

> I was already deeply moved by the splendid panorama, and now on top of it all came this book which in the most condensed fashion and with unsurpassable vividness throws at one's head the whole trashy world. It calls up not only the great problems of knowledge, but the real riddles of life, all the conflicts of feelings and impulses; and it confirms the awareness of our perplexity in the mysteriousness that reigns everywhere. (qtd. in Jones I: 174–175)

Freud was Jewish, but Austro-German Jewish, and as a good Austro-German, he follows previous commentators by making an allusion to Goethe's *Faust*, and in particular its scene of the Witches' Sabbath, the "Walpurgisnacht." Freud finds such a Walpurgisnacht in *La Tentation de saint Antoine* and praises "the vividness of the hallucinations, the way in which the same impressions surge up, transform themselves, and suddenly disappear" (qtd. in Brown 481–2). With these statements, Freud dramatically, if unconsciously (!), signals a new kind of novel, the psychological novel, such as would be taken up in the twentieth century by Marcel Proust and James Joyce. The implication is that Flaubert was there first.

By contrast, in 1898, the Irish poet W.B. Yeats takes a backward glance, naming *La Tentation de saint Antoine* as "the last great dramatic invention of the old romanticism" (Yeats 38). From whatever angle one looked at it, Flaubert's novel clearly marked a turning-point in Western literature. Oddly, Henry James, who was to make his own contribution to the psychological novel, was unimpressed by the book, which he found to be all spice and no meat: "the human mind, even in indifferent health, does after all need to be *nourished*, and thrives but scantily on a regimen of pigments and sauces" (James, *Literary Reviews* 150). So much for culinary metaphors.

Trois contes was not spared hostile reviews, as from the formidable Ferdinand Brunetière, and Flaubert grumbled that Francisque Sarcey and other critics had found "Hérodias" "trop fort pour eux" (Flaubert, *Correspondance* 5: 239). However, the book was, on the whole, well received. The reliably sympathetic Théodore de Banville remarked that "les *Trois contes* ne sont pas cependant des contes détachés; ils sont unis au contraire par un lien étroit, qui est l'exaltation de la charité, de la bonté inconsciente et surnaturelle" (Banville, *Trois contes passim*). For Henry Houssaye, Flaubert in "Un Cœur simple" proved that an artist could create a marvel out of the most banal raw material: "Le limon devient marbre sous l'ébauchoir du sculpteur" (Houssaye *passim*).

The Scottish poet James Thomson, the "laureate of pessimism," who wrote *The City of Dreadful Night* (1874) was nevertheless upbeat in his assessment of "La Légende de Saint Julien l'Hospitalier," praising its "wonderful power and fertility as well as intensity of imagination" (Thomson 104). Thomson's own masterpiece possessed a visionary, hallucinatory quality, so he was likely to be well-disposed towards Flaubert's atmospheric tale, and in spite of the fact that as a staunch atheist Thomson was responding to the representation of a saint. Thomson's was one of many favorable accounts of the piece; moreover, "Hérodias" drew from Ernest Drumont this enthusiastic assessment: "Une page d'histoire se déroule ainsi devant le lecteur, étourdissante de mouvement, admirablement restituée jusqu'au moindre détail, instructive, terrible, émouvante. Dans cette composition magnifique, tout a sa place, sa signification, son importance [...]" (Drumont *passim*). There developed a consensus that "Un Cœur simple" miniaturized similar material to that of *Madame Bovary*; "La Légende de Saint Jean l'Hospitalier" to that of *La Tentation de saint Antoine*; "Hérodias" to that of *Salammbô*.

As for an emerging consensus on *Bouvard et Pécuchet*, Flaubert would not live to follow that, though he might well have felt a sense of vindication. Inevitably, there was much bemused dismissal. Henry James considered Flaubert's last, unfinished novel to be "a work as sad as something perverse and puerile done for a wager" (James 183); there is unconscious irony in this, given that Baudelaire had praised *Madame Bovary* for being just that, a wager, a piece of risk-taking, as the necessary existential prerequisite for a true work of art. Three other non-French critics, the Englishman George Saintsbury, the Irish-born Lafcadio Hearn, and the German Paul Ernst, compared *Bouvard et Pécuchet* to Jonathan Swift's *Gulliver's Travels*; Hearn and Ernst found Flaubert's satire to be as horrific as Swift's, if not more so (Saintsbury 377; Hearn 262–3; Ernst, qtd. in Freienmuth 31). D.F. Hannigan, who made the first English translation of *Bouvard et Pécuchet*, clearly found it a labor of love: "Never has the tragi-comedy of life more luminously revealed than it has been in this marvelous book." Hannigan opened his introduction by pointing out that the two books on which Flaubert worked with the greatest "pains" and "anxiety" were *La Tentation de saint Antoine* and *Bouvard et Pécuchet*; "no two books could, in many respects," he went on, "be more dissimilar" but they resembled each other in their "undercurrent of irony." (Hannigan x, ix). Another resemblance—if an ironic one— would be their common roots in the Faust legend, and indeed there is a strong case for the view that *Bouvard et Pécuchet* is a parody of Faust. The legendary German scholar traversed all areas of knowledge and concluded that his labors were pointless; Flaubert's two clerks, pursuing their researches in their amateurish, half-baked manner, reach the inevitable disillusionment. Lacking a Mephistopheles to tempt them towards grand sin, with even greater tragedy and redemption to follow, Bouvard and Pécuchet return to their former routine, in all its petty-bourgeois banality: "*Copier comme autrefois*" (Flaubert, *Œuvres* completes 987).

The most eloquent early piece on *Bouvard et Pécuchet* is by Flaubert's young protégé and fellow Norman, Guy de Maupassant:

De toutes les œuvres du magnifique écrivain, [he wrote in April 1881, just under a year after his friend's death,] celle-ci est assurément la plus profonde, la plus fouillée, la plus large; mais, pour ces raisons mêmes, elle sera peut-être la moins comprise. [...] C'est l'histoire de la faiblesse de l'intelligence humaine, une promenade dans le labyrinthe infini de l'érudition avec un fil dans la main; ce fil est la grande ironie d'un merveilleux penseur qui constate sans cesse, en tout, l'éternelle et universelle bêtise (Maupassant 201, 202).

By the turn of the nineteenth century, Flaubert criticism had moved on from the not unrelated complaints against him of (1) lack of moral compass; (2) a supposed realism that dwelt on unpleasant subjects to the exclusion of anything pleasant. More sophisticated responses took the place of such commonplaces (though not quite entirely): it was Flaubert's art, above all, that was admired. The publication of his correspondence aided this process, as it was there that Flaubert took his private (and, now, public) readers into his workshop. Henry James, himself someone who brooded much on his own practice, dubbed Flaubert "a writer's writer" (James, *Selected* 173). The master's doctrine of impersonality, and the satisfying precision of his style, were coming to the fore. Of the first, the German "anti-philosopher" Friedrich Nietzsche objected to its anti-egoism: the supposedly "selfless" devotion to *art* was a denial of *life*, and was therefore decadent (Nietzsche 67–68). Of the second, it was Maupassant who so well summed up Flaubert's uncompromising dedication to perfection: "Obsédé par cette croyance absolue qu'il n'existe qu'une manière d'exprimer une chose, un mot pour la dire, un adjectif pour la qualifier et un verbe pour l'animer, il se livrait à un labeur surhumain pour découvrir, à chaque phrase, ce mot, cette épithète et ce verbe. Il croyait ainsi à une harmonie mystérieuse des expressions [...]" (Maupassant qtd. in Flaubert, *Lettres de Gustave Flaubert* lxii). The English critic Walter Pater translated Maupassant's utterance in the course of an essay on "Style," where he devoted several pages to Flaubert. For Pater, the essence of style is found not only in knowing what to put in, but also in what to leave out: "For in truth all art does but consist in the removal of surplusage, from the last finish of the gem-engraver blowing away the last particle of invisible dust, back to the earliest divination of the finished work to be, lying somewhere, according to Michelangelo's fancy, in the rough-hewn block of stone" (Pater 16).

This assertion of a lapidary scrupulousness in the choice of words was part of the growing insistence that a novelist was as much an *artist* as were a composer, painter, and sculptor (as well as a craftsman, like the jeweler). In the first full-length monograph on Flaubert in English, J.C. Tarver remarked that "the novel, from being the resource of idle moments, the dissipation of indolent minds, a thing to be preached against, and put away on Sundays, has become the chosen instrument of the gravest thinkers of our age" (Tarver 63–4).

Of this Flaubert was the great exemplar. Flaubert's early works, *Memoires d'un fou*, *Novembre*, and the first *L'Éducation sentimentale*, at last received serious attention on the 1914 publication of Algernon Coleman's doctoral dissertation for John Hopkins University (Coleman 1914). Academics are generally the first people to recover a writer's beginnings, and though their commentaries may have little impact beyond the campuses, it could still be said that almost the full corpus of Flaubert's work had come into its own within a hundred years of his birth in 1821.

The centenary year of 1921 coincided with Proust's *Á la recherché du temps perdu* (1913–27) and Joyce's *Ulysses*. Twentieth-century criticism would yield fresh perspectives from Jean-Paul Sartre, Roland Barthes, Victor Brombert, Jonathan Culler, and a host of others, including contributors to the present volume. However, the basic tools and concepts were provided by the body of responses during the sixty-plus years from the controversial appearance of *Madame Bovary* in 1857.

Works Cited

Arnold, Matthew. *Essays in Criticism: Second Series*. London: Macmillan, 1888.

Banville, Théodore de. *Critiques*. Paris: Fasquelle, 1917.

_____. "*Trois contes* [...] par Gustave Flaubert." *Le National* (14 mai 1877).

Baudelaire, Charles. *Œuvres*. Paris: Gallimard, 1958.

_____. *Œuvres*. Paris: Gallimard, 1975.

Berlioz, Hector. "Théâtre-lyrique." *Journal des débats* (23 décembre 1862).

Brombert, Victor. *The Novels of Flaubert: A Study of Themes and Techniques*. Princeton, NJ: Princeton UP, 1966.

Brown, Frederick. *Flaubert: A Life*. New York: Little, Brown, 2006.

Coleman, A[lgernon]. *Flaubert's Literary Development in the Light of His Mémoires d'un fou, Novembre, and Éducation sentimentale (version of 1845)*. Baltimore: John Hopkins Press, 1914.

Drumont, Édouard. "Hommages et choses: Gustave Flaubert et son dernier livre." *La Liberté* (23 mai 1877).

Duranty, [Louis-Edmond]. "Nouvelles diverses." *Réalisme* (15 mars 1857).

Faguet, Émile. *Flaubert*. Paris: Hachette, 1899.

Flaubert, Gustave. *Correspondance*. Ed. Jean Bruneau. 5 vols. Paris: Gallimard, 1973–2007.

_____. *Lettres de Gustave Flaubert à George Sand. Précédées d'une étude par Guy de Maupassant*. Paris: Charpentier, 1884.

_____. *Œuvres complétes*. Vol. 3. 1851–1862. Paris: Gallimard, 2013.

Freienmuth von Helms, E.E. *German Criticism of Gustave Flaubert 1857–1930*. New York: Columbia UP, 1939.

Gautier, Théophile. "*Salammbô*, par M. Gustave Flaubert." *Le Moniteur officiel* (22 décembre 1862).

Goncourt, Edmond & Jules. *Journal des Goncourts*. Vol. 1. Paris: Charpentier, 1887.

Hannigan, D.F. "Introduction" [to his translation:] *Bouvard and Pécuchet*. London: H.S. Nichols, 1896: x–xii.

Hearn, Lafcadio. *Life and Literature*. New York: Dodd, Mead, 1917.

Houssaye, Henry. "Variétés. *Trois contes* par M. Gustave Flaubert." *Journal des débats* (21 juillet 1877).

James, Henry. *French Poets and Novelists*. London: Macmillan, 1878.

_____. *Literary Reviews and Essays on American, English and French Literature*. Ed. Albert Mordell. New York: Grove Press, 1979.

_____. *Selected Literary Criticism*. Ed. Morris Shapira. Harmondsworth: Penguin Books, 1968.

Jones, Ernest. *The Life and Work of Sigmund Freud*. 3 vols. New York: Basic Books, 1953–57.

Maupassant, Guy de. *Chroniques 1: 22 octobre 1876–23 février 1882*. Paris: 10/18, 1980.

Moore, George. "A Tragic Novel." *Cosmopolis* 7 (July 1897): 38–59.

Nietzsche, Friedrich. *The Complete Works [...]*. Vol. 8: *The Case of Wagner [etc.]*. New York: Macmillan, 1911.

Pater, Walter. *Appreciations*. London: Macmillan, 1889.

Proust, Marcel. *Contre Sainte-Beuve [...] suivi de Essais et articles*. Paris: Gallimard, 1978.

Rolph, C.H., ed. *The Trial of Lady Chatterley: Regina v. Penguin Books Limited*. Harmondsworth: Penguin Books, 1990.

Sainte-Beuve, Charles. "Causeries du lundi: *Madame Bovary* par Gustave Flaubert." *Le Moniteur universel* (4 mai 1857).

_____. "*Salammbô*, par M. Gustave Flaubert." *Le Constitutionnel* (8, 15, 22 Décembre 1862).

Saintsbury, George. *Essays on French Novelists*. London: Percival, 1891.

Scherer, Edmond. "Variétés: Le Roman de M. Flaubert." *Le Temps* (7 décembre 1869).

Stevenson, Robert Louis. *Essays Literary and Critical*. Tusitala Edition. London: Heinemann [1924].

Tarver, J.C. *Gustave Flaubert As Seen in His Works and Correspondence*. Westminster: Constable, 1895.

Thomson, James. "*Trois contes*." *The Secular Review and Secularist* (July 21, 1877): 103–4.

Yeats, W.B. *Selected Criticism*. Ed. A. Norman Jeffares. London: Macmillan, 1964.

Zola, Émile. "Causeries." *La Tribune* (28 novembre 1869).

Anna Karenina: Tolstoy's Polemic with *Madame Bovary*

Priscilla Meyer

> Rousseau and the Gospels have been the two great and beneficent influences of my life. (Lev Tolstoy, letter to Bernard Bouvier, 1905)

The richness and ambiguity of *Anna Karenina* arises from the conflict between its sympathy with both the adulteress and the family. In his novel, Tolstoy at once empathizes with Anna and reaffirms the biblical understanding of adultery as sinful, while including a vision of family that could prevent it. Tolstoy's antidote to the decadence he found in the French novel of adultery is made up of the ideals of Rousseau and the eternal authority of the Gospels; he needed both to answer the question that increasingly tormented him as he was writing *Anna Karenina*—the meaning of life, and how to live. In his novel, Tolstoy sets this conflict into dialogue against the background of a variety of literary, philosophical and sacred texts; he builds his response by recasting the most minute details of each work in such a way that the novel both forgives Anna and enshrines the holy ideal of the family.

Since *Les Liaisons Dangeureuses* first appeared, adultery has been a particularly French theme. To portray an adulteress, Tolstoy, who followed French prose closely throughout his life, drew from Rousseau as well as from French works published during the twenty years preceding his writing *Anna Karenina*. Tolstoy's novel of adultery in the European style became a "philosophico-moral" one as he set the relationship among Karenin, Anna, and Vronsky into dialogue with the ideas of a range of French novels. Tolstoy's counterexample to the adulterous triangle, the story of the successful marriage of Kitty and Levin, explicitly contradicts these French models and uses the Gospels to suggest the mysteries of the sacrament of marriage.

The novel of adultery was a widespread genre in European literature of the nineteenth century, sharing many features: adulteresses go mad or, more often, die—by disease, in childbirth, or by murder, while adulterous men perish on the battlefield, in a train crash, in exile, and a child often serves as a source of grace (Armstrong 121–137). The problem of a woman's role in marriage becomes a paradigm for the problems created by interrelating patterns, with marriage as mediator attempting to harmonize the natural, the familial, the social, the religious, and the transcendental realms (Tanner 15–17). As Tony Tanner puts it in *Adultery and the Novel*, "The tension between [Old Testament] law and [New Testament] sympathy... holds the great bourgeois novel together" (14). While marriage brings harmony in a mythologized society such as those depicted by Shakespeare, in nineteenth-century Western European society, marriage is the mythology that the novel of adultery demythologizes. The generic commonalities, however, are insufficient to explain Tolstoy's highly specific response to particular representatives of the genre. Of the many literary sources for *Anna Karenina*, Tolstoy used French material as a base line against which to consider adultery; he builds the relationship among Karenin, Anna, and Vronsky in dialog with Rousseau, Dumas, Zola, and Flaubert.

Most of the French subtexts for *Anna Karenina* address the problem of the adulteress from the point of view of the betrayed husband. Only Flaubert's *Madame Bovary* conveys the adulteress's experience predominantly from her point of view, which contributes to making it the most important of the novel's subtexts. Did Tolstoy intend a dialog with Flaubert's *Madame Bovary* when he wrote *Anna Karenina*? Eikhenbaum quotes S. de Pirelée's "Léon Tolstoy" as an example of judgments widespread in the French press that *Anna Karenina* "makes one recall" *Madame Bovary*. George Steiner, adducing several important parallels, concluded that "[a]ll that can be said is that *Anna Karenina* was written in some awareness of its predecessor" (48). But the evidence of that awareness is so abundant and suggestive that it is worth examining the possibility of a more detailed dialectic than Eikhenbaum and Steiner propose.[1]

Tolstoy arrived in Paris on February 21 (N.S.), 1857. Less than a month earlier, on January 29, Flaubert and the editors of *La Revue de Paris* had been taken to court for "outrage to public and religious morals and to morality" (Lotman 137). The defendants were acquitted of all charges, a verdict that was announced on February 7 (Lotman 137). Tolstoy alludes to none of this in his diary, noting on the day of his arrival, "spent a lot of money, saw absolutely nothing. Diarrhea" (47, 113).[2] In Paris, he spent a lot of time with Turgenev, went frequently to the opera, and admired the many plays of Molière he attended. He also read a lot of Balzac—*Cousine Bette*, as well as the foreword to the *Human Comedy*, which he finds "petty and arrogant" (April 10, 1857), and deplores Balzac's "depravity" (April 20). At the time that Tolstoy was reviling Balzac, Michel Levy brought out *Madame Bovary* in book form (in mid-April), which was followed by a flurry of reviews in all the major journals as well as in Sainte-Beuve's regular Monday column for *Le Moniteur universel*; later, there were responses by George Sand, Baudelaire, and many others. Fifteen thousand copies of the novel were sold in two months. As Francis Steegmuller put it, "since the death of Balzac, no novel had so impressed the public" (286).

But Tolstoy says nothing about all this in his diaries. In fact, he who says so much about so many things over so many decades says almost nothing about Flaubert's novel.[3] When G. A. Rusanov spent two days talking about literature with him in August of 1883, he mentioned Flaubert: "*Madame Bovary* T. had forgotten, but he remembers that when he read it, he had 'liked it.'[4] Forgotten it!"

Tolstoy did, however, express his admiration for Flaubert years later. In an interview with a French journalist in 1904, he said, "One of my most favorite writers is your incomparable Flaubert. There is a truly magnificent artist, strong, exact, harmonious, full-blooded, perfect. His style is filled with the purest beauty. Can one say this of many writers?" (Bourdon, 15 March). Furthermore, Tolstoy's library contained a copy of the Russian translation of *Madame Bovary* published in *Biblioteka dlia chteniia* in 1858. Interestingly, it had been torn out of the journal and bound together with Shakespeare's *Othello*, suggesting that Tolstoy did indeed read Flaubert's novel in the context of the adultery question that so occupied him in the early 1870s.

The fact that both Flaubert's and Tolstoy's novels belong to the genre of the adultery novel could account for some of the similarities of plot line: a woman in her twenties with a young child is married to a man she finds dull (and who becomes ludicrous and pitiful in her eyes once betrayed); she takes a passionate lover, and the relationship deteriorates into sensuality, in part due to its illicit nature. The women begin to imagine the decline of their lovers' ardor; with Emma Bovary it is her second lover, Léon, who brings out her fears of losing him—like Anna, Emma becomes more and more demanding, increasing her lover's alienation. Both Léon's and Vronsky's mothers oppose their sons' liaisons—the women are jeopardizing their sons' careers. The adulteress tries to be ever more physically alluring, but becomes jealous and desperate as she feels she is losing her lover. With nothing meaningful left, she commits suicide in a moment of frenzy. The novel passes judgment on her— she has broken both divine and human law, but she has our sympathy inasmuch as we are made to consider society's complicity in the adulteress's unresolvable dilemma.

No doubt it is this fairly elaborate and precise set of parallels that has led many critics to note, *en passant*, certain similar features between the two novels—the whole description of the decline in the relationships between Emma and Léon and Anna and Vronsky, for example. But none of them has proposed an overall relationship of *Anna Karenina* to *Madame Bovary*. Steiner, for all his initial disavowal that no more can be said, seems to be nursing a suspicion: he writes that Anna's inability to focus on reading her book on the train ride home to Petersburg "seems to derive directly from Tolstoy's remembrance of *Madame Bovary*." And when Anna suddenly notices the absurdity of Karenin's ears at the station, Steiner queries: "Is this not Tolstoy's version of Emma Bovary's discovery that Charles makes uncouth noises while eating?" (Steiner 67).

It is worth pursuing Steiner's speculation that Tolstoy incorporates remembered details of Flaubert's novel into *Anna Karenina*. The two sets Steiner mentions cannot be said to be central in themselves. Given the extensive congruence of the novels' plots, it would be unlikely that these would be the only details to correspond in over eight hundred (English) pages. There are remarkable parallels between the two novels not only in theme and plot line, but in character description, motifs, and central emblems, suggesting a carefully structured polemic.

Heroines

There are several similarities in appearance between Emma and Anna, though they may carry different meanings in the text; it will be possible to infer what Tolstoy might be suggesting by these parallels once they are sketched out. Emma surprises Rodolphe by being "de la tournure comme une Parisienne" (161)[5]; her elegance of dress and manner is noted by all throughout the book. She moves "comme un oiseau" (263, 313) and has dark hair. At her father's farm, "le grand air l'entourait, levant pêle-mêle les petits cheveux follets de sa nuque" (51). "Ce qu'elle avait de beau, c'étaient les yeux; quoiqu'ils fussent bruns, ils semblaient noirs à cause des cils (49). During her relationship with Rodolphe, Emma is repeatedly described with narrowed eyelids or half-closed eyes. These features will recall Anna's elegance of figure, light tread, black hair with "the willful little curls that always escaped... on the nape of her neck" (72), and her habit, which grows after she enters into adultery, of narrowing her eyes, squinting through her "thick lashes" (56).

The break in the heroines' lives is located in a ballroom scene. The Viscount's ball at La Vaubyessard gives Emma her fatal taste for luxury, aristocracy, and sensuality, emblematized by the greenness of the silk border on the cigar case Charles finds in the road on the way home to Tostes. This green is related to the color of both of Emma's lovers' coats: Rodolphe is wearing "une redingote de velours vert" when Emma first sees him (159), and Léon wears a green coat to his tryst with Emma at the Rouen cathedral, which leads to the infamous carriage ride. An elegant ball also determines Anna's fate: there Vronsky forsakes Kitty for her. The ball scenes are naturally characterized by luxuriousness, which in both is indicated by hothouse plants: it is winter in Moscow when Kitty wears a rose in her hair (70), and Anna has pansies at her wrist (72); the landing with the mirror at which Kitty pauses is lined with "growing plants," and the staircase is "flower-decked" (70). The ladies at La Vaubyessard wear in their hair "des myosotis, du jasmin, des fleurs de grenadier, des épis ou des bleuets" (84), while Emma, like Kitty, wears a rose in her chignon; the guests are served pomegranates and pineapple. The elegant foreign influences in Moscow are French or English, while Anna wears Venetian lace; in France the old chateau at La Vaubyessard has been torn down and a modern building "de construction moderne, à l'Italienne" (81) erected in its place. Emma's fatal dance is a sensual waltz with the Viscount, which leaves her dizzy and panting; the waltz is the determining dance for both Anna and Kitty, for it is the dance that makes Vronsky's preference for Anna clear to Kitty.[6]

Anna shares another determining scene with Emma: the opera. Both Flaubert and Tolstoy maintain an ironic distance from the opera, describing it as the meeting place of the best society. Flaubert stresses the provincialism of the audience and the performance of the celebrated tenor Lagardy, who combines elements "du coiffeur et du toreador" (249). Tolstoy focuses on the hypocrisy and affectation of members of high society who condemn Anna for crimes they themselves commit. The performance by Patti is incidental, but the apparently random bit of social chitchat that closes the scene echoes Flaubert's Lagardy: Vronsky's friend Stremov says to Anna, "There are no more tenors. *Le moule en est brisé*" (499). The opera scene determines Emma's next adulterous affair: from being in love with the legend of the tenor Lagardy, she begins to imagine herself his mistress; at that point, Léon appears in her box, and her fantasy devolves to him. The failure of Emma's second attempt to find love leads to her demise. For Anna, her evening at the opera reveals conclusively the impossibility of her position in society, which contributes to her final tragedy.

There are more similarities. For example, the way their husbands summon them to bed: Charles says "Viens donc, Emma, disait-il, il est temps" (197), while she is waiting for Rodolphe; Karenin comes in to Anna's room at midnight in his bedroom slippers and says

---

"Time for bed now" with a "special smile," and Anna, thinking of how Vronsky looked at Karenin at the station, goes into the bedroom with her usual fire "quenched or hidden far away" (103). We can add to Steiner's soup-slurping/ears protruding parallel Charles' "doigts aussi carrés" (215) and Karenin's habit of cracking his knuckles, Charles' "esprit aussi lourd" (215) and Karenin's pedantic one.

Tolstoy uses several motifs to characterize Anna that Flaubert had used for Emma. Vronsky's relations with his racehorse Frou Frou are clearly meant to relate to his affair with Anna; Emma's affair with Rodolphe begins when they go riding together on his horses. The horses and heroines are linked by a bird motif: In Tolstoy's novel, after Frou Frou falls, she begins "fluttering on the ground... like a wounded bird" (182), while Anna in the stands is described a few pages later as "fluttering like a caged bird" (192). Emma moves "comme un oiseau" (263), swallows dart by when Emma comes to Abbé Bournisien for spiritual guidance; Rodolphe's house has "deux girouettes à queue-d'aronde se découpaient en noir sur le crépuscule pale" (192); and Emma's dreams "tomb[e]nt dans la boue comme des hirondelles blessés" (212). Flaubert names the coach that takes Emma to Rouen for her trysts with Léon the Hirondelle, "swallow" in French. Thus the bird motif connects the heroines to their adulterous affairs.

Anna and Emma share another motif—fog, haze, mist. When Emma takes Rodolphe as her first lover she is ecstatic: "une immensité bleuâtre l'entourait" (191). The scene of her first tryst with Rodolphe is surrounded by mist: (171) "Il y avait du brouillard sur la campagne. Des vapeurs s'allongeaient à l'horizon, entre le contour des collines" (187). Emma's features are discernible through her blue veil "à travers son voile,... on distinguait son visage dans une transparence bleuâtre, comme si elle eût nagé sous des flots d'azur" (188);[7] her vision of eloping with Rodolphe hovered "à l'horizon, bleuâtre... et couvert de soleil" (224).[8] Flaubert's narrator is the creator of the motif, while in Tolstoy's novel, Anna herself speaks of the blue haze, associating it with the innocence of first love: "'I remember that blue haze, like the haze on the mountains in Switzerland. That haze which envelops everything at that blissful time when childhood is just coming to an end and its huge merry circle narrows to a path which one treads gaily yet with dread into life's corridor'...Kitty smiled...'How did she go through it? How I should like to know the whole romance of her life!' she thought, recalling the unromantic exterior of Anna's husband" (67). Tolstoy uses the Russian word *tuman* in all instances of the motif, sometimes assigning a color. We can use "haze" throughout except for Levin's fields (*tuman* is sometimes rendered both as "haze" and "mist" within a single translation). The motif appears again when Kitty realizes the growing attraction between Anna and Vronsky at the ball and "a haze spread(s) over the ball and the whole world in Kitty's soul" (74). Tolstoy uses the blue haze for what he deems a genuine form of ecstatic love; by contrast, the violent break of the natural order through adultery he associates with the shrieking, whirling snowstorm surrounding the future lovers' meeting on the platform, though Vronsky's pursuit produces "joyful, glowing and exhilarating" visions in Anna (95), similar to Emma's delight at her new role of adulteress. Tolstoy's recasting of the haze motif is hinted at just before Kitty refuses Levin: for her "a future with Levin appeared wrapped in haze" (43), which appears at this point in the novel to be a neutral image. Tolstoy reserves grey mist for another kind of bliss on Levin's estate (138), of which more in a moment.

These similarities between Anna and Emma not only make us aware of their resemblance, but underscore how very dissimilar they are. Emma is hopelessly shallow and selfish, as is shown by her relationship to her daughter Berthe. Anna before her affair with Vronsky is intelligent, direct, unpretentious, and a devoted mother. Emma's downfall, like Tatiana's in *Eugene Onegin*, is caused not by reading romantic novels, as her mother-in-law suggests, but rather by misreading them, identifying with their heroines in a particularly sensual and indiscriminate way. Anna, by contrast (here is Steiner's parallel again), is unable to read her English novel on her train ride home after dancing with Vronsky. "She was too eager to live herself. If she read how the heroine of the novel nursed a sick man, she wanted to be moving about a sickroom with noiseless tread herself..." (115). When she does identify, it is to make an unconscious moral judgement: "The hero of the novel had nearly attained to his English happiness of a baronetcy... and Anna wanted to go to the estate with him, when she suddenly felt that he must have been ashamed, and that she was ashamed for the same reason" (92). It is only the trivial Betsy Tverskaya and her circle who read like Emma and project role-playing onto Anna. Betsy reports that Liza Merkalov "raves" about Anna, who is "like a real heroine out of a novel" (271).

And this suggests Tolstoy's idea: Emma is conceived by Flaubert as an imitation, the product of *idées reçues*, of undigested clichés drawn from a hodgepodge of literature. After Emma first enters into adultery, "elle se rappela les héroïnes des livres qu'elle avait lus, et la légion lyrique de ces femmes adultères se mit à chanter dans sa mémoire avec des voix de soeurs qui la charmaient" (191).

But Tolstoy wants to consider the dilemmas faced by the adulteress at the deepest level possible, and to do that, he has his appealing heroine reject the accepted practice of deceiving her husband. The change from the early drafts of *Anna Karenina*, where Tolstoy described his adulteress as unattractive both physically and morally, suggests that as the novel evolved, he came to identify with her need for passionate love (to which his story *The Devil* testifies so vividly that it was only published after his death, in 1911). Her stature grew as his sympathy (and desire for complexity) increased.[9]

It is possible to understand Anna as an ideal version of Emma. Emma admires and imitates luxury; Anna already has it. Emma wants a passionate aristocratic dashing lover, but finds only imitations of one; Anna gets Emma's wish in Vronsky.[10] Emma wants to be the heroine of a novel; Anna is seen as one by her peers. Emma fantasizes eloping to Italy with the pseudo-aristocrat Rodolphe (who clenches his teeth in predatory passion [173]); Anna and the truly aristocratic Vronsky (of the "regular" [160], "compact" [164] teeth) actually do elope to Italy. In this way, Tolstoy isolates and distills the moral and psychological aspects of adultery for a young married woman, purifying it of the concern with social status and material luxury that obsess Emma and positing an intelligent, self-aware heroine.

The unfulfilled young woman with small child and uninspiring husband who takes a passionate lover and commits suicide is the obvious point of contact between the two novels. But Tolstoy incorporates a large array of more complex details and structures that show he had *Madame Bovary* in mind while writing *Anna Karenina*. An analysis of them will reveal Tolstoy's subtle reading and reinterpretation of Flaubert's novel.

Emblems

Much has been written about the centrality of the railroad to Tolstoy's novel.[11] Anna and Vronsky meet at the Moscow station where a peasant is killed by a train; their understanding is sealed during the snowstorm on the platform on the return trip; Anna throws herself under a train; and we see Vronsky for the last time on his way to war back again at the Moscow station. The train from the outset is associated with metallic clanking, with incipient romantic passion, and with the peasant's death, in which Anna sees an omen. Anna and Vronsky both dream of a dirty peasant with a matted beard, and oddly in both their dreams, he is speaking French. Vronsky "vividly recalled the peasant again and the incomprehensible French words the man had muttered, and a chill of horror ran down his spine" (324). In her dream, Anna can make out the words "il faut le battre, le fer; le broyer, le pétrir…" (329). And as Anna falls to the rails, "A little peasant muttering something was working at the rails" (695). The grotesqueness of the dream has to do in part with the incongruity of the *muzhik*, that essence of Russianness, speaking French. Throughout the novel, the corrupt characters speak or read French, while the innocent ones are distorted by having to use French in elegant society, starting with the Tatar waiter who translates Levin's soup and kasha into "kasha à la Russe" (47). Like the French language, the railroad is an artificial foreign graft onto Russia causing, among other things, exaggerated centralization in the cities, as Levin says (510). The city in *Anna Karenina* is associated with luxury and debauchery; Levin has called Moscow a Babylon, as the Countess Nordston tauntingly reminds him at Kitty's (45). And Flaubert does the same with Rouen: "that ancient Norman city lay outspread beneath [Emma's] eyes, like an enormous metropolis, a Babylon awaiting her" (274).

The Yonville priest Bournisien warns against Emma's proposed trip to the opera in Rouen: "ces personnes de sexe différent réunies dans un appartement enchanteur, orné de pompes mondaines, et puis ces déguisements païens,... tout cela doit finir par engendrer un certain libertinage d'esprit et vous donner des pensées déshonnêtes, des tentations impures" (243–44).

The Hirondelle is the conveyance that makes impure temptations available to Emma Bovary. From the outset, the carriage has ominous dimensions, marking key moments in Emma's decline toward suicide. Charles and Emma arrive in Yonville on the Hirondelle to meet the members of the cast assembled at the Golden Lion. The Hirondelle passes as Léon brings Emma a cactus and while Rodolphe begins his verbal seduction of Emma at the fair. Like the railroad, the Hirondelle is accompanied by the "rattle of old iron" (340). Tanner makes this connection too, noting that iron is "an inexplicably ominous part of [Emma's] surroundings."[12]

The railroad for Anna is associated with the French-speaking peasant; an analogous figure follows Emma alongside the Hirondelle:

Il y avait dans la côte un pauvre diable vagabondant avec son bâton, tout au milieu des diligences. Un amas de guenilles lui recouvrait les épaules, et un vieux castor défoncé, s'arrondissant en cuvette, lui cachait la figure; mais, quand il le retirait, il découvrait, à la place des paupières, deux orbites béantes tout ensanglantées. La chair s'effiloquait par lambeaux rouges; et il en coulait des liquides qui se figeaient en gales vertes jusqu'au nez, dont les narines noires reniflaient convulsivement. Pour vous parler, il se renversait la tête avec un rire idiot; – alors ses prunelles bleuâtres, roulant d'un mouvement continu, allaient se cogner, vers les tempes, sur le bord de la plaie vive.

Il chantait une petite chanson en suivant les voitures

Souvent la chaleur d'un beau jour
Fait rêver fillette à l'amour.

Et il y avait dans tout le reste des oiseaux, du soleil et du feuillage. (291)

The love song is in grotesque contrast to the revolting beggar, like the *muzhik* and the French-speaking world. The heroines' quests for romantic love are far removed from the reality of the world around them. The heart of both novels is contained in this emblem of adulteress, conveyance, and grotesque peasant; components of the image map the novels' denouements.

Anna feels right away when she first meets Vronsky that the death of the peasant under the train is an omen. Emma too begins to sense something uncanny when the hideous beggar appears:

> Quelquefois, il apparaissait tout à coup derrière Emma, tête nue. Elle se retirait avec un cri.
>
> Souvent, on était en marche, lorsque son chapeau, d'un mouvement brusque entrait dans la diligence par le vasistas, tandis qu'il se cramponnait, de l'autre bras, sur le marchepied, entre l'éclaboussure des roues. Sa voix, faible d'abord et vagissante, devenait aiguë. Elle se traînait dans la nuit, comme l'indistincte lamentation d'une vague détresse ; et, à travers la sonnerie des grelots, le murmure des arbres et le ronflement de la boîte creuse, elle avait quelque chose de lointain qui bouleversait Emma. Cela lui descendait au fond de l'âme comme un tourbillon dans un abîme, et l'emportait parmi les espaces d'une mélancolie sans bornes. Mais Hivert, qui s'apercevait d'un contrepoids, allongeait à l'aveugle de grands coups avec son fouet. La mèche le cinglait sur ses plaies, et il tombait dans la boue en poussant un hurlement. (291)

The jingling horse bells are part of a motif that culminates in the tolling of the church bells at Emma's death, just as the motifs of clanking metal accompany Anna's trajectory toward death. The *muzhik* reappears at Anna's death, and it is ambiguous whether she sees him in reality, or in her imagination:

> She tried to get up, to throw herself back; but something huge and relentless struck her on the head and dragged her back. "God forgive me everything!" she murmured, feeling the impossibility of

struggling. A little peasant muttering something was working at the rails. And the candle by which she had been reading the book filled with trouble and deceit, sorrow and evil, flared up with a brighter light, illuminating for her everything that before had been enshrouded in darkness, flickered, grew dim, and went out forever. (695)

Emma's peasant also reappears at her deathbed scene just before the darkness:

Tout à coup, on entendit sur le trottoir un bruit de gros sabots, avec le frôlement d'un bâton; et une voix s'éleva, une voix rauque, qui chantait:

Souvent la chaleur d'un beau jour
Fait rêver fillette à l'amour.

Emma se releva comme un cadavre que l'on galvanise, les cheveux dénoués, la prunelle fixe, béante.

Pour amasser diligemment
Les épis que la faux moissonne
Ma Nanette va s'inclinant
Vers le sillon qui nous les donne.

– L'Aveugle s'écria-t-elle.
Et Emma se mit à rire, d'un rire atroce, frénétique, désespéré, croyant voir la face hideuse du misérable, qui se dressait dans les ténèbres éternelles comme un épouvantement.

Il souffla bien fort ce jour-là
Et le jupon court s'envola !

Une convulsion la rabattit sur le matelas. Tous s'approchèrent. Elle n'existait plus. (344)

The song traces Emma's descent into gross carnality. By the end of the novel, the final realist image of Nanette bending over with no petticoat has replaced the earlier romantic "thoughts of love" and "all the rest... about birds, sun and leafiness." Tolstoy emphasizes the difference between Anna and Emma in his choice of the recurring image associated with Anna's death. Anna reacts with compassion and dread when the peasant is killed by the train. Her dream is associated with the guilt she feels from the beginning of her relationship with Vronsky, despite the real possibility of marriage to him, and the presence of the peasant at her death is emblematic of "the book filled with trouble and deceit, sorrow and evil" that her life has become. Unlike Emma, Anna has never deluded herself. Emma has no desire to marry either of her lovers and feels no sense of sin or remorse; Anna's honesty and conscience keep her from accepting the breach of the sacrament of marriage and doom her from the start.

Flaubert and Rousseau

Tolstoy began his novel with the adultery story, but was discontented with it and set it aside, even after having sent it off to the printer. Gradually he built what he called the novel's "scaffolding," the story of Levin. What "scaffolding" does his story provide, and can a relationship be found here, too, to Flaubert's novel?

When the poet Fet read the first installment of *Anna Karenina*, he wrote Tolstoy, "Fools will carry on about Flaubert's realism, but here everything is ideal." Indeed, this is why the novel resists any dramatic rendition that perforce focuses on the plot line; Anna's story seems merely to echo Emma's, but throughout *Anna Karenina*, Tolstoy infuses his ideals into every aspect of the life he depicts. His impulse is not to show the low aspect of the everyday, the evidence of a falling away from an ideal world, but a Matisse-like distillation of what its beauty consists of—Dolly's love and care of her children, Levin's cherishing of family tradition and farming his land, Karenin's dutiful government service and well-ordered life; the beautiful, loving embodiment of the life force in Anna and even in its undercut form in the jovial, kindly Oblonsky. *Anna Karenina* moves us particularly because it presents an *almost* ideal world of decent members of the Russian aristocracy, a portrait that is the opposite of Flaubert's ironic rejection of the restrictive pettiness of provincial France.

From the catalog of similarities that point to differences between Flaubert's novel and Tolstoy's, it appears that Tolstoy restores the ideals that Flaubert shows are being lost. Both authors seem to locate the formulation of these ideals in Rousseau's work. As Milan Markovitch has noted, several of the incidents in *Anna Karenina* may have their source in *Julie*: like Levin, Wolmar works with his peasants, struggles with the question of faith, and begins to lose some of his skepticism when faced with the possibility of his wife's death.[13] With Rousseau's ideals so much in mind, how might Tolstoy have read *Madame Bovary*?

Flaubert lampoons Rousseau, displaying the degradation of Rousseau's ideals. Charles' first wife, the scrawny widow Dubuc, is named Héloise, but is the antithesis of either a romantic lover or a wifely ideal, neither *une ancienne* or *nouvelle* Héloise. Homais invokes a confused version of Rousseau's ideas about education from *Emile* when he encourages Charles to agree to Emma's piano lessons so that she can teach her daughter: "Moi, je trouve que les mères doivent instruire elles-mêmes leurs enfants. C'est une idée de Rousseau, peut-être un peu neuve encore, mais qui finira par triompher, j'en suis sûr, comme l'allaitement maternel et la vaccination" (285). The lessons, of course, are a cover for Emma's adulterous trysts; and the novel shows romantic literature to be the source of her malaise.[14] Another of Rousseau's views travestied is his argument against the theater made in his *Lettre à d'Alembert*: Flaubert puts it in the mouth of the inadequate priest Bournisien, where it is trivialized, but proven in some sense to be valid—Emma *is* corrupted by going to the theater.

Flaubert shows the absence of Rousseau's ideas in contemporary French life. In *Madame Bovary*, the reader can infer the possibility of Rousseauian ideals, in religion, in art, in true science and in nature, through their travesty by the shallow characters' actions. Léon's seduction of Emma begins in the glorious Rouen cathedral, making a travesty of religious ideals. The only place these ideals are present in positive form in the novel is in the perfection of Flaubert's verbal medium, which he famously agonized over. Not the characters, but the author finds meaning in *Madame Bovary*, as in this impersonal evocation of natural beauty seen from the hill over Yonville: "L'eau qui court au bord de l'herbe sépare d'une raie blanche la couleur des prés et celle des sillons, et la campagne ainsi ressemble à un grand manteau déplié qui a un collet de velours vert, bordé d'un galon d'argent" (105). The green and the velvet that had betokened luxury and romance for Emma and that Charles therefore uses for Emma's shroud occurs in its only pure role in Flaubert's narration; here, the green velvet carries no pretensions, but rather functions as a metaphor that creates a synthesis between man and nature in artistic prose. Man plants the meadow, but God makes it grow; the novelist, "like God in the universe,"[15] makes the metaphor, and divine inspiration assists it to unify the novel's levels of meaning.

While Flaubert leaves the glories of nature and his own description of them beyond the ken of his characters, Tolstoy uses Levin's world as scaffolding to integrate the ideals contained in *Julie* and *Émile* into the life of the Russian landowner. Flaubert's location of meaning in his own artistic synthesis is antithetical to Tolstoy's views, but Flaubert's green velvet fields are the point of origin of Levin's quest for meaning:

> On the Thursday the wind fell and a thick grey mist [*tuman*] rose as if to hide the secret of the changes nature was carrying on. Beneath the mist the snow-waters rushed down, the ice on the river cracked and moved, and the turbid, foaming torrents flowed quicker, until on the first Sunday after Easter toward evening the mists dissolved, the clouds broke into fleecy cloudlets and dispersed, the sky cleared, and real spring was there... Last year's grass grew green again and the young grass thrust up its tiny blades[...]Invisible larks broke into song above the velvety green fields [*nad barkhatom zelenei*] and the ice-covered stubble-land... Spring had really come. (138–9)

This is the description of spring on Levin's estate, where, after Kitty has refused his offer of marriage, Levin locates his hopes for the future, first without Kitty, but by the end of the novel, together with her. Like Levin's economic analysis, in which agriculture is the basis of the wealth of a nation, his spiritual analysis bases moral existence in working his land.

The scene of Levin's joy on that spring morning brings together several motifs that are crucial to both novels: green, velvet, haze/mist, and cigars. All four motifs depict Emma's moral decline throughout *Madame Bovary*; Tolstoy redeploys them. In this scene, the first three motifs convey the joy of man's cooperation with nature, while the fourth, cigars, is made to travesty the first three as well as the morals that Tolstoy associates with Levin's farming.

Tolstoy continues the long description of Levin's spring with another "vast expanse of smooth, velvety green carpet" [*barkhatnym kovrom zelenia*] spreading before Levin as he goes about his estate planning to get the manuring done before the first planting (142). And then Oblonsky arrives: "[Levin] showed his guest into the spare bedroom, where Oblonsky's things—his bag, a gun in a case, and a satchel for cigars—were also brought" (145).

In *Madame Bovary*, cigars are a motif connoting worldliness, luxury, and sensuality, originating in the aforementioned viscount's cigar case found on the road after the ball.[16]: the priest has tobacco stains on his chest; Rodolphe smokes a cigar after he first seduces Emma in the woods; Emma gives Rodolphe "un porte-cigares tout pareil à celui du Vicomte" (218); Léon lights a cigar while waiting for Emma at the cathedral before their carriage ride. Emma goes out on the street in Rouen with a cigarette in her mouth, which marks her moral decline.

In *Anna Karenina*, cigars play a similar role, and it is Oblonsky who is most frequently found smoking them. He calls them "the crown and hall-mark of pleasure" (147). He lights one after dinner at Levin's, when he opines that "a pretty maid is better than an old nurse" (145). It is part of his moral blindness: Oblonsky "enjoyed his newspaper, as he did his after-dinner cigar, for the slight haze it produced in his brain" (6). This reminds us of his sister, who, as we have seen, associates blue haze with young love. So it is emblematic that Oblonsky should arrive at Levin's with an entire separate satchel for cigars, which, against the background of the twice-mentioned green velvet fields, is perceived by the reader as their antithesis. In this way, the luxury that Flaubert associates with the Viscount's green-trimmed cigar case is transferred in *Anna Karenina* to the true source of well-being, the well-tended fruit of Levin's honest toil. Anna acquires a tortoise-shell cigar case by the time she meets Levin (631); it contains the cigarettes she now smokes, associating her with Oblonsky's sensuality and thereby tracing her decline as cigarettes do Emma's.

The two novels share the motifs of haze, green, velvet, and cigars. In *Madame Bovary*, all these motifs are associated with Emma's descent into debauchery, but Tolstoy redistributes them: The first three are transferred to Levin's estate,[17] while Oblonsky obtrudes upon them with his own tobacco haze. Interestingly, the drafts for this scene do not combine the "green" with the "velvet," nor do they contain Oblonsky's satchel for cigars.[18] Instead of the latter, Tolstoy had only "[Oblonsky's] elegant things—straps, suitcase, bag, gun—were carried in."[19] Later Tolstoy gave Oblonsky a cigar case (*"sigarochnitsa"*), which became a satchel (*"sumka dlia sigar"*) only when he prepared the first edition of the novel for publication as a separate book.[20] Anna's tortoise shell cigar case is also absent from the published drafts of the scene.[21] The late addition of this system of details, which links the shared sensual aspect of the brother's and sister's personalities, suggests the importance of the motif for Tolstoy and his awareness of Flaubert's famous cigar case.

Another motif focuses the essential difference between Flaubert's and Tolstoy's novels: manure. Dmitri Merezhkovsky connects Tolstoy's love of manure to Rousseau in *Tolstoy as Man and Artist*: "The idyllic perfume of manure moved [...] Jean-Jacques Rousseau almost to tears. Leo, too, loves its savour" (Merezhkovsky 64).

Levin's joy in the mystery of spring in the scene is coupled with his concern that the manuring be done properly, and the word *manure* is repeated three times in two pages, in perfect keeping with the elevation of Levin's soul and our fresh amazement at nature's miraculous self-renewal. It is the same juxtaposition that had gotten Wordsworth and then Pushkin, into such trouble years earlier, that of the lofty with the lowly.[22]

Flaubert plays with this juxtaposition, also using manure, but to comic effect. Rodolphe begins his seduction of Emma at the

Agricultural Fair in Yonville. He entrances her with talk of souls ordained to meet by Fate against the counterpoint of the speeches from the Fair's tribunal. Both lines in the counterpoint are made up of horrendous clichés, each set designed to manipulate their audience. Romantic love and political idealism are equally travestied:

> – Ainsi, nous, disait-il, pourquoi nous sommes-nous connus ? quel hasard l'a voulu? C'est qu'à travers l'éloignement, sans doute, comme deux fleuves qui coulent pour se rejoindre, nos pentes particulières nous avaient poussés l'un vers l'autre.
> Et il saisit sa main; elle ne la retira pas.
> "Ensemble de bonnes cultures!" cria le président.–
> Tantôt, par exemple, quand je suis venu chez vous...
> "À M. Bizet, de Quincampoix."
> – Savais-je que je vous accompagnerais?
> "Soixante et dix francs!"
> – Cent fois même j'ai voulu partir, et je vous ai suivie, je suis resté.
> "Fumiers." (178)

Manure and fertilizers are mentioned three times in as many pages from the Yonville tribunal: "Work above all at the improvement of the soil, at producing rich fertilizers, at breeding horses, cows, sheep, pigs! (*les races chevalines, bovines, ovines et porcines!*)" (160/177).

What Flaubert uses to mock cynical political exploitation of a bovine peasantry Tolstoy makes the basis of Levin's faith, Levin who thinks joyfully of his future herd of cows bred from Pava even during his despair over Kitty's refusal. In Tolstoy's drafts for *Anna Karenina*, Levin was to have come to Moscow not to propose to Kitty, but to show Pava at an agricultural fair. Oblonsky was to have met him there by chance, in the company of one of his mistresses.[23] In the draft we have the same intersplicing of the adulterous couple with the agricultural concerns as in *Madame Bovary*, with the same redistribution of censure: while Flaubert mocks both, Tolstoy shows the agricultural, marked by the manure motif, to embody an elevated moral ideal, while adulterous love is a travesty of the ideal of married love that is based in nature and ordained by God.

Thus in *Anna Karenina*, Tolstoy examines the question of what men live by in order to consider the problem of adultery, returning to Rousseau for a basis. Anna's great tragedy is that she is condemned by the very honesty that constitutes Levin's virtue: both characters adhere to Tolstoy's Rousseauian ideals by refusing to abide by public opinion and meaningless social convention. But while Levin flouts the frivolous conventions of society, he comes to accept the wisdom of those related to God; Anna flouts both and is repaid accordingly.

Flaubert does not make this distinction; the villain of his novel is his bête noir, the *idée reçue*, the cliché, the unexamined view, and all the damage it can do. *Madame Bovary* ends not when Emma dies, but after the chemist of Yonville, Monsieur Homais, has received the Légion d'honneur.

Homais is the chief agent of events in the novel. He talks Charles into performing the operation on the clubfoot Hippolyte because he has read about a new method in the newspapers. Homais talks Charles into taking Emma to the theater in Rouen. It is among Homais' chemist supplies that Emma finds the arsenic to kill herself. Finally, it is Homais who tells the blind beggar to come to Yonville so that Homais can apply ointment to his eyes, which culminates in Homais having him imprisoned. Homais and the pseudo-science he preaches are a parody of Him who would make the lame walk and the blind see.

In *Anna Karenina*, Oblonsky acts as go-between, the agent of all the important interactions of the novel:[24] he summons Anna to Moscow; brings Kitty and Levin together; obtains Karenin's consent for a divorce; and introduces Levin to Anna, to mention the most important. He corresponds in many ways to Homais and even has the same number of children (six). Tolstoy endows Oblonsky with many loveable characteristics, so that the reader tends to accept him as uncritically as Oblonsky's friends do, but nonetheless shows that he lives without any moral basis for his actions and lacks the capacity for independent thought.[25]

Oblonsky is also a purveyor of the accepted view. A materialist like Homais, he gets all his opinions from the newspapers:

And although he was not particularly interested in science, art or politics, on all such subjects he adhered firmly to the views of the majority, as expressed by his paper [...] The Liberal Party said, or rather assumed, that religion was only good as a curb on the barbarous part of the population; and indeed Oblonsky could not stand through even a short church service without aching feet, or understand the point of all that dreadful, high-flown talk about the other world, when living in this one would be very pleasant. (6)

Homais as a man of science has no use for religion and constantly baits Bournisien. Homais is a chemist, while Oblonsky is head of a government board, but the language describing him smacks of the pseudo-medical: Oblonsky, "who had a leaning towards physiology," is said to act "'by a reflex action of the brain'" (2)[26] and to "have a physical effect" on the people he meets (13).[27]

Homais and Oblonsky are linked by a shellfish motif. In Moscow, Oblonsky takes Levin to dinner against his will at a restaurant whose elegance seems to defile Levin's feelings for Kitty. They have three dozen oysters, described so as to emphasize Oblonsky's sensuality: "'Not bad,' he said, tearing the quivering oysters from their pearly shells with a silver fork and swallowing them one after another. 'Not bad,' he repeated, turning his moist and glittering eyes now to Levin, now to the Tatar" (32).

Homais arrives in Rouen and drags Léon off to a long lunch at a pretentious restaurant. Léon is in despair because he knows Emma is waiting for him, but is forced to listen to Homais "expound immoral theories on women" (62). Red lobster claws had lain over the edge of the platter at La Vaubyessard as part of the abundant luxury; by the end of the book via a series of permutations, the crustacean motif, like other motifs in the book connoting luxury, has descended along with Emma to become a ludicrously defiled token of elegance and romance: "... près d'eux [Homais and Léon], derrière le vitrage, en plein soleil, un petit jet d'eau gargouillait dans un bassin de marbre où, parmi du cresson et des asperges, trois homards engourdis s'allongeaient jusqu'à des cailles, toutes couchées en pile, sur le flanc" (302).

Madame Bovary closes with Homais' reward for his destructive meddling. In the final Part 8 of *Anna Karenina*, we learn that Oblonsky has won the post at eight thousand rubles a year that he has been discreetly lobbying for. He is to be secretary of the committee of the consolidated agency of credit balance of the southern railways, which he describes to Karenin in Homais-like journalese as "a new institution of undoubted utility" (653). Given the role of railways in the novel and Levin's view that their premature proliferation is detrimental to agriculture, Oblonsky's post and the entire agency suggests that its utility is precisely dubious and that Oblonsky's phrase is a ready-made piece of high-flown obfuscation. He is rewarded with the post for his readiness to employ the ready-made phrase, idea, way of life unquestioningly, while the railroads that will supply him extra income have also been the means of his sister's destruction.

Homais is master of the cliché, which he assembles with demonic rapidity for the articles he writes for the local newspaper, the Rouen *Beacon*. "–Ah ! c'est là la question ! Telle est effectivement la question: *That is the question!* comme je lisais dernièrement dans le journal," he prattles, immune to the irrelevant (to him) source of his tag line (235). In *Anna Karenina*, it is Vronsky's friend Petritsky who uses "That is the question!" fatuously (163), but Oblonsky also uses ready-made tags, quoting Levin (33–4) the same verses about a young man in love[28] that he later repeats to Vronsky (53). In both books, there is ironic meaning for the reader. But while Homais cannot know that Hamlet's suicide soliloquy pertains to Emma, Oblonsky does know that Levin and Vronsky are apparently both in love with the same woman and, therefore, bears moral responsibility for his utterance, though it has no consequence. Flaubert's characters are his victims; Tolstoy's are autonomous moral beings.

If Emma's story illustrates the tragic results of acting out her projective reading of romances, Homais displays the destruction caused by misapplied materialism, embodied in his apothecary's faith in science. Emma is a degraded version of Chateaubriand's René; she devalues his romantic quest for an ideal by embodying it in tawdry reality; Homais, on the other hand, presents the degradation of Rousseau's progressive views and of Enlightenment ideas. Emma is guided by sensuality, Homais unrestrained by any moral principle. Oblonsky combines these features. As Anna is the best possible adulteress, he is the best possible sensualist, enjoying oysters, women, hunting, and his friends with appealing good health, energy, and bonhomie. But he is nonetheless the Enemy; he represents the destructive force of Tolstoy's novel, for it is this life force and sensual appetite, unrestrained by any moral principles, that precipitates Anna's ruin.

Tolstoy's polemic with European literature, focused on the "woman question" and the novel of adultery, is, as Eikhenbaum wrote, "a dialectic unity, the result of a complex mental process" (152). That complexity includes applying values absorbed from Rousseau to the problem of adultery, values that were elaborated specifically in dialogue with Flaubert.

The parallels between *Madame Bovary* and *Anna Karenina* show both authors to be concerned with the decline of cherished values; emblematized by the adulteress in the conveyance accompanied by the grotesque peasant with his inappropriate language, a people is shown to betray its own best nature and traditions through shallow understanding of them. Instead of Flaubert's trivial heroine, Tolstoy posits the best possible case, but Anna is, no less than Emma, doomed by the inherent contradictions both of her society[29] and especially of adultery itself.

Tolstoy, then, may be said to be restoring Rousseau's views by giving them a dignity, freeing them from the parody with which Flaubert degrades them. Levin is a true Emile, learning from his own experience the cost of luxury, the superiority of things made by oneself, the freedom to enjoy black bread and not to be a slave to public opinion (Rousseau 163). Instead of allowing Oblonsky's Homais-like success to dominate part 8, Tolstoy rewards Levin with a son and a revelation about the nature of human existence. This is Tolstoy's antidote to adultery, an evolving answer to the question of how to live a meaningful life.

Answering the French novels of adultery with Rousseau and the Gospels, Tolstoy is able to reinfuse idealism into the realist novel, which he felt had become distressingly naturalistic, as his remarks about Balzac and responses to Zola suggest. While the romantics insisted on the unattainability of a Platonic Ideal in the real world, and materialists denied the existence of God, Tolstoy shows another possibility: the continuous approach toward the ideal and the divine in the everyday. Both the romantic and the holy ideal of the beloved can be united, painfully and gradually, with the actual wife: the "strange, limp, red creature" (650) that is his son can reveal the divinity in the everyday, and the novel of adultery can be transformed into a *profession de foi*.

Notes

1. Other critics have rejected this possibility. Several French opinions are collected in *Literaturnoe nasledstvo*, 2 vols., Moscow, 1965. For example, Romain Rolland: "The effect of Tolstoy's art does not depend on stylistic contrivance as does Flaubert's" (189); André Maurois, "What does Tolstoy owe to Balzac, Flaubert? He read them, but it does not seem to us that he learned writing technique from them. His realism does not resemble that of our naturalists... Elegant literary devices in the spirit of Flaubert are foreign to him" (219–220); and Jean Jaurès: "Tolstoy is most concerned with moral problems. You cannot compare him in this respect with Balzac, Sand, Flaubert, Zola... Flaubert cares most about artistic form, but feels a scornful pity for the unhappy and grey human race!" (580).

2. *Pss* 47, 113.

3. Michel Cadot points out that Tolstoy wrote to his wife in 1892, "*Madame Bovary* has great qualities and is not for nothing highly regarded by the French" (*Pss* 84, 505). See Michel Cadot, "La Mort comme évenement social et comme destin personnel: remarques sur *Madame Bovary* et *Anna Karenine*," 31–40.

4. In a letter to Strakhov (April 22, 1877) Tolstoy called *Flaubert's The Catholic Legend of Saint Julian the Hospitaller* "an abomination" (merzost') and "disgusting filth" (*vozmutitel'naia gadost'*) (Ibid. 472). But in a later letter to Strakhov (1881), he called *Anna Karenina* "merzost" as well (63, 61).

5. *Madame Bovary,* Garnier-Flammarion, Paris, 1966. Citations will be drawn from this edition.

6. In his *Dictionary of Accepted Ideas,* Flaubert facetiously calls the waltz "[a] lascivious impure dance" (84).

7. Flaubert also uses a blue haze in *A Simple Heart.* The story is a kind of complement to *Madame Bovary,* as Tolstoy's later stories "The Kreutzer Sonata" and "The Devil" are to *Anna Karenina.* Flaubert wanted to answer the charge that he was inhuman in his novel by writing the touching tale of Félicité's truly ideal loves. Her religious fervor is associated with a blue cloud of incense when, on her deathbed, Félicité achieves the religious exaltation that Emma had only imitated. Félicité associates cigar smoke with her nephew because she learns he is in Havana. The motifs that had denoted corrupt, empty sensuality in *Madame Bovary* are used to connote ideal love in *A Simple Heart.*

8. Tanner traces the motif of mist, fog and vapors, connecting it to the "fog in Emma's head," 312–14.

9. Like Gary Saul Morson ("Prosaics and *Anna Karenina*" 8), I think that the book condemns Anna, but rather for her breach of the sacrament of marriage than for the self-indulgence for which Richard Gustafson berates her. See Richard F. Gustafson, *Leo Tolstoy. Resident and Stranger,* especially 118–132.

10. Judith Armstrong says that Vronsky is not a seducer "of the Rodolphe type" (84).

11. See, for example, Sydney Schulze, *The Structure of Anna Karenina,* 117–122; Elisabeth Stenbock-Fermor, *The Architecture of Anna Karenina,* especially 66–71.

12. Tanner traces the iron motif (316–317), connecting the whirring of Binet's lathe and a passing cart "loaded with iron rods" (303) to the Hirondelle.

13. See Markovitch, 48–50, for further parallels.

14. Flaubert said of *Madame Bovary,* "It was in hatred of realism that I undertook this book. But I equally despise that false brand of idealism which is such a hollow mockery in the present age" (*Correspondence* 4: 134, letter to Madame Roger des Genettes, October or November 1856).

15. As Flaubert says he should be, "present everywhere, and visible nowhere." Flaubert, *Correspondance* 2: 155.

16. Here Flaubert (unkindly) refers to the jeweled and inscribed cigar holder Louise Colet gave him. (Frances Steegmuller, *Flaubert and Madame Bovary* 300).

17. In The *Lady of the Camellias* the motifs connote opposites: (corrupt) Paris in the distance is "in the mist" (110) while the cottage in Bougival where Marguerite returns to rural innocence has "a green lawn, smooth as velvet" (112). Alexandre Dumas-fils, trans. Edmund Gosse; Sainte-Beuve and other reviewers saw Emma Bovary as a version of Marguerite Gautier (Steegmuller 297).

18. *Pss*, 20, 214, 217. In the draft for the long paragraph about spring (Part II, Chapter XII), mist (*tuman*) is mentioned once. In the final version, it appears three times in a way that emphasizes the miraculous aspect of nature's rebirth. The draft uses both green and velvet, but separated by two sentences, whereas the final version breaks the paragraph into two sections, each of which combine them. *Anna Karenina*, ed. V. Zhdanov & E. Zaidenshnur, 133, 136.

19. *Pss* 20, 217.

20. The correction was made in Tolstoy's handwriting. I am grateful to Tatiana Georgievna Nikiforova of the Tolstoy Museum archive in Moscow for her help in discovering this.

21. *Pss* 20, 505–6.

22. Tolstoy uses the motif again later in "The Devil," assigning it the opposite meaning: the phosphates that Irtenev has been fertilizing the fields with are associated with his peasant mistress, who has borne him a child (a point made by Elliott Mossman in "Plus s'accuse, plus s'excuse: Confession in Tolstoy," paper delivered at the annual AATSEEL convention, December 1992, New York). The motif thus carries the opposition between ideal wedded love and the lust that undermines it. This suggests that in Tolstoy's creative process, Anna's adultery becomes the necessary complement to Levin's wedded bliss, serving to purge it of the illicit passion that destroys her.

23. *Pss* 20, 52–57.

24. Schulze also makes this point, 151.

25. Gary Saul Morson agrees: "Stiva is the villain of the book, its representative of what evil is" ("Prosaics and *Anna Karenina*" 6), as does Dostoevsky, whom he cites.

26. *Refleksy golovnogo mozga* is the title of a book by Professor Sechenov, who carried on a polemic with another scientist in the periodicals Oblonsky would have read. See Louise and Aylmer Maude, trans. *Anna Karenina*, London, 1939, 2 vols., 1: 495.

27. "Bylo chto-to, fizicheski deistvovavshee druzheliubno i veselo na liudei, vstrechavshikhsia s nim" (Part I, Chapter V). Rosemary Edmonds translates this "acts like a tonic" (27). The Maudes have "had a physical effect on" (17).

28. Pushkin's translation of Anacreon's fifty-fifth ode.

29. As Stenbock-Fermor puts it, Anna is "entrapped by mistaken culture with its machinery, dances, provocative dresses, and all the artificial comforts and social conventions" (70).

Works Cited

Armstrong, Judith. *The Novel of Adultery*. London: Macmillan, 1976.

Bourdon, George Henri. "En écoutant Tolstoi." *Le Figaro* (15 Mar. 1904).

Cadot, Michel. "La Mort comme évenement social et comme destin personnel: remarques sur *Madame Bovary* et *Anna Karenine.*" *Études comparatives, Cahiers Léon Tolstoi* 3, Institut d'études slaves, Paris (1986): 31–40.

Flaubert, Gustave. *Dictionary of Accepted Ideas*. Trans. Jacques Barzun. Norfolk, CT: New Directions, 1954.

_____. *Madame Bovary*. Trans. Alan Russell. Harmondsworth: Penguin, 1950.

_____. *Madame Bovary*. Paris: Garnier-Flammarion, 1966.

_____. *Correspondence*. Ed. Eugene Pasquelle. Paris, 1900.

Gustafson, Richard. *Leo Tolstoy, Resident and Stranger: A Study in Fiction and Theology*. Princeton, NJ: Princeton UP, 1986.

Lottman, Herbert. *Flaubert*. London: Methuen, 1989.

Markovitch, Milan. *Jean-Jacques Rousseau et Tolstoi*. Paris: Librairie ancienne Honoré Campion Paris, 1928.

Merejkowsky, Dmitri. *Tolstoi as Man and Artist*. London: Archibald Constable, 1902.

Morson, Gary Saul. "Prosaics and Anna Karenina." *Tolstoy Studies Journal* 1 (1988): 1–12.

Riffaterre, Michael. "Flaubert's Presuppositions." *Diacritics* XI.4 (Winter 1981): 2–11.

Rousseau, Jean-Jacques. Émile. New York: Dutton, 1974.

Schulze, Sydney. *The Structure of Anna Karenina*. Ann Arbor, MI: Ardis, 1982.

Steegmuller, Frances. *Flaubert and Madame Bovary*. London: Collins, 1947.

Steiner, George. *Tolstoy or Dostoevsky*. London: Faber & Faber, 1959.

Stenbock-Fermor, Elisabeth. *The Architecture of Anna Karenina*. Lisse: Peter de Ridder Press, 1975.

Tanner, Tony. *Adultery and the Novel*. Baltimore, MD: Johns Hopkins UP, 1979.

Tolstoy, Leo. *Anna Karenina*. 2 vols. Trans. Louise & Aylmer Maude. London: Oxford UP, 1939.

Tolstoi, Lev Nikolaevich, *Anna Karenina*. Eds. V. Zhdanov & E. Zaidenshnur. Moscow: Nauka, 1970.

_____. *Polnoe sobranie sochinenii*. 90 vols. Moscow: Khudozhestvennaia *literatura*, 1928–1964.

Orientalism -- in Theory -- *Salammbô* and the Orient of Style _____

Beryl F. Schlossman

In the *Prison Notebooks*, Gramsci says: "The starting point in critical elaboration is the consciousness of what one really is [...] as a product of the historical process to date, which has deposited in you an infinity of traces, without leaving an inventory" [...] Gramsci's Italian text concludes [that] "therefore it is imperative at the outset to compile such an inventory."... In many ways my study of Orientalism has been an attempt to inventory the traces upon me, the Oriental subject, of the culture whose domination has been so powerful a factor in the life of all Orientals. (Said, *Orientalism* 25)

* * *

This image of language as the enemy of experience, this assertion that representation is always-already a misrepresentation, this shallow pathos about the impossibility of truthful human communication, is of course a familiar Romantic trope, which has undergone much aggrandizement—first in those irrationalist philosophies of the late nineteenth century and the early twentieth, which preceded the rise of fascism and then again, on a much wider scale, in the reactionary anti-humanisms which have dominated many strands in contemporary avant-gardist thought. (Ahmad, *In Theory* 194)

* * *

The task of this essay is to explore Edward W. Said's *Orientalism* as a critical lens applicable to the study of *Salammbô*. What are the features of Said's conception of Orientalism, and are they relevant to Flaubert? How might the discourse of *Orientalism* inform an analysis of the discourse at work in *Salammbô,* or an interpretive reading of Flaubert's Carthaginian novel? In the first part of the essay, I will examine Said's application of Orientalism in the context of Flaubert and mention several of the many responses to Said's book as they relate to an Orientalist understanding of *Salammbô.*

The second part of this essay will examine whether or not the novel offers some form of resistance to nineteenth-century Orientalism. If Flaubert's Orient of style (my own term) can be interpreted as a trans-romantic project—the working-through of romanticism that offers an alternative to overwhelmingly corrosive doctrines and clichés—then it might be possible to attribute a more nuanced role to Flaubert's literary construction of the Orient than Said granted to it. This may or may not be the case, given the evidence of the novel itself, as well as theoretical responses to Orientalism.

Flaubert is prominent as a prestigious figure in Said's discussions of nineteenth-century French literature as key evidence for the book's thesis. Flaubert's most successful novel about the Orient receives only brief treatment, however. I would propose, then, to return to *Salammbô* in the terms of Said's analysis and examine if the novel fits its assigned role. My point of departure in my own work is an alternative view of Flaubert's Orient that I explore in *Objects of Desire: The Madonnas of Modernism,* and *The Orient of Style: Modernist Allegories of Conversion.*

Are Flaubert's aesthetic criteria viable? One hundred and thirty years of critical judgments of *Salammbô*—by Sainte-Beuve and more recently, Lukács, followed by Foucault, Donato, Bernal, and Said—have been harsh. Flaubert's astonishingly violent novel is accused of decadence, abjection, false claims of experience, lifeless decoration, and unredeemed horror. Aside from the popularity of the novel in 1862 and Flaubert's enduring reputation, *Salammbô* receives much less attention than *Madame Bovary* or *L'Éducation sentimentale.* In addition, *Salammbô* was viewed in a particular way—and here, one could make two arguments for a nuanced form of Orientalism, as follows. First, the popularity of Flaubert's invented figure of the languorous virginal priestess of Tanit was seen as an exotic version of French femininity, and the more or less isolated figure of the heroine thus took on a role across the arts (painting, opera, theater, and fashion). Second, as if *Salammbô* were a variation on *Madame Bovary*, the novel's historical discourse was viewed as a commentary on events in France, and a view of Carthage as merely a figure for the Second Empire took root in Flaubert scholarship.

As concerns the novel's focus on the city of Carthage, destroyed by the Roman empire in 146 BCE, protests against the novel's alterity began with Sainte-Beuve, who questioned the choice of Carthage over Rome, celebrated in terms of empire, racism, and identification by the influential historians, Michelet and Renan. Flaubert deeply admired both of them; it would be impossible to claim that his Carthage owes nothing to Michelet's conclusions (Bernal 355). But for literary reasons if not for cultural ones, the novel appears to dissolve contemporary racial and racist perspectives in favor of portraying Oriental antiquity. Flaubert was absorbed in researching and reconstructing the Phoenician culture of Carthage and in representing the city through fiction (borrowed, rewritten, and invented) in the Orient of style. The novel's alterity (or Otherness) is related to the mode of allegory that is used to reveal Carthage rather than to a disguised melodrama about France (Neefs, Schlossman). The problems begin, however, with the novel's contrasts between race and subjectivity, refinement and violence.

Since the publication of *Orientalism* in 1978, Said's powerful exploration of the West's uses and misuses of the Orient continues to shape major discussions of racism, colonialism, imperialism, and cultural representation. A revered teacher, intellectual, and scholar as well as a courageous and indefatigable activist, Said was the author of many distinguished works of political, cultural, and literary criticism, essays, and memoirs. After 1978, writings on Palestine and especially essays in *The World, the Text, and the Critic*; *Culture and Imperialism*; *Reflections on Exile*; and the memoir titled *Out of Place* continued to defend or to reflect on aspects of the earlier book. *Orientalism* radically changed the tone of Said's writing and decisively injected it with the voices of subjects. The book appeared at a critical moment of finality and historical closure. Its reception was sensational, for reasons that have marked and transformed theory across disciplines. *Orientalism* earned its author celebrity as well as death threats. A tone of passionate engagement characterizes Said's writing on a topic related to what he calls the Palestinian's "uniquely punishing destiny," presented as his own. *Orientalism* and later works combine Said's writing on the politics of the Orient with the author's expertise in philology and comparative literature, a field so to speak rescued from Nazi Germany by a small group of exiled refugees, including Leo Spitzer, the Frankfurt School, and (most importantly for Said) Erich Auerbach.

Early in *Orientalism*, Said filters the evocation of historical process through an intriguing quotation from Antonio Gramsci (quoted in my epigraph). Said's reference to Gramsci's incarceration (by the Italian fascists who feared his influence) anticipates his selective evocation of the exile of Erich Auerbach, who found shelter from the Nazis in Istanbul before coming to the US. Each of these two prestigious writers—the founding political figure and the founding literary critic—becomes a witness to Said's stake in the book. For the author then steps forward as "the Oriental subject," while aspects of the two founding figures that Said finds less likeable are left in the shadows. In any case, Gramsci's formulation of "traces without an inventory" strikingly recalls Freud's revolutionary view of the unconscious, and it anticipates concepts that would enter the writings of Foucault, Lacan, Lévi-Strauss, Lyotard, and Derrida, among others. Said adds *Orientalism* to Gramsci's conscious construction of an inventory: the Italian phrase that Said mentions without quoting it is "occorre fare inizialmente un tale inventario" (Gramsci 1376). The two anecdotes give some insight into Said's perspectives. In this context, an observation (quoted in my epigraph) by the writer and theorist Aijaz Ahmad on the use of theory to deny the Orientalist's capacity for experience also speaks to the deprivation of experience that Ahmad aptly attributes to refugees lacking the substantial material, institutional, and metropolitan comforts that Said adapts to his view of the Oriental subject. Said's selective responses to serious objections to the book did not alter the critic's construction of those comforts (Ahmad).

Said begins the introduction to *Orientalism* with a French journalist's remark that the war-ravaged downtown of Beirut "had once seemed to belong to… the Orient of Chateaubriand and Nerval" (1). The civil war of 1975 and 1976 is seen through the lens of European representation (or ownership) of the Orient, rather than through Beiruti and Lebanese perspectives. The Orient disappears into the Orientalist's gaze—reading replaces a reality that outsiders cannot experience. At the same time, the text posits the echo of loss and destruction sustained by the victims themselves. Wartime, a ruined homeland, and the anticipation of exile are placed on one side of the scale; romantic evocations of Beirut are placed on the other. The journalist's remark illustrates some unconscious effects of the European dominance and paternalism that are at the core of Said's inquiry. In the definitions that follow, the ambiguous role of French literature in Orientalism enters Said's argument. One might recall Walter Benjamin's writing on the loss of experience in modernity, were it not for the confusion that lingers about uses of power and knowledge. The opening paragraph resonates with losses and exiles that are presented as strictly Oriental, in part because the injuries sustained are attributed to the domination of an Occident.

Said's opening definitions shape the book's theoretical problems (Ahmad, Clifford). The first definition posits the Orient as an object of study by an Orientalist, who produces the work of discourse described as Orientalism across a range of essentially modern disciplines (2). Said adds that "Orientalism is a style of thought based upon an ontological and epistemological distinction made between 'the Orient' and (most of the time) 'the Occident'" including Aeschylus, Dante, Victor Hugo, and Marx (3). The third definition locates the starting-point of the discourse of Orientalism in the late eighteenth century "as a Western style for dominating, restructuring, and having authority over the Orient" (3). The Orient is the Other; the Orientalist is guilty of essentializing it. The Orient and the Oriental per se become invisible under the pressure of European (French, English, and later, American) discourses.

Aijaz Ahmad explores major topics relevant to Orientalism through questions of immigration, literature, and identity in his book titled *In Theory: Classes, Nations, Literatures*. The book discusses Said's perspectives on Marxism, history, feminism, literature, and theory in the chapter titled "Orientalism and After: Ambivalence and Metropolitan Location in the Work of Edward Said." James Clifford discusses his objections to Said's categories and especially to his use of Foucault in *The Predicament of Culture*. Rajagopalan

Radhakrishnan's *A Said Dictionary* places Said's Orientalism in context; Elleke Boehmer and Lisa Low confront theory with the role of women; Nicolas Harrison looks at Flaubert and Nerval in Said's book, and Christopher Prendergast returns to Clifford's findings. Said's later essays in *Reflections on Exile* revisit Orientalism and its reception. Said's filtering of Flaubert in *Orientalism* raises questions that enter into dialogue with other critical responses; Said's specific treatment of *Salammbô* is of interest to Lowe, Harrison, and the present essay.

Ahmad and Clifford ask about Said's choices of works and discourses placed within the territory of Orientalism. Briefly, these two influential critics take issue with the broadness as well as with the ambiguities of the book's central thesis that Orientalism is a discourse of representation used by the West at the expense of the East. (Said speaks of "West" and "white Occidentalism" in contrast to "East" and "colored Orientalism"). Another question relates to the book's almost exclusive engagement with Arab countries; the book does not explore the more positive Indian perspective on Orientalism (as the use of languages other than English) versus Anglicism, or German and Russian Orientalist scholarship (independent of directly imperialist contexts).

Ahmad and Clifford view Said's methodological deployment of Foucault's concept of discourse as a source of some confusion about issues of power and knowledge. *Orientalism* does not propose a method or a trope to differentiate how discourse operates, nor does the book offer a critique of ideology to reveal economic determinants behind a set of thoughts, hidden meanings, or duplicities, in a space where Marx and Freud come together. In addition, Said's ambivalence about the Orientalist qualities of works by several writers, including Flaubert, shifts the argument away from textual analysis to evidence of nineteenth-century travel. Genre and the status of the texts in question are treated as irrelevant (Harrison, Prendergast).

Said's explicit references to Foucault include an influential essay, "La Bibliothèque fantastique" that evokes the role of the Orient in Flaubert. Said mentions the Alexandrian-American theorist,

Eugenio Donato, who also refers to Foucault's essay. Written as an introduction to the German translation of *La Tentation de saint Antoine*, Foucault's essay was published at least twice in French during the author's lifetime, and several times after the author's death. Foucault's essay interestingly anticipates Said's thesis about Orientalist reading as opposed to experience. Even more strikingly, Foucault echoes standard reductive terminology opposing West and East, the dangerous clichés that Said denounces.

In contrast to Jean Seznec's Orientalist scholarship on Flaubert, noted by Foucault (33) and in another context by Bernal (157–158), Foucault divides the world according to Flaubert into an advanced, lively, and forward-looking West and an old-fashioned moribund East. Science and knowledge (the West in the future) are contrasted with religion and mysticism (the East viewed as the past). At the beginning of the essay, Foucault writes: "That which was 'temptation' in the ruins of an ancient world still inhabited by ghosts became 'education' through the prose of the modern world" (5). Toward the end of the essay, the saint's moment in Christian Egypt is described as the zero point where "Antiquity totters and collapses upon itself" at "the modern world's germinal point, with the promises of infinite knowledge" (Foucault 23). Foucault does not mention that this was the moment when Egyptian culture was attacked, its influence erased, and the temple and library of Alexandria burned by Christian mobs. In other words, it was the moment when the Dark Ages began—a zero point indeed, but not in the way that Foucault evokes it.

One could suppose that Foucault had some good reasons for not altering the remarks quoted above and several others in the same vein, although he made corrections for the publication of the essay in French and republished it unchanged, except for the title. It remains an interesting essay for other reasons. I quote it primarily to illustrate Said's predicament as an anti-Orientalist admirer of Foucault, whose method he proclaims and applies to the topic of the book. This predicament is related to the question of Flaubert's so-called decadence, essential to Donato's argument and Said's commentary on Flaubert. Based on his reading of *La Tentation*,

Donato's hypothesis concurs with Mario Praz's famous view of the excesses of romanticism. The label of decadent seems to confirm a view of Flaubert as entrenched within some of the least pleasant French notions of race and empire (as well as articulated obscene fantasies that had an extraordinary impact on modernism, e.g., the Nighttown chapter of Joyce's *Ulysses*).

Foucault refers to Seznec's scholarship on Flaubert's sources in the *Tentation* as evidence for the claim that Flaubert's work reflects the impact of books rather than experience. This claim appears to have had a formative impact on Said (who also attentively cites the Foucault essay as a source on Flaubert, in addition to other quotations and conceptual borrowings from Foucault's discourse analysis). Readers of *Orientalism* will recognize one of Said's basic theses: writing, reading, and texts replace authentic experience as the Orientalist falsifies the truth of the Orient, or indeed misrepresents something he—the Orientalist—could never represent with any kind of truth because he is caught within a discourse of power and knowledge.

Foucault's claim is reprised by Donato in several essays on Flaubert, religion, and philosophy. Donato explores some Gnostic sources consulted by Flaubert for the *Tentation* in an attempt to read Flaubert as a decadent, a judgment that interests Said. Foucault's claim about the impact of books on Flaubert is seductive to Said for two reasons, one related to the Western misrepresentation of the East, and the other related to the high costs of exile. Said therefore dismisses the experience of Westerners as substitutive, tainted, banal, and brutal. Thus discourse allows the substitution of Kuchuk-Hanem, for example, for the figures in Flaubert's second novel, *Salammbô*, and in addition, the strange symptoms of *Salammbô*'s disappearance in Foucault as well as Donato. (Perhaps Auerbach is to blame for this disappearance, after all? That would have a certain poetic justice.) The novel goes underground, swallows invisible ink, or something of the kind. Only Lukács, then, articulates the complaints that lead several generations of critics away from *Salammbô*. Lukács's criticism, according to Donato, concurs with Sainte-Beuve's criticism of Flaubert. In itself that is extraordinary, since it would be hard to imagine a more conservative voice than Sainte-Beuve reading *Salammbô*, with the single exception perhaps of the Orientalist Ernest Froehner, who labored and scratched away at Flaubert's novel with such pedantic rage that Flaubert (who generally kept his distance from what he considered the vulgarity of journalism) found it necessary to respond publically. At the end of detailed rebuttals, Flaubert sarcastically concluded that Froehner made him doubt he had ever actually been to Carthage.

Foucault's essay on Flaubert's *Tentation* quotes only a letter from Flaubert's correspondence and some notes on structure as specific textual references. The essay states that the *Tentation* is the source for all of Flaubert's writing—without any evidence to that effect. Foucault pairs the old saint with a metropolitan young man in another novel, also without evidence (5). Like most of Flaubert's sympathetic characters, Saint Antoine and Frédéric suffer from melancholy and desire. Foucault claims for Flaubert, as for Cervantes and Sade: "The library is on fire" (10). The allusion to the library of Alexandria might be relevant. It would have been the perfect moment to evoke *Salammbô*, with its display of eroticism and solitude, its bloody flames, its burning deserts, and the destruction of young boys and barbarian soldiers in the fires of the god Moloch and the strategies of war. But Foucault only mentions the sculpted decors of *Salammbô*'s opening scene (6).

Salammbô continued to be a problem, as it already had been for Sainte-Beuve and Lukács. In an essay briefly mentioned by Said in a footnote, Eugenio Donato explores the impact of Flaubert's Orient in the context of Foucault's summary of Flaubert's writing on the Orient as the product of a "fantastic library," reading carried away, "the library on fire." This judgment coincides interestingly with Said's larger judgment of Orientalism as the product of books rather than experience. Foucault's widely cited essay on Flaubert becomes a secret sharer of Orientalism and plays a role on the level of the text's unconscious.

In other places, I have explored the set of discursive practices and their interpretive results in impersonal modern style, conceptualized through the notion of the Orient, as well as the fictional creation of an Other as a "madonna of modernism," a virginal figure that allows for an identification of erotics and poetics together. Flaubert's methods, his combination of lived experience, travel, scholarship, and the transformative adventures of style shape his own modern response to a repressive and imperial world that he dismissed as hopelessly bourgeois, philistine, and disgustingly vulgar. Some of the resulting rage that seethes in the pages of the novel takes the form of shocking and horrible imagery. While many of these images come from Flaubert's sources, his use of them is occasionally attributed to Flaubert's "decadence."

Said's academic expertise is connected with the figure of Erich Auerbach, whose influence on Said's work complicates the Foucauldian method of the book. According to Aijaz Ahmad, some of the book's fundamental ambivalence is rooted in the underlying conflict between the methodological approaches that Said draws from Foucault's discourse analysis and Auerbach's masterful studies of Western humanist tradition expressed in his literary scholarship (Ahmad 162–170). I would add that Auerbach's firm categorizations of "Western" tradition begin to be subtly undermined by his own questioning, and they leave traces within the works of an exile from Nazi Germany whose work on the surface appears to be conservative of the "Western" value system that Said reveres in a literary context and blames for ignoring the Other, the Orient, in a political context. This sense of Otherness and compromise, interestingly, is duplicated not only in Said's own arguments, but also in the absence of a feminine (not even feminist, but simply feminine) partaker of the experience of the Oriental. This was already the case in Foucault's essay, with its marked division between West and East. But Flaubert, a bourgeois atheist obsessed with religion, mixes East and West. Following Foucault, perhaps, Said and even Donato turn away from the book and take up the (Christian) *Tentation de saint Antoine*. This avoids the ancient gods and rituals, Flaubert's Oriental fiction of the feminine, and especially, the troubling questions of culture and race that Bernal explores in relation to the Phoenician world of Carthage (Bernal 337–366).

Salammbô is Flaubert's most intense and quasi-experimental exploration of the Orient and of the Other. In this novel, Flaubert elaborates a representation of an imagined and experienced lifelike reality out of several thousand written and visual fragments, but he also bases it on his own experience, travel, and very dark view of culture. The troubling forms of violence in Flaubert's novel recall the questions of ritual sacrifice that still preoccupy historians. Bernal's comments on *Salammbô* suggest that Rome's imperial genocides (including the destruction of Carthage in the spring of 146 BCE) are considered less horrific than sacrifices to Moloch supposed to have taken place at the troubling "tophet of Salammbô" (Bernal 355–359). Roman violence, by contrast, does not seem to disturb anyone (357). The allegory of Flaubert's novel is anchored in the documentation of the Phoenician goddess, Tanit, whom Salammbô serves. Flaubert inventively associates the divine powers of destruction represented by the god Moloch with the historical figure of Mâtho, borrowed from Polybius and entwined with Salammbô in a fictional love story. The historical aspect is the result of the Carthaginian sacrifice of the Mercenaries, on the economic and military levels, and the fiction invents a fatal attraction between the mercenary leader and the virginal priestess who solemnly (and bizarrely) serves wine to him. This gesture of appeasement or seduction marks the (fictional) feast that launches the (historical) war.

Flaubert's private joke is that a Gallic soldier points out that the wine marks Mâtho's betrothal to the priestess. Spendius translates the soldier's jovial pleasantry to Mâtho, whom he has slapped on the shoulder: "'Quelles noces?'—'Les tiennes! car chez nous,' dit le Gaulois, 'lorsqu'une femme fait boire un soldat, c'est qu'elle lui offre sa couche.'"(Flaubert, *Salammbô* 16). Against the racist distinctions drawn by his contemporaries, Flaubert includes a few Gauls among the foreign "barbarian" soldiers. They are the only trace of modern France in the novel.

In the background of this fatal detail is an echo of *Madame Bovary*. The same emblematic eroticism appears in Charles Bovary's courtship of Emma, or perhaps one could say her courtship of him, since she insists on serving him a glass of curaçao—the liqueur named (in Portuguese, like the island), for the heart! Like Sappho's Eros, curaçao is bittersweet, exotic, and romantically reminiscent of Otherness. Emma fills Charles's glass and serves herself almost nothing: "Comme il était presque vide, elle se renversait pour boire; et, la tête en arrière, les lèvres avancées, le cou tendu, elle riait de ne rien sentir" (Flaubert, *Madame Bovary* 23). This trivial incident foreshadows the melancholic reality of the marriage, whereas the incident in Salammbô constructs a somewhat different "fatality"— Charles's last word on adultery and his own broken heart, an echo of the letter Rodolphe had sent Emma.

The pure Salammbô, priestess of Tanit, does not drink wine; her gesture at the feast echoes the allegorically resonant detail of Emma's empty glass in *Madame Bovary*. The virginity of both characters is significant for Flaubert. These details converge, ineluctably, with the author's rage and his trans-romantic perspective. He ends the novel with the combination of the lovers' last encounter (at a distance) and the bloody fictionalized scene of the Carthaginian victory against the Mercenaries in 241 BC. In Flaubert's last paragraphs, Schahabarim finishes off the hideously tortured Mâtho: the high priest literally cuts the mercenary soldier's heart out of his chest. Flaubert added this gory detail of Aztec sacrifice to the representation of Carthage on the verge of disappearing in the Roman genocide of 146 BCE. The description of the priest lifting up Mâtho's dripping heart to show the crowd irresistibly recalls the caricature of Flaubert spearing Emma's heart and his claim—in writing—that he himself was Madame Bovary (Schlossman, *Orient of Style* 134–135).

In evoking Flaubert's accounts of the Orient, Said quotes from the travel journal rather than from fictional works (*Orientalism* 186–188). Said understandably finds passages on disease and prostitution to be demeaning and even horrifying, although if the passages in question were compared to Flaubert's comments on Europeans—even some remarks in his publications—it might be difficult to make the point that Flaubert is more condescending to Asians or North Africans than to his "own." But aside from Flaubert's particular mentality, Said effectively draws our attention to the abusive contexts of early tourism and to the ambiguities of Flaubert's nights with prostitutes, including several fondly cherished memories of Egypt.

Given the imperialist tendencies of mid-century travelers, one may still require some comfort after revisiting Flaubert's journal entries about entertainers and prostitutes (including minors) visited in between Maxime Du Camp's culturally ambitious photo shoots with underpaid natives. Flaubert gives detailed accounts of witnessing the buying and selling of human beings and, more personally, of the two "cawadjas" giving alms to servants, *slaves*, and beggars; the journal is horrifying and casual in its indications of the banality of slavery and the conditions of the poor (women, workers, prostitutes, entertainers, the sick, and especially children). Said quotes Flaubert's Egyptian journal as evidence for his argument about imperial superiority, although the journal could be compared with other examples of Flaubert's writing that are not obviously connected to Orientalism. That may be the effect of Said's talents as a reader, on the one hand, and the unconscious presence of Orientalist thinking on the other. But of all nineteenth-century travelers, Flaubert most wanted (apparently) to converse with the almehs he slept with, since he sometimes brought an interpreter into the room. It is not obvious that Flaubert was less sensitive to the woman's situation than an "Oriental" man would have been, for that matter. Class and gender, the visible and the invisible, affect one's considerations of the Other. Said takes his reading of Flaubert into places where few readers will want to follow.

The greater difficulty in these passages is that Said argues about the attitudes of Flaubert's writing without making clear distinctions between the private journal and the published fiction. There is a similar and uncomfortable blurring of boundaries when he discusses Nerval and Flaubert together, and it adds to the confusion about literature. At least since Montaigne, the status of originality in travel literature may deserve some particular attention: scholars of travel literature are aware of borrowed or plagiarized materials used by travelers primarily with the notion of publishing their travel journals after their return home. Flaubert, on the other hand, and for obvious reasons, kept his journals private. The circumstances of Gérard de

Nerval, Théophile Gautier, and others mentioned by Said are quite different from those of Flaubert, who appears to have decided early in the trip to keep a journal that would not have escaped censorship or worse. In the years of writing *Salammbô*, he never forgot the infamous trial of *Madame Bovary* in 1857. In any case, the journal does not explain or illustrate the novel.

As discussed so far in this essay, the complexity of Flaubert's Carthaginian novel does not enter the field of vision presented through Said's use of Foucault's discourse analysis—it eludes the question of differences among texts and writers. The common complaint that Said's three arguments make it impossible to enter into the terms of his argument is evident in the example of Flaubert. Said's reader must assume the novel conforms to Said's criteria. But Flaubert's unusual passion for Egypt and Carthage sets him apart from his contemporaries, even Nerval. Flaubert's prominence in *Orientalism* can be compared with the role of Dante in the book: Dante is strategically placed in relation to Auerbach's emphasis, in *Mimesis* in particular, on Flaubert's extraordinary writing and his aesthetic of realism. Aijaz Ahmad analyzes the problem of Said's revision of Auerbach's view of Dante, including a racist portrait of Mohammed in the *Commedia* (170).

An additional problem in Said's discussion of these iconic authors is that Flaubert's fictional portraits are not obvious products of the modern racism found in the works of Renan, Gobineau, and Michelet (Flaubert's "dear Master"), whose poison permeates many literary and cultural works of the period. While Said's reading of passages in Flaubert's journal would make it tempting to see Flaubert's fiction as a product of the same kind of reasoning that exuberantly portrays the exploits of the two "cawadjas" on the prowl, the connection between the fictional character's lost virginity and the realities of Egyptian almehs as sex workers is exaggerated. It is something of a shock to read Said's claim that Kuchuk-Hanem is a source for the character of Salammbô, although his reasoning is clear.

There is a tension between Said's two arguments about Orientalism in the writing of geniuses (Said's term). Given that they are the descendants of Napoleon, their use of library sources means they do not engage with the true Orient; their status as wealthy European travelers led to typically imperialist behavior toward the subjects they encountered on their travels. They are simultaneously inside and outside of the authentic experience that leads us to read them regardless of what their works teach us about the Orient. There are many contradictions of this type throughout the book.

There is one explicit discourse at work in *Orientalism*, and another that hovers in the wings, and the feminine does not have much of a place in either one. The question of Said's view of *Salammbô*, then, is twofold: what can be drawn from *Orientalism* to give insight into Flaubert's discursive practice or into his use of modes of literary representation? One would anticipate that Flaubert's successful and aesthetically accomplished novel situated in ancient Carthage (near present-day Tunis) would have a prominent place in the book, along with many nineteenth-century works that play a role in Western representations and historical studies of the Orient. While Said's later works continue to mention Flaubert (or Conrad, or even Lane), *Salammbô* never reappears.

In suggesting that something happens in a singular act of literature to transform the tourist's banal brutality into an art of the Other, I do not deny the facts and damaging effects of colonial power, racism, sexism, or other institutionalized forms of violence. The overwhelming evidence of Second Empire culture (including the legacy of Gobineau, Renan, Michelet, Cousin, and many others) supports a less ambivalent reading of French nineteenth-century Orientalism. After nearly two hundred pages that regularly mention the names of the two French writers, Said proposes his view of Flaubert and Nerval in the East as one of the book's high points. (For reasons of space, I cannot explore the fascinating case of Nerval in this essay.) Said's pages on Flaubert, however, are filled with contradictions and dismissals (Lowe, Harrison). Evoked as a chauvinist traveler, a pedantic Orientalist researcher, a cliché-ridden romantic in search of home, and a sadist, Said's Flaubert is also a genius—but a genius worth reading for his self-portrait, not for his portrayals of others (Said 179–186). I propose instead to read *Salammbô* in part as a kind of protest against the power of empire. A forthcoming essay will explore this perspective—and its consequences for historically-based narration—in a reading of Flaubert's portrait of Carthage in antiquity and modern style.

Flaubert's *Salammbô* is a means of approach to the Orient and an apprehension of the Other as suggested by the sources, including writing, reading, travel, and experience. Unlike many Orientalist works, the novel explores the Orient in terms that transform an army of clichés into a surprisingly innovative work of literature. Against all the odds, Flaubert manages to leave the West out of the equation—as much as it is possible for a "white male bourgeois" writer living in the repressive (and bogus, for Marx and others) Second Empire to write beyond the clichés and facts of empire.

If this accomplishment actually took place, it is not obvious how it could have occurred. Without invoking the notion of the miracle of style that Proust's reading of Flaubert presents—an accomplishment that Proust records in terms borrowed from theology, although without supposing any particular divinity at their source—one might observe that Flaubert's *Salammbô* combines the contributions of life and art, the traces of history and the reading and writing that confront them within a particular frame of space-time that presents the West uniquely as the enemy. The novel attributes a wide range of perspectives to Carthaginians and unpaid mercenary soldiers who rebel against Carthage following the First Punic War. Carthage and the mercenaries as well are under the shadow of Rome and the threat of imperial destruction. In the Phoenicians' future is the end of the empire and Rome's complete destruction of Carthage in the spring of 146 BCE. The specific moment of antiquity that interests Flaubert in his invented characters and a carefully documented historical framework is presented as an encounter among many forms of Otherness, a highly allegorical work of quasi-baroque splendor and suffering. The inhabitants of Carthage are part of a venerable "Oriental" realm that will be erased and all of its citizens killed or enslaved. The little chain ("la chaînette") worn by Salammbô (like other young women of good Carthaginian families) is broken into two snake-like fragments: the chain is a rhythmic modulator of movement, described as a device to preserve virginity, but is also an ornament of enslavement. In the novel's allegorical structure, Salammbô represents Carthage as well as the goddess. Her death at the end of the novel is a figure for the end of the Oriental city at the hands of the West.

Unlike most journals and literary works about the Orient, Flaubert's novel does not contain any traces of modern England or France. Who is the narrator, then, when all traces of the West have been erased? There is nothing similar in the writing of other writers quoted by Said. Foucault's Flaubert remains steadfast in the West, Eugenio Donato's Flaubert locates the most nauseating images attributed to Gnostic texts on the horizon of the Christian Saint Anthony, and Flaubert himself, of course, could not write as other than a Frenchman steeped in books as well as personal experiences (some better, some worse, as far as his personal Orientalism is concerned).

Salammbô—perhaps Flaubert's most challenging work of fiction—is the most unusual case of Orientalist literature. Strangely, it receives little attention in Said's study or in his later writing. The example of *La Tentation de saint Antoine*, another famously difficult work, raises somewhat different questions about the split between East and West, and its perspective on Christian cultures of the Orient is more in line with Said's criteria of Orientalism. But Said emphasizes the role of the travel journals for Flaubert and Gérard de Nerval to deflect the absence of the novel of Carthage from *Orientalism*. As Said uses one of Erich Auerbach's favorite techniques in simultaneously discussing the work of two writers with something essential in common, the disappearance of the novel from the discourse of Orientalism takes effect. In its place, is the frequently discussed episode of Flaubert's Egyptian escapade with the courtesan, Kuchuk-Hanem, singled out from a vast quantity of encounters with prostitutes detailed in Flaubert's notes. Said argues that Kuchuk-Hanem is the prototype for the fictional character of Salammbô and that both are sterile in contrast to the "omniféconde" goddess Tanit (Said 186–188). Said argues consistently against the funereal portrayal of colonial Egypt that appears in many English

---

and French responses and seems to interpret the attributed sterility of the two women in that context. (Salammbô is a virgin for most of the novel, and no one knows about Kuchuk-Hanem's personal life.) But Said also underestimates the almeh's effect on Flaubert and the impact of Egyptian dancers on his work (Schlossman, *Objects of Desire*).

The violence and horror of Flaubert's novel *Salammbô*, with its figures of excess and Otherness, required a portrayal of the feminine as an aesthetic alternative and counterpart to the bloody, sadistic, and imperial world of Moloch. The question of the status of allegory in a work of modern realist literature (in contrast to Renaissance allegory, for example) is crucial. How does Flaubert intend the reader to negotiate the evocation of the priestess of Tanit, dressed in blue harem pants covered with silver stars—a virginal figure, an incarnation of the goddess, and the moon in the sky, at the same time? Flaubert's explicit use of allegory might explain the disappearance of the novel in Foucault, Donato, and Said—and possibly Auerbach as well.

Flaubert's major figures of the feminine emerge from the three early projects, as follows: the woman loved by Don Juan, the Flemish virgin, and the Egyptian woman offering herself to a god (Schlossman, *Orient of Style* 71–139, 225–260). The virginal priestess wrapped in translucent colored veils enters the scene of fiction from Flaubert's view of art and the feminine. Genetic studies indicate the importance of the veil in Flaubert's thinking about the novel and the structures that gradually emerge, from the heroine's costumes to the "zaïmph," the veil-like garment of the goddess Tanit that Flaubert strategically moves through the novel (Le Calvez, Neefs).

The accomplishment of the novel is in Flaubert's vivid portrayal of subjects in the world, and of subjectivity—artfully constructed through a trans-romantic art of the impersonal that continued to shape modern prose fiction for at least a century after the author's death. The nearly magical restraint of Flaubert's aesthetic combines with the baroque waves and curves of precisely articulated violence and poetic sensibility in *Salammbô*. Although mannered dialogue occasionally threatens to topple into kitsch, most of the novel maintains the sense of vividness and the effects of perception, apprehension, emotion, and experience that are at the heart of Flaubert's accomplishments across his best works. Barthes's theory of the reality effects that occur in the pages of *Madame Bovary* also gives the reader a sense of Flaubert's powers in the prose of *Salammbô*—on the condition, of course, that the reader is not intimidated, angered, or bored by Flaubert's use of an unfamiliar vocabulary that does not reflect Second Empire culture. The novel portrays a vivid, violent Orient that Flaubert scripted as an alternative to the world in which he lived, Madame Bovary and all.*

*The author gratefully acknowledges research support from the University of California, Irvine.

Works Cited

Ahmad, Aijaz. *In Theory: Classes, Nations, Literatures.* London & New York: Verso, 1992.

Bancquart, Marie-Claire, Ed. *Flaubert, la femme, la ville.* Paris: PUF, 1982.

Barthes, Roland. *Le Degré zéro de l'*écriture suivi de Nouveaux essais critiques. Paris: Seuil, 1973.

Boehmer, Elleke. "Edward Saïd and (the Postcolonial Occlusion of) Gender." Ed. Ranjan Ghosh. *Edward Said and the Literary, Social, and Political World.* New York & Oxford: Routledge, 2009. 124–136.

Bernal, Martin. *Black Athena: The Afroasiatic Roots of Classical Civilization.* Vol. 1. New Brunswick: Rutgers UP, 1987.

Clifford, James. *The Predicament of Culture: Twentieth-Century Ethnography, Literature, and Art.* Cambridge, MA: Harvard UP, 1988.

Culler, Jonathan. *Flaubert: The Uses of Uncertainty.* Aurora: Davies Group, 2006.

_____. "The Realism of *Madame Bovary*." *Modern Language Notes* 122.4 (2007): 683–96.

Donato, Eugenio. *The Script of Decadence.* Oxford: Oxford UP, 1993.

Flaubert, Gustave. *Salammbô.* Ed. G. Séginger. Paris: Flammarion, 2001.

_____. *Madame Bovary*. Ed. Cl. Gothot-Mersch. Paris: Flammarion, 1965.

_____. *Salammbô*. Ed. E. Maynial. Paris: Garnier Frères, 1961.

_____. *Voyage en Egypte*. Ed. Pierre-Marc de Biasi. Paris: Grasset, 1983.

Foucault, Michel. *La Bibliothèque fantastique*. Paris: Seuil, 1983.

Gramsci, Antonio. *Quaderni del carcere*. Vol. 1. Torino: G. Einaudi, 1975.

Harrison, Nicholas. "'A Roomy Place Full of Possibility': Said's Orientalism and the Literary." Ed. Ranjan Ghosh. *Edward Said and the Literary, Social, and Political World*. New York & Oxford: Routledge, 2009: 3-18.

Le Calvez, Éric. *Genèses flaubertiennes*. Amsterdam & New York: Rodopi, 2009.

Lowe, Lisa. *Critical Terrains: French and British Orientalisms*. Ithaca: Cornell UP, 1991.

Neefs, Jacques. "Le Parcours du zaïmph." Ed. Cl. Gothot-Mersch. *La Production du sens chez Flaubert*. Paris: UGE, 1975: 227–251.

_____. "*Salammbô*, textes critiques." *Littérature* 15 (1974): 52–64.

_____. "Allegro Barbaro, la violence en prose." *Modern Language Notes* 128:4 (2013): 744–760.

Prendergast, Christopher. *The Triangle of Representation*. New York: Columbia UP, 2000.

Radhakrishnan, Rajagopalan. *A Said Dictionary*. London: John Wiley, 2012.

Said, Edward W. *Culture and Imperialism*. Cambridge: Harvard UP, 1983.

_____. *Orientalism*. New York: Random House, 1978.

_____. *Out of Place: A Memoir*. New York: Random House, 2000.

_____. *Reflections on Exile and Other Works*. Cambridge: Harvard UP, 2000.

_____. *The World, the Text, and the Critic*. New York: A. Knopf, 1993.

Schlossman, Beryl. *The Orient of Style: Modernist Allegories of Conversion [On Flaubert, Proust, Baudelaire]*. Durham & London: Duke UP, 1991.

_____. *Objects of Desire: The Madonnas of Modernism [On Joyce, Flaubert, Baudelaire, Stevens]*. Ithaca & London: Cornell UP, 1999.

Séginger, Gisèle. *Flaubert: Une Poétique de l'histoire*. Strasbourg: Strasbourg UP, 2000.

CRITICAL
READINGS

Memoirs of a Madman

Germaine Greer

There was never a time when Gustave Flaubert did not think of himself as a writer. He had thirty playlets to his credit before he was ten years old. At boarding school in Rouen from the age of eleven, he whiled away the long evenings by writing all kinds of short fictions, "opuscules historiques" and another play, spun out of his escapist reading and the morbid fantasies of his loneliness. *Memoirs of a Madman*, written before he was sixteen, is his twenty-fifth surviving work. His hero is a younger version of himself and the narrator an older version of that self, but the disillusionment and disgust that he gives vent to can be found in the letters written to his chum Ernest Charpentier by Flaubert when he was not yet fourteen.

During his life Flaubert forbade the publication of his juvenilia; the text of *Memoirs of a Madman* was not published until December 1900, since which time academics have mined it for information about the personality of a great artist, using it as the kind of factual account of events that might be extracted during sessions with a psychoanalyst, rather than understanding not only that the sixteen-year-old Flaubert shaped his account in a self-consciously literary fashion, but that he had been modelling his actual behavior on literary precedents for years. "I recall with what intense pleasure I devoured, at that time, the pages of Byron and of *Werther*, with what transports I read *Hamlet, Romeo*, and the most ardent productions of our period, all those works, in a word, which make the soul melt with rapture or set it afire with enthusiasm."

The boy who was in Trouville on a family holiday in 1836 had already cast himself as a Hamlet figure, "like John-a-dreams," condemned by his own "bourgeoisophobia" to inhabit a fantasy world of superior pleasures. In Chapter 10 of *Memoirs of a Madman* he recounts how, instead of playing with other children, he went for long Byronic walks along the shore and just happened to find himself beyond the village, at the place where bathers of both sexes came to the beach in bathrobes, which they left at the water's edge while they swam in their underwear. At the water's edge he finds a red pelisse with black stripes and moves it out of reach of the water. The artfulness of his way of recounting the series of events is worth noting: "That day a charming red pelisse with black stripes had been left on the shore. The tide was rising—the shore was festooned with foam—already a stronger wave had wet the silk fringes of this coat. I picked it up to move it away, its material was soft and light. It was a woman's coat."

The process of discovery first that the pelisse was charming, then that the fringe was silk, then that the garment was a woman's is not nature but art. The woman, Elisa Schlésinger, was real enough, but her rising from the sea to dazzle an innocent boy has more to do with Venus Anadyomene than with any actual bourgeois who went on holiday in 1836. Flaubert wants us to think that he happened upon the bathing spot innocently and "par hazard," but he certainly knew where the bathing place was because he had swum there with his family two summers before. On his return from Trouville in 1834, still six months shy of his thirteenth birthday, he wrote to Chevalier, his elder by a year:

> We went for a dip in the sea several times over three days. One of the other people bathing was a lady, oh, a pretty lady, innocent although married, pure although she was twenty-two. Oh, how beautiful she was with her pretty blue eyes! The day before, we saw her laughing on the beach as her husband read to her, and the following day… we learnt… that she had been drowned yes, drowned, dear Ernest, in less than quarter of an hour the wave had swept her away… her husband who had stayed behind on the beach to watch her bathing saw her disappear.

He speaks of the young woman to his friend as if he were already a disillusioned roué, tacitly disparaging both marriage and women's virtue. The lifelong pose was already taken. He does not tell this story in *Memoirs of a Madman*; instead we are told of a dream in which he is walking by a river with his mother who suddenly falls into the water; he sees the water bubble up and ripples spread, but she does not resurface. He hears her calling, but when he throws himself down and peers into the water, he can see nothing: "The water flowed on, flowed limpidly on, and that voice I could hear from the depths of the river plunged me into despair and rage..."

It is only to be expected that a child on the brink of his teens should recycle the tragic death of a young wife as a nightmare with himself in the position of the helpless husband. In *Memoirs of a Madman*, he elaborates the motif of the male on dry land and the female in the water. Although he went every day to watch his Venus bathe, he never thought of getting closer to her by becoming a bather himself. He remains in the position of the helpless husband, but this time the subject of his gaze does not disappear. Though the water can hardly have been as limpid as that of his dream-river, he can see Maria, as he calls her, "de loin" from a distance, immersed in the water, and envies the wavelet "lapping against her sides and covering with foam that heaving breast." There is no need to unpack this description of its sexual content because the erotic sequence is knowingly contrived. If the researchers who hunted down the real-life original of Maria had tried to watch swimmers "de loin," they would have realized at once that what Flaubert claims to have seen cannot be seen. The sexual stimuli that shower from Maria, her exotic appearance, her scent, the burning heat of her flesh, her engorged breast, her voice, her foam-flecked panting bosom, all are imagined. The climax, an idyllic boat-trip by night, is pure E. T. A. Hoffmann. The vividness of the constructed fantasies is the best evidence that the boy did spend a sleepless night watching his bedside candle burning down and torturing himself with imagining his goddess and her "vulgar and jovial" husband making love. And there are no prizes for identifying the melting candle with the post-masturbatory penis. Though Madame Schlésinger was a real person, the Maria of *Memoirs of a Madman* is an imaginary construct to which Flaubert would return again and again.

At eighteen, Flaubert did go swimming in the sea off Marseilles; this time his wet body caught the eye of a beautiful thirty-five-year-old woman who came to his hotel room and introduced him to "an orgy of delights," which left him detumescent, miserable, and utterly disgusted with himself and her. Like Maria, she was dark, with the same aquiline nose and features *à l'antique*, with even the same dark down on her upper lip. For six months after their encounter, Flaubert, who had no interest in seeing the woman again, made love to her by letter. The pleasure was not in the sex, but in writing about it.

Seduced by the cunning of the telling, commentators have allowed themselves to take at face value Flaubert's claims that Madame Schlésinger was his only love. In fact the distant, unattainable, fleshly goddess has been the only successful love object since the beginning of literature, which is about neither cohabitation nor copulation, but courtship. A woman enjoyed is a goddess destroyed. Flaubert liked to say that Lesbos was his native land; he could have learnt the imagery of unslaked desire from Sappho, who described it six centuries before the birth of Christ or, closer to home, in medieval Provençal lyrics. In following the creed that (in Keats' words) "Heard memories are sweet, but those unheard are sweeter." Flaubert is simply romantic. What has changed for him and contemporaries like Baudelaire, the De Goncourt brothers, Daudet, and De Maupassant, is that they put the notion to the test by exploring physical, even criminal pleasures, and minutely recording their disgust. Even in this, they followed in the footsteps of Ovid, Martial, Petronius, and Juvenal. Flaubert's narrator/hero is the lineal descendant of a long line of despairing young men, of the speaker of Rochester's "Satire upon Reason and Mankind," say, or Byron's *Childe Harold* or Goethe's *Werther*; he is also the forebear of the narrator of Sartre's *Nausea*. In his dreamy love idealism, his fastidious rejection of the everyday, and his desperate unhappiness, he is also Emma Bovary.

As Flaubert says, everyone would rather be a madman than a fool. Every day young men set up "madman" personal websites on the internet where other madmen may visit them and swap rants against conformism, bourgeois society, and pop culture. There are diaries of madmen on video, film, and vinyl. Their disgust, like the disgust that Flaubert cultivated from his childhood, is an artefact. Flaubert lived his revulsion; he elaborated it into the habit of mind that we now call "bovarism" and wrote a sublime novel about its female victim. The pose is still compelling; most of the young people who adopt it will abandon it, accept bourgeoisification, and join the consumer culture. For those who don't—few or none of whom will have Flaubert's obsessive devotion to his craft—misery, ill-health, and ultimate self-destruction are more likely outcomes than the creation of a masterpiece.

The Irony of Irony in *Madame Bovary*_____

Vaheed Ramazani

As early as 1838, in his *Mémoires d'un fou*, Flaubert articulates a thematic irony that many years later will prove to be central to his mature work as well: the inadequacy of language as a means of self-expression; the tragic gap between the artist's unique, ineffable self and the anonymous social discourse by which, as Jean-Paul Sartre says, he is "spoken" (1:33). It is not, however, until the writing of *Madame Bovary* that Flaubert will hazard a stylistic solution to the philosophical problem, which the narrator of the *Mémoires* formulates as follows: "comment rendre par la parole cette harmonie qui s'élève dans le cœur du poète, et les pensées de géant qui font ployer les phrases? . . . Par quels échelons descendre de l'infini au positif?" (*Œuvres complètes* 1: 231).

In her quest to live out an impossible ideal culled from her reading of popular fiction, Emma Bovary serves as a self-reflexive figure for the author's own desire to fashion an authentic, individual identity from within an alienating symbolic system—that preexistent, secondhand communicative medium which, if we credit Sartre's thesis in *L'Idiot de la famille,* Flaubert experienced, from early childhood on, as a violation of his private, original essence: "La Culture, pour lui [Flaubert], c'est le vol: elle réduit l'indécise et vaste conscience naturelle à son être-autre, cela veut dire: à ce qu'elle est pour les autres... [L]'âme, cette fièvre cosmique et particulière, devient un lieu commun" (Sartre 1: 40). Yet while Emma finds neither self-knowledge nor self-fulfillment in her desperate attempts to discover real-life referents for the kitschy tableaux and sentimental abstractions "qui lui avaient paru si beaux dans les livres" (Flaubert, *Œuvres complètes* 1: 586), Flaubert's use of an uncertain irony ("une ironie frappée d'incertitude" [Barthes 146]) enables him to rescue a distinctive sense of self from within the already said by creating a narrative voice whose originality lies, paradoxically, in its partial relinquishment of narrative authority, its ironization of the

_____

114

very project of individualization that the narrator shares with his ill-fated heroine. The reader's sense that irony, or the potential for irony, hovers not only over the world, of the novel, but also over the novel, as the *writing* of a world is in large measure a function of this relinquishment of authority, this openness of the text to the *bêtise* of the Other, to saturation by familiar forms of everyday social discourse. Insofar as no decidable countermeaning emerges from the novel's ironic subversion of the implicit assumptions informing these discursive codes, any attempt to assign to the narrator an alternative system of positive values seems arbitrary. Whatever amorphous narratorial identity may be produced by our act of reading, it can be inferred only negatively, as *not* being commensurable with the plethora of clichés that the text reproduces with apparent passivity. The irony of Flaubert's irony is that readers generally do, despite the dearth of textual and contextual cues, attribute an ironic vision to an implicit narrator, however resistant to positive characterization (other than by its implacable irony) that narrator's voice may be. More often than not, as we shall see, readers grasp the implied authority of an irony of relinquished authority—an irony requiring that they actively dissociate the worldview of an elusive narrator from that of his fictional characters while nevertheless remaining aware that the narrator, the characters, and the fictional world they share are but second-order effects of a style that is beautiful in and of itself, independent of its subject or of the story it tells.

The narrator's general inscrutability notwithstanding, stable ironies do abound in the novel, in its satirical citation (its pastiche, really) of conventional discourses of the bourgeoisie: Homais's pseudoscientific jargon, the priest Bournisien's physiological rather than spiritual vocabulary, Rodolphe's cynical deployment of the language of eternal love, the bombastic orations at the agricultural fair, and of course Emma and Léon's trading of sentimental clichés. In each one of these cases, quotation and paraphrase are unambiguously antiphrastic and depreciatory; that is to say, they are readily intelligible as the narrator's transparent (i.e., ironic) pretense of complicity with his characters' mediocrity, egoism, and so on. What distinguishes these particular ironies from more traditionally instrumental and polemical uses of language is that they arise in a narrative context that leaves open the question (famously posed by Roland Barthes [146]) "*Qui parle?*"—*who* is speaking, and in the name of *what* (what intellectual, moral, or ideological position)? It is not that potentially credible answers are lacking, but that there may be too many of them for the reader to choose from. The lineaments of plot, theme, and narrative voice do not offer us clear signposts for interpretive closure, for arresting the negative spiral of an irony that, once set in motion, threatens to undercut virtually anything we may say about the text (including, especially, about its irony). In the absence of a delineable narratorial identity that would frame and thereby limit the play of semiosis, what begins as the hermeneutically secure affirmation of the cognitive superiority of both the (implied) author and the (implied) reader to the conventional ways of thinking and speaking that are embodied in specific characters becomes readable as well as a kind of metairony—an irony that takes the reader, the author, *and* their irony as illocutionary objects of its endlessly "self-escalating act of consciousness" (de Man 220).

This overarching sense of unstable irony is inseparable, then, from Flaubert's celebrated doctrine of impersonality, according to which, we recall, the narrator must inhabit his fictional world "comme Dieu dans l'univers, présent partout, et visible nulle part" (Flaubert, *Correspondance* 2: 204). What this means, however, is not that the narrator is somehow "absent" from his fictional world, never calling attention to himself or to his attitude toward what he is at a given moment representing, but that the narrating voice is too diffuse, too self-contradictory to be naturalized as the enunciation of a knowable persona, a subject with a coherent, definable personality. At times, the narrator in *Madame Bovary* constructs lapidary aphorisms and ponderous metaphors, expressing overtly what we surmise are "his" own opinions and moral judgments regarding characters and events in his story. But such interventions are part of a broader strategy of ironic distanciation from the fictional world, a panoply of techniques by means of which the narrator foregrounds the artifactual nature of his novelistic writing, reminding us thereby that he, unlike his heroine, is aware of the difference between an autonomous system of linguistic signs and the world to which the signs refer.

The textual devices of ironic estrangement include a continual shifting of narrative distance and point of view—passages, for example, where limited, but anonymous, focalizations mingle with "omniscient" information and knowledge; where the immediate impression of an unidentified participant-observer alternates with detached and uncontextualized aesthetic commentary; or where descriptions of events equivocate between the singulative and the iterative. Additional peculiarities of Flaubert's autotelic style were first and most famously noted by Proust, for whom the rhythmical effects of prepositions and adverbs, the "éternel imparfait," and the "style indirect" work to convey a timeless, homogeneous vision, a structural and tonal unity that Flaubert himself called "une manière absolue de voir les choses" (*Correspondance* 2: 31). Sartre refers to the rhythms and sonorities of Flaubert's prose (which Proust had compared to the mechanical murmur of a "trottoir roulant" [194]) as the text's "nonsignifying elements," arguing that, for Flaubert, these texturing elements of style are invested with all of the metaphysical nostalgia that in his correspondence he associates with terms like *Truth, Beauty*, and the *Ideal*: "*son* style," says Sartre, "se forgera par l'utilisation systématique des éléments non-signifiants du discours pour rendre marginalement l'indisable" (2: 1981). "L'indisable"— Flaubert's personal coinage for "the unsayable" or "the ineffable"— designates, accordingly, a mystical experience arising, for narrator and narratee alike, from the connotative suggestiveness of a poeticized prose—a prose dominated by the phonetic and structural principle of equivalence that Roman Jakobson calls the "poetic function," and that he likens to the signifying process of metaphor. As Charles Bernheimer points out, when the principle of equivalence is applied to a text or a speech act,

> the semantic content of words is made secondary to their similarity in sound, and / or rhythm, hence to their sensuous, material qualities... Metaphor thus comes to be associated with a structural effect in literary art that tends to erase meaning by suggesting the substitutability

and reiterability of the linguistic units in any particular sequence. (Bernheimer 32)

Flaubert's avowed hope was that this activity of linguistic designification might arouse in his readers both astonishment and incomprehension, "une espèce d'ébahissement" (*Correspondance* 2: 204) or, as Sartre describes it, a pleasurable stupor—indeed, a kind of stupidity (*idiotie*)—that would release the mind into dream-filled serenity. Great works of art are "sans fond, infini, multiple," says Flaubert; they give rise to sensations of awe, exaltation, or impassive meditation: "Ce qui me semble, à moi, le plus haut dans l'Art (et le plus difficile), ce n'est ni de faire rire, ni de faire pleurer, ni de vous mettre en rut ou en fureur, mais d'agir à la façon de la nature, c'est-à-dire de *faire rêver*: Aussi les très belles oeuvres ont ce caractère. Elles sont sereines d'aspect et incompréhensibles" (*Correspondance* 2: 417).

Thus, the nonsignifying yet subjectively and subliminally evocative "music" of Flaubert's novelistic prose, in combination with the self-referential instabilities of point of view and narrative voice mentioned above, comprise the basic textual strategies of a transcendental ironism by means of which the author seeks to forge for himself, from within the alienating discourse of the Other, a sense of creative agency and of ontological plenitude such as will remain unavailable to Emma, his fictional alter ego. Flaubert's text, says Leo Bersani, "has kept traces of being continuously worked over," thus calling attention to "its own strategies, sounds and designs;" and, "while this gives something awkward and heavy to his writing... a certain stylistic opacity is Flaubert's decisive refutation of Emma's confused argument for a literature of pure sensation" ("Emma Bovary" 103). That is, Flaubert's retort to his protagonist's literature of easy and sensationalistic identification—a literature that would, in the author's own words, merely "faire rire" or "faire pleurer"—is a style rendered "incompréhensible" by its formal opacity, by the metaironic "strategies, sounds and designs" that for him represent "le plus haut dans l'Art" *precisely because* they are also "le plus difficile" (*Correspondance* 2: 417).

Flaubert insists on this caveat of difficulty in a letter to Ernest Feydeau, in which he asserts, grandiosely: "les livres ne se font pas comme les enfants, mais comme les pyramides, avec un dessin prémédité, et en apportant des grands blocs l'un par-dessus l'autre, à force de reins, de temps et de sueur, et ça ne sert à rien!" (*Correspondance* 2: 783). Literary monuments are not "made" in the same manner as children (that is, we surmise, in the heat of passion, or through an uncontrolled labor akin to giving birth); rather, they are *built*—built up over time, through a slow and deliberate artistic ascesis. Correlatively, a book that is not only difficult to write, but also in some sense difficult to read is a mere commodity. Effortlessly consumable and instantly gratifying, it requires of the reader, Flaubert suggests, no ethos of discipline, postponement, or restraint. Not surprisingly, then, Emma—to whom, we learn early on in the novel, "la discipline...était quelque chose d'antipathique" (*Œuvres complètes* 1: 587)—is a model of precisely that market-driven hedonism that is antithetical to her creator's cult of pure art. Both the untroubled representationalism of Emma's favorite books and her naive surrender to the illusion of mimesis deprive her, implicitly, of the hard-won pleasures of detached contemplation, rewarding her instead with the proverbial "cheap thrill"—"une sorte de profit personnel; et elle rejetait comme inutile tout ce qui ne contribuait pas à la consommation immédiate de son cœur" (1: 586). To underscore the shallowness of Emma's literary escapism, Flaubert depicts her fantasies as crude distillations of any and all of the literature she may have read: in the novel's extensive portrayals of Emma's inner menagerie, "good" and "bad" avatars of romanticism alike are reduced to a compendium, a phantasmagoric catalogue of contextless clichés. The "great romantic talents," as Bersani says, "have been filtered through a process which leaves only a sediment of anonymous, parodically simplified images. Originality has become a popular commodity and therefore resembles the conventional" ("Flaubert" 160).

The commodification of art and the rise of consumer culture are, of course, key elements of both plot and theme in *Madame Bovary*; and insofar as they implicate the author's will to distinction

---

in and through his protagonist's fatal *bovarysme*, they are also powerful motivating tropes for much of the text's irony. What inescapably binds Flaubert and his heroine, after all, is that in their respective roles as reader and writer, consumer and producer, they are mutually condemned to express their desire through the defiles of an economy—linguistic and commercial—where desire is recoverable only as cliché. *Madame Bovary* throws into relief, consequently, the historical coincidence and structural affinity of two cultural phenomena, the commodity and the cliché. Both concepts "grew up," as it were, in the nineteenth century, the figurative use of the term *cliché* emerging from its association with techniques and technologies of mechanical reproduction that had been introduced by the modern industry of printing (Amossy & Rosen 5–9). As a writer, Flaubert was acutely aware of the commercial nature of the medium through which he sought to express his individualistic vision. His tragic sense of linguistic dispossession could only be heightened by his anticipation of the inevitable commodification of his art, the originality of which would forfeit attention from even a limited, elite readership, unless his creation were physically disowned, subject, that is, to the depersonalizing processes of industrial production and mass distribution. With the diversification and relativization of public discourses that followed the social upheaval of 1789, any figure of speech was susceptible to devaluation as a result of its promiscuous circulation in the public domain. In the fundamentally verbal medium of literature, then, the threat of repeating an *idée reçue* was doubled by the published work's inevitable loss of "aura" (Benjamin 223), a loss that, in the wake of technological advances in photography and printing, haunted not only the visual arts, but *any* mechanically duplicable object of consumption.

In *Madame Bovary*, the connection between repetition, copying, and the loss of meaning (or aura) is pointedly illustrated by a variety of scenes and leitmotivs, including, most notably: Binet duplicating mechanically (i.e., on his lathe) a vast accumulation of identical napkin rings; the young student Charles copying the verb *ridiculus sum* twenty times over; Léon copying a sonnet from a keepsake, in counterfeit compliance with Emma's request that he write love poems for her. But, of course, it is Emma's own relentless pursuit of signs that best emblematizes the homology and the reciprocity of the commodity and the commonplace, of consumption and cliché.

The books that Emma Bovary so insatiably consumes are commodities that do exactly what good commodities are supposed to do—incite the desire for further commodities, in this case, not just more (and more intensely stimulating) books, but also the many glamorous things they describe. For Emma, love and wealth are two symbiotic components of a vital organic totality, two interdependent parts in a relation of metonymy: "Ne fallait-il pas à l'amour, comme aux plantes indiennes, des terrains préparés, une température particuliére?" (*Œuvres complètes* 1: 594). In her confusion of "les sensualités de luxe avec les joies du cœur, l'élégance des habitudes et les délicatesses du sentiment" (1: 594), she acquires luxury objects as if by possessing them she were possessing as well the elusive love she presumes they embody. Keepsake images, religious artifacts, the viscount's cigar case, and Lheureux's tempting wares all seem to hold for her a talismanic power. As Bersani remarks, Emma "dreams of 'persecuted ladies fainting in lonely pavilions' and of 'nightingales in thickets' as if they *were* romantic passion" ("Emma Bovary" 96).

Read ironically, this magical belief in the consubstantiality of words with things, and of things with emotional and conceptual abstractions (*"félicité," "passion," "ivresse,"* for example [*Œuvres complètes* 1: 586]), suggests that clichés and commodities alike are signs devoid of referential "content," arbitrary symbols that derive their meaning from an abstract network of differential relations—whether a commercial market or a linguistic system—and that are emptied, through processes of circulation and exchange, of their material specificity or use-value. As Emma attempts to bend the world to language, she discovers that language mirrors only itself, each signifier finding meaning not in reality, but in its diacritical relation to other signifiers. Perpetually displaced and deferred in this way, meaning cannot come to rest on an authenticating exterior, on a reality that, by governing the play of signs from without, would guarantee their referential truthfulness, their mimetic transparency.

Emma is trapped in a linguistic hall of mirrors in which words refer not to stabilizing referents (referents that would be adequate to her preconceived ideas), but only to other words in a chain of substitutions; words, she learns, neither determine reality nor are determined by it. Likewise, her commodities mirror only one another, producing value, as Marx has shown (54–75), through a series of reflections, each commodity shedding its material particularities in its relation of exchange with other commodities and ultimately with the "universal equivalent" of money.

The relation of these intersecting thematic and theoretical elements—specularity and iteration; mimesis and commodity fetishism—to the production of irony in *Madame Bovary* may be illustrated by brief analysis of a passage in which Emma, recently returned from her idyll with Rodolphe in the misty forests above Yonville, meditates on her own image as she sees it reflected in her bedroom mirror:

> Mais, en s'apercevant dans la glace, elle s'étonna de son visage. Jamais elle n'avait eu les yeux si grands, si noirs, ni d'une telle profondeur. Quelque chose de subtil épandu sur sa personne la transfigurait.
>
> Elle se répétait: "J'ai un amant! Un amant!" se délectant à cette idée comme à celle d'une autre puberté qui lui serait survenue. Elle allait donc posséder enfin ces joies de l'amour, cette fièvre de bonheur dont elle avait désespéré. Elle entrait dans quelque chose de merveilleux où tout serait passion, extase, délire; une immensité bleuâtre l'entourait, les sommets du sentiment étincelaient sous sa pensée, l'existence ordinaire n'apparaissait qu'au loin, tout en bas, dans l'ombre, entre les intervalles de ces hauteurs.
>
> Alors elle se rappela les héroïnes des livres qu'elle avait lus, et la légion lyrique de ces femmes adultères se mit à chanter dans sa mémoire avec des voix de soeurs qui la charmaient. (1: 629)

Here, in what resembles a rehearsal of the process of ego-formation as it is theorized by Lacan in his parable of the mirror stage, Emma "puts on" her ideal self-image, like a department store customer trying on an apparel to ensure that its objectified transformative effects are visibly in harmony with her desired social identity—

with, that is, an appropriated *image* that she makes her own through a gestalt-configuring dialectic of introjection and projection. But of course, the identity that Emma now wants to make her own is not a priori of her own making. Like the language she speaks, and through which she so relentlessly affirms her individuality, "her" image comes to her from a distant outside, an alien space she does not control. Emma's relation to her mirror image suggests, accordingly, that neither the words in her books nor any of the *other* objects she buys and consumes are the spontaneous expression of her true, inner self; they are the signs by means of which a preexisting ideological code confers on her a readymade social identity—not an authentic self, but an identification, a self-alienating desire for and of the Other.

Thus, Emma's introjection of the bookish convention of "la légion lyrique de ces femmes adultères" symbolically reiterates the fall into language, reenacting (or in Freudian terms, retranscribing) the archetypal severance from oceanic bliss, from the primordial feelings of unity and omnipotence experienced in connection with the body of the mother. In this textual allegory of infantile trauma, words, the fragmenting and repressive agents of culture, promise to fill the void they themselves have created with the plenitude of "des voix de sœurs qui la charmaient"— with, that is, more books, more words, and more material objects, which in turn create more loss, more nostalgia, more desire, in a never-ending cycle of compulsive consumption. In this context, Emma's incantation ("J'ai un amant! Un amant!") becomes readable as an index of her fetishistic belief that in uttering the word she possesses the thing; whereas what she in fact possesses are only more words, more empty signifiers ("ces joies de l'amour, cette fièvre de bonheur") that, as the deictic elements ("ces," "cette") suggest, derive primarily from her book-fed assumptions and that, as the proleptic liminality of the verb tense makes clear, still remain to be experienced and coherently defined ("Elle *allait donc posséder*" [my emphasis]).

At one level, then, irony arises from the reader's perception of a series of reversals: of possessor and possessed, active and passive, original and banal. Yet irony does not simply "correct"

Emma's *bovarysme*; by its repetitive gesture of distancing and self-distancing, it points as well to the author's *bovarysme*, as faith in the magical power of signs is transferred from their referential to their self-referential function. What this irony accomplishes, in sociolinguistic terms, is the reader's estrangement from modes of perception and praxis that, in Flaubert's time, were coming to be seen as natural, self-evident. The fragmentation of daily experience that was becoming normalized under modern industrial culture is restaged, in *Madame Bovary*, in a style that duplicates (as it must) the impersonal grammars of language and commerce, while at the same time signaling the text's distance from them. The text does not thereby transcend these social and historical structures; it ironizes, through the desiring figure of Emma, the fetishization of commodities and signs, yet by this very recourse to the fetish of irony, it acknowledges as well the impossibility of escaping, of avoiding altogether, the homogenizing effects of modern capitalism—a culture in which, as we have seen, the desire for originality cannot readily be distinguished from the desire for novelty, for a newness to be consumed and rapidly "re-newed."

In the passage at hand, an ironic reading of Emma's transformation—of, that is, her perception of herself, or of her reflected image, as profoundly changed or remarkably "new"—depends on our recognition that the transformation itself is doubly specular, taking place through the detour not only of a reflection, but also of the character's reflection on that reflection, through, in other words, a consciousness that "reflects," faithfully or not, the literary images by which it is colonized. Our (ironic) sense that the "new" Madame Bovary may not be so new, so original as she thinks, is in part a function of a general thematic context (her confusion of luxury, leisure, and love; her position as the third in a series of Madame Bovarys [first, Charles' mother; second, Charles' first wife Héloïse; and finally, Emma]) that is itself an effect of a "naïve" mimetic reading not unlike that by which Emma is seduced; yet this same sense of irony is overwritten and destabilized by narrative uncertainties that problematize the very mimesis on which it and its context both depend.

This brings us to consideration of that particular feature of Flaubert's style that is, I think, largely responsible for the mimetic indeterminacy that often attends narration of Emma's thought and speech. Brief quotation of her speech notwithstanding, we have very little textual evidence—not only in this passage, but throughout the novel—as to how Emma Bovary "really" speaks, whether silently, to herself, or out loud, to others (or sometimes, as here, to herself alone). We know only that "romanticism" is spoken on her behalf, *through* her, as it were, by a voice so monolithic that "she" and her subjectivity seem to be mere pretexts for irony directed against the romantic code itself. The sustained uniformity of narrative style and register frequently makes it difficult, if not impossible, to say just where the heroine's voice leaves off and where the voice of the narrator may begin, or indeed (and in consequence of the foregoing ambiguity) whether what is being narrated is the character's voice at all, or instead some kind of pre-articulate, nonverbal mental matter: impressions, sensations, perceptions, or intuitions; dreams, daydreams, hallucinations, and so on.

In the mirror scene quoted above, for example, it is unclear whether the opening sentences are to be construed as the purely "objective" narratorial report of a vague impression—one that, in the mind of the character, lies prior to or beneath verbal formulation—for instead as predominantly neutral narration that nonetheless is tinged with words for which Emma (or her conscious thought processes) may be the source, unspoken words such as might cross her mind as she apprehends, or imagines, her transfiguration. The next sentence is an example of *style indirect libre,* or free indirect discourse, which critics often hail as a hallmark of Flaubert's stylistic innovation. By eliding the introductory verb and subordinating conjunction that are typical of indirect discourse (e.g., "She said that" or "She thought that") and blending the grammar of third-person narration with lexical and emotive features attributable to the character's speech (or manner of speaking), free indirect discourse becomes interpretable as a particularly subtle form of (potentially ironic) narratorial mimicry of the character's "voice." Unambiguous instances of free indirect discourse—such as this one, "Elle allait donc posséder…"—are, however, less prevalent in Flaubert's major work than is commonly assumed, not because free indirect discourse is an inherently ambiguous fusion and confusion of narrating and narrated perspectives, but because whatever ambiguity may result from the technique's comingling of third- and first-person voices, the *dominant* voice, in free indirect discourse proper, is that of the character. That is, the reader's recognition of free indirect discourse is, by definition, his or her contextually enabled inference, or "extraction," of an imagined, yet verisimilar, simulacrum of the *character's discourse* from "behind" or "within" the narrating discourse (this despite the reader's implicit understanding that, due to the third-person narrative embedding, what is audible "beneath" the narrator's voice may be only an approximation of the "real" words spoken, or thought, by the focalized character).

An example of the more typically Flaubertian—as well as, it seems to me, the more pragmatically ambiguous and aesthetically significant—mode for rendering the character's inner life is offered by the closing sentence of our quoted passage above. The first part of this long coda equivocates between free indirect discourse and the narration of preverbal psychic material, as we wonder whether "Elle entrait dans quelque chose de merveilleux" is an unsubordinated and narratively camouflaged reproduction of the character's conscious thought or instead a superordinate narrator's representation of an emotional state that for the character remains only latently articulable. Similarly, we can only speculate as to whether the ensuing parataxis— "passion, extase, délire"—reports words that "actually" occur to Emma or instead merely compiles, to hyperbolic effect, terms such as would be found in her personal library, terms broadly emblematic of a literary code that *already* suffers from hyperinflation, and whose status as cliché serves to remind us, more generally, of the inherent inadequacy of language to the description of objects. (As the narrator will interject later on in the novel, apropos of words exchanged between Léon and Emma, "la parole est un laminoir qui allonge toujours les sentiments" [*Œuvres complètes* 1: 653]). The sentence concludes with a highly plastic tableau offering a metaphorical distillate of the joyful anticipation that the paragraph

---

126

as a whole is designed to portray. This visual spatialization of abstract emotions and concepts unfolds to the rhythm of three asyndetic verbal phrases ("l'entourait," "étincelaient," "n'apparaissait"), the last of which declines its series of prepositional phrases through four measured periods, each marked by a *coupe*. The language is traversed as well by a cascade of *voyelles graves* and *consonnes liquides* that lends a solemn splendor to an image that seems otherwise clumsy and trite. Indeed, the prosodic elements of Flaubert's style here may arouse in readers aesthetic and emotive effects that are consonant with the heroine's lyrical effusion and that therefore may be felt to soften the attendant irony. Particularly in the absence of reporting tags, such as "She saw" or "She felt," which, by explicitly indexing the narrator's distance from the image, would unambiguously demarcate his role as its architect from the delusional perspective it so poetically represents, readers must work actively to infer textual irony, to dissociate narrator and narratee alike from a perspective that, despite its evident naïveté, takes on something of the authority and the value of the "absolute" style that enshrines it. This irony, once decoded, "feels" less definitive, less negative or judgmental, than it would were its object not cast in a prose that so elaborately displays the hand of the craftsman.

In its ideal form, this ironic-poetic style was envisioned by Flaubert as autonomous, self-contained, entirely freestanding: "ce que je voudrais faire, c'est un livre sur rien, un livre sans attache extérieure, qui se tiendrait de lui-même par la force interne de son style" (*Correspondance* 2: 31). Of course, style in *Madame Bovary* attains no such purity; nor does it pretend to. It equivocates, instead, between mimesis and opacity, irony and empathy, refusing Emma's fetishism of commodities and of signs, while also acknowledging, through this figural and tonal ambivalence, its inevitable complicity with those same structures of power to which Emma succumbs without reservation. In this context, the uncertainties of perspective and narrative voice that we have been discussing may be read as the text's ironic emulation of the contradictory logic of "organized disorganization" (Terdiman 117–146)—the commercially motivated fragmentation of the consumer's time and space that in the nineteenth century was already manifest in the collage-like layout of the newspaper page, with its disjunctive arrangement of unrelated articles; in the jolting sights and sounds of advertising and display; and in the disorienting floor plans of the new department stores. The ordered disorder of everyday life is registered, in *Madame Bovary*, not only in the incongruous historical and cultural eclecticism of the heroine's keepsakes but also in the kaleidoscopic narrative shifting between detachment and immediacy, proximity and distance, anonymity and identity that, as we have seen, is the distinctive mark of Flaubert's "impersonality." Yet this same style imposes its own rigorous order on the heterogeneous objects and perspectives it presents, foregrounding formal and compositional devices that reinforce our ironic distance from the tropes of easy reading and easy consumption, while at the same time suggesting that this very margin of distance is inherently compromised, the irony of the text's irony being that irony itself is a product of the medium and of the media that it nonetheless tirelessly continues to critique.

Works Cited or Consulted

Amossy, Ruth & Elisheva Rosen. *Les discours du cliché*. Paris: CDU et SEDES Reunis, 1982.

Barthes, Roland. *S/Z*. Paris: Seuil, 1970.

Baudrillard, Jean. *La Société de consommation*. Paris: Gallimard, 1974.

Benjamin, Walter. "The Work of Art in the Age of Mechanical Reproduction." *Illuminations* by Walter Benjamin. Ed. Hannah Arendt. Trans. Harry Zohn. London: Fontana, 1973.

Bernheimer, Charles. *Flaubert and Kafka: Studies in Psychopoetic Structure*. New Haven: Yale UP, 1982.

Bersani, Leo. "Emma Bovary and the Sense of Sex." *A Future for Astyanax*. By Leo Bersani. Boston: Little, Brown & Co., 1976.

_____. "Flaubert and the Threats of Imagination." *Balzac to Beckett: Center and Circumference in French Fiction*. By Leo Bersani. New York: Oxford UP, 1970.

Booth, Wayne C. *A Rhetoric of Irony*. Chicago: U of Chicago P, 1961.

Bowlby, Rachel. *Just Looking: Consumer Culture in Dreiser, Gissing, and Zola*. New York: Methuen, 1985.

Brombert, Victor. *The Novels of Flaubert: A Study of Themes and Techniques*. Princeton, NJ: Princeton UP, 1966.

Chambers, Ross. "Repetition and Irony." *The Writing of Melancholy: Modes of Opposition in Early French Modernism*. By Ross Chambers. Trans. Mary Seidman Trouille. Chicago: U of Chicago P, 1993.

Chatman, Seymour. *Story and Discourse: Narrative Structure in Fiction and Film*. Ithaca: Cornell UP, 1978.

Cohn, Dorrit. *Transparent Minds: Narrative Modes for Presenting Consciousness in Fiction*. Princeton, NJ: Princeton UP, 1978.

Culler, Jonathan. *Flaubert: The Uses of Uncertainty*. Ithaca: Cornell UP, 1975.

de Gaultier, Jules. *Le Bovarysme*. Paris: Mercure de France, 1921.

de Man, Paul. "The Rhetoric of Temporality." *Blindness and Insight* by Paul de Man. *Theory and History of Literature*. Vol. 7. 2nd ed. Minneapolis: U of Minnesota P, 1983.

Flaubert, Gustave. *Correspondance*. Ed. Jean Bruneau. 5 vols. *Bibliothèque de la Pléiade*. Paris: Gallimard, 1973–2007.

_____. *Œuvres complètes*. 2 vols. Paris: Seuil, 1964.

Freud, Sigmund. "Fetishism." *Three Essays on the Theory of Sexuality*. By Sigmund Freud. Trans. and ed. James Strachey. New York: Penguin Books, 1977.

Genette, Gérard. *Figures III*. Paris: Seuil, 1972.

Jakobson, Roman. "Linguistics and Poetics." *The Structuralists from Marx to Lévi-Strauss*. Ed. Richard T. De George & Ferdinande M. De George. New York: Doubleday, 1972.

Lacan, Jacques. "Le Stade du mirroir comme formateur du fonction du Je." *Ecrits*. By Jacques Lacan. Paris: Seuil, 1966.

Mannoni, Octave. *Clefs pour l'imaginaire ou l'autre scène*. Paris: Seuil, 1969.

Marx, Karl. *Capital: A Critique of Political Economy*. Trans. Samuel Moore & Edward Aveling. New York: International Publishers, 1967.

McHale, Brian. "Free Indirect Discourse: A Survey of Recent Accounts." *PTL: A Journal for Descriptive Poetics and Theory of Literature* 3 (1978): 249–287.

Muecke, Douglas C. *The Compass of Irony*. London: Methuen, 1969.

Proust, Marcel. "A Propos du 'style' de Flaubert." *Chroniques*. Paris, Gallimard, 1972.

Riffaterre, Michael. "Flaubert's Presuppositions." *Flaubert and Postmodernism*. Ed. Naomi Schor & Henry F. Majewski. Lincoln: U of Nebraska P, 1984.

Sartre, Jean-Paul. *L'Idiot de la famille*. 3 vols. Paris: Gallimard, 1971–72.

Sperber, Dan & Deirdre Wilson. "Les Ironies comme mentions." *Poétique* 8 (1978): 399–412.

Tanner, Tony. "Flaubert's *Madame Bovary*." *Adultery in the Novel: Contract and Transgression*. By Tony Tanner. Baltimore, MD: Johns Hopkins UP, 1979.

Terdiman, Richard. *Discourse/Counter-discourse: The Theory and Practice of Symbolic Resistance in Nineteenth-Century France*. Ithaca, NY: Cornell UP, 1985.

Flaubert in Trans-medial and Trans-national Contexts: Adapting and Translating *Madame Bovary*

Élodie Laügt

> Isn't the most reliable form of pleasure, Flaubert implies, the pleasure of anticipation? (Julian Barnes, *Flaubert's Parrot* 13)

The dialog between literature and other art forms constitutes an important aspect of literary criticism. From the notion of *ekphrasis* to the ways in which painters, composers, playwrights, and film directors have, for centuries, drawn their subject matter from literary sources, literary criticism has had to engage with, and conceptualize, spaces of encounter with what literature is not or what is not it. The very idea of literature is thus intimately tied to the question of its own limits as a mode of expression and has to be thought in relation to the question of what it can and cannot do. It is within this context that our understanding of literary texts—and perhaps Flaubert's œuvre more than any other—has been enriched by the development of adaptation studies. Adaptation studies constitutes a field of research concerned not only, as is perhaps most immediately thought, with the transposition of literary works onto the screen, but also with a whole range of rewriting practices, thanks to which texts travel from one genre, or medium, to another: novels can be adapted for theatrical performances, poems can become songs, stories can also be retold from different characters' perspectives, texts can be interpreted into art works, screenplays can be turned into novels, and, with the development of new interactive technologies, novels are increasingly used as the basis for video games. Adaptation studies, therefore, deals with the constant redefinition of boundaries between genres and media through innovative artistic practices and the ways in which they interact and inform each other. While the notion that the meaning of a text may be created by one person has been strongly challenged since the 1960s, particularly in the wake of Barthes's formulation of the 'death of the author,' the practice of adaptation presents us with the possibility of better understanding the relations and interplays between author and reader as well as the connections between reading and writing. Reading can thus be conceptualized as a way of countersigning or co-writing a text, and adaptation may be seen as the performance of a particular reading or interpretation of a given text.

Nineteenth-century literature, and more specifically the novel, constitute an extremely fertile ground for adaptation, in particular filmic adaptation: from Charles Dickens to Jane Austen and Emily Brontë, via Tolstoy and Balzac, to name but a few of the authors whose novels are given new lives by filmmakers themselves belonging to a wide range of filmic traditions or schools, from the French New Wave to Hollywood. These novels are frequently built around well-known story lines with which the public is familiar and from which they can, therefore, derive "part of [their] pleasure [...] from repetition with variation, from the comfort of ritual combined with the piquancy of surprise," as Linda Hutcheon puts it (*A Theory of Adaptation* 4). This is partly why, within the French literary tradition, Flaubert's *Madame Bovary* is among the novels which have been most often adapted, rewritten and used as what Gérard Genette calls hypotext, that is, a starting point for new theatrical, cinematic, and literary creations.[1] In an article in which she analyses how successive interpretations of *Madame Bovary* have been informed by, and have contributed to, the evolution of feminist theories, Suzanne Leonard notes that the novel "has inspired a veritable culture industry" and highlights the fact that "the past fifteen years have witnessed a marked surge of interest in rewriting or reimagining the original text" (Leonard 647). As I am writing this chapter, two new films have just premiered in the United States, in addition to—or perhaps one should say despite—the many already existing, including versions by Jean Renoir (1934), Vincente Minnelli (1949), and Claude Chabrol (1991): Sophie Barthes' *Madame Bovary*, starring Mia Wasikowska, and Anne Fontaine's adaptation of *Gemma Bovery*, the graphic novel by Posy Simmonds, in which Flaubert's Emma is reincarnated into an English illustrator who decides to leave London in order to settle in a small Normandy town with her new husband Charles Bovery.[2]

The unfaltering attraction that *Madame Bovary* has exerted on film directors and cinema audiences can be explained by the canonical status of the novel, a status that the multiplication of adaptations in turn reinforces. However, if Flaubert's first novel continues to speak to us across time and space, in French and in translation, perhaps more insistently than some and as uniquely as other texts (such as Homer's Odysseus or Shakespeare's plays) it may be because it articulates in a very singular way questions about its own status as an art form exploring the possibility of adaptation. By exemplifying the way in which literature in its modern sense raises the question of its own definition, Flaubert's novel both marks and contributes to shaping a particular moment in French literary history that continues to inform the way in which we conceive not only of literature, but of arts and culture more generally. In the present essay, I will suggest that the novel's contemporaneity and the reason why it continues to be read, rewritten, translated, and adapted, lie in the very possibility that it keeps creating for us, to engage imaginatively with words (written or spoken) and images (verbal or not), that is, with the way in which we perform our cultural heritage. In addition, the novel's many journeys across languages and media enable us to question the very notion of "cultural heritage." Seen through the lens of adaptation, as well as in relation to questions of propriety and appropriation raised by various re-writing practices, this notion of cultural heritage requires that we ask to whom or to what *Madame Bovary* belongs. More broadly, the very notion of literature's "belonging" must be questioned since, as has already been hinted here through references to artworks produced and performed in other languages and countries than French or France, engaging with adaptation means first of all being prepared to challenge the categories of what may be referred to as national literatures.

As the narrator of Julian Barnes's *Flaubert's Parrot* is visiting Normandy, where Flaubert famously lived and set some of his stories, he plays with the idea that the parrot in *Un cœur simple* (1877) may be a metaphor for the writer's voice. However, as he visits the novelist's hometown of Rouen, he comes across two different stuffed parrots, both thought to have served Flaubert as models depending on whom you listen to: the *gardien* at the Hôtel Dieu or the *gardienne* at the Croisset pavilion. Beyond the questions of both the authenticity of the objects and whether asserting which one is the right one matters at all, this "duplication" of parrots prompts the narrator to ask: "The writer's voice—what makes you think it can be located that easily?" (Barnes 22). The question of the possibility of locating Flaubert's voice seems to have been at stake from the very moment *Madame Bovary* was published in 1857. At the time, the story of an adulterous woman who leads her husband to ruin and disrepute before eventually herself committing suicide, sees its author prosecuted for "offense to public morals and to religion." The literary critic Sainte-Beuve expresses his criticism of the novel in the following terms in the *Moniteur universel* (4 May 1857): "un reproche que je fais à son livre c'est que le bien est trop absent; pas un personnage ne le représente...." As LaCapra has argued, the problem for the authorities at the time, and the reason why they condemned the book, is that according to them, the author adopts too impersonal an attitude and does not judge his characters explicitly. However, what is perceived as a fault of the novel is in fact precisely what Flaubert wants to achieve: his own disappearance as author. As he wrote to Louise Colet on February 8, 1852: "Je veux qu'il n'y ait pas dans mon livre un seul mouvement, ni une seule réflexion de l'auteur." The following month, he explains to another correspondent, Mlle Leroy de Chantepie (March 18, 1857), what he is striving to achieve, that is to be "dans son œuvre comme Dieu dans la création, invisible et tout-puissant." Beyond the first chapter, which is narrated from the perspective of one of the children whom Charles Bovary joins when he starts at school, any identifiable narrator disappears, and the narration is carried through what is referred to as indirect free style and has come to be seen as one of Flaubert's hallmarks, as Stephen Heath as shown. The effect that indirect free style has on the narration constitutes an interesting starting point when thinking about adaptation. The multiplicity of perspectives rendered within the text to the exclusion of a clearly identifiable narrator's viewpoint is paralleled by the fact that the very possibility of locating the author's voice is at the heart of the question of adaptation. Although the narrator must not be confused with the author, the shifting perspectives of the narration in Flaubert's text anticipate the relation analysed by Rancière in *La Fable cinématographique*, between the 'objective eye' of the camera and the subjective gaze of the director.

There are various ways to explore this issue. One of them consists of approaching literature itself as an adaptive process. From this point of view, if the so-called voice of the writer is difficult and even impossible to locate, it may be because it was never only one voice in the first place, but rather, it always already consisted of a "mosaic" of perspectives. This is what Andrew Watts suggests in his analysis of *Madame Bovary* in *Adapting Nineteenth-Century France: Literature in Film, Theatre, Television, Radio, and Print*. Drawing from Julia Kristeva's definition of intertextuality and Julie Sander's theorization of adaptation, Watts examines Flaubert's own "adaptive method" in order to show how the novelist drew from a number of texts ranging from the medieval tradition to romantic novels and journalistic accounts in order to piece together or "assemble" his own text. Watts writes: "*Madame Bovary* appears as a textual mosaic that selects from and rewrites earlier fictions, resulting in a work that is simultaneously past and present" (93). The tension identified by Watts here concerns the fact that "[i]n contrast to the plot of *Madame Bovary*, which reflects an authorial sensitivity to the dangers of adaptation, Flaubert's own adaptive method demonstrates the potential for rewriting an array of earlier sources and texts" (86). This approach contributes to our understanding of the "timelessness" of the novel insofar as it is built on an ensemble of texts whose canonical status is both confirmed by, and rubbed onto, Flaubert's novel. From that perspective, *Madame Bovary* constitutes a particular reading of the literary tradition from which it stems and in which it partakes: it mocks a certain kind of romanticism by making its main protagonist the victim of her own readings and of the fantasies and aspirations that they entertained in her mind, making her discontented with, and spiteful of, what she perceives as too common and dull a life. Through Emma as a reader, Flaubert offers us his reading of the literary tradition. He not only sketches a literary landscape with which his contemporary readers would be familiar and that we in turn inherited, but he does so critically by making his protagonist a "bad" reader who has herself no critical distance *vis-à-vis* what she is reading, mostly romantic works whose heroines she longs to resemble.

Another way of engaging with the question of the author's voice in the context of adaptation consists of paying attention to devices that directors have used in order to somehow retain the figure of Flaubert in their adaptations of his work. It is partly to that effect that Vincente Minnelli frames Emma's story by having it recounted by Flaubert during his trial so as to give him the opportunity to explain himself in front of prosecutor Ernest Pinard. While Minnelli is thus addressing issues of censorship that could arise because of the Motion Picture Code in place at the very end of the 1940s in relation to the subject matter, the representation of Flaubert himself reinforces the sense that, in this film, Emma's story can be viewed as co-authored not only by Minnelli and the author of the screenplay, Robert Ardrey, but also by Flaubert. There are undoubtedly some issues with the way in which Flaubert's authorial voice is thus brought to the fore, not least because it goes against what Flaubert himself was trying to achieve with free indirect style, and this is one of the criticisms levelled at Minnelli by George Bluestone. As he puts it, "[f]or Flaubert, who spent so many agonized years trying to refine himself out of his work, this retailing of Emma's story would seem appalling" (Bluestone 50). At another level, the use that Chabrol makes in his own adaptation starring Isabelle Huppert, of a voiceover whose lines are most often lifted directly from Flaubert's text, contributes to maintaining Flaubert's ghostly presence in the film, while giving the audience the chance to enjoy again both the poetic qualities and the irony of his prose. A particularly good example of this occurs as Emma and Charles have settled into life as a married couple. The voice of François Périer comments on how "à mesure que se serrait davantage l'intimité de leur vie, un détachement intérieur se faisait qui la déliait de lui. La conversation de Charles était plate comme un trottoir de rue, les idées de tout le monde y défilaient dans leur costume ordinaire, sans exciter d'émotion, de rire ou de rêverie." (Flaubert, *Œuvres Complètes* 1: 328). Flaubert's irony is enhanced by the weaving of the poetic way in which he describes the boredom inspired by Charles's conversation and actual snatches of Charles's conversation flatly delivered by Jean-François Balmer.

Chabrol's decision to quote Flaubert's text directly or to imitate his style has been amply analyzed, which is indicative of the fact that style constitutes one of the major challenges for anyone trying to adapt a literary text for the screen or the stage. This is very much a problem that writers adapting novels share with translators: how do you deal with the novelist's style and what happens to it in the process of adaptation? What can you do in order to translate a literary style into another medium or another language? And should you always try to translate it? Such is the set of issues raised by Julian Barnes in his review of Lydia Davis's translation of *Madame Bovary* published in the *London Review of Books*. Barnes considers whether good translators are themselves good writers in the first place or even if good writers can make good translators, asking: "[W]ould you rather have your great novel translated by a good writer or a less good one?," before explaining his question as follows:

> This is not as idle a question as it seems. That perfect translator must be a writer able to subsume him or herself into the greater writer's text and identity. Writer-translators with their own style and worldview might become fretful at the necessary self-abnegation; on the other hand, disguising oneself as another writer is an act of the imagination, and perhaps easier for the better writer. (Barnes, "Writer's Writer and Writer's Writer's Writer")

The problem that Barnes then identifies with Davis's translation concerns the way in which, in order to be "faithful" to Flaubert, to retain his sentences' structures and as many expressive nuances as possible, she tends to introduce some "clunkiness" into the English version, which is the exact opposite of what Flaubert achieves in his prose. As Barnes puts it: "This is the paradox and bind of translation. If to be 'faithful' is to be 'clunky', then it is also to be unfaithful, because Flaubert was not a 'clunky' writer." This seems all the more problematic since, if Flaubert has long been considered to occupy a position at the heart of modernity, it is precisely because of the importance that he grants to style and the departure that his writing constitutes from a conception of literature whose focus is on the plot. Style, for Flaubert must take precedence over plot. His ambition is, famously, to write a book about nothing, a book in which language is not put at the service of a story but, rather, constitutes the very matter of the book. "Art for art's sake" or the notion of "pure art" lies partly in the way in which literature is not conceived as a window through which one can see or access the world, but is seen as that which is accessed when reading. Language is not seen as a transparent communication tool that would convey a pre-existing meaning. On the contrary, its materiality is poetic insofar as it itself produces meaning. This particular way in which Flaubert inherits the first German romantics' conception of literature of 1798 to 1804, has been analyzed by Jacques Rancière, in particular in *The Politics of Literature*. Rancière articulates what he sees as a shift operated in *Madame Bovary* in terms of reversal of the hierarchies of representation as established by Aristotle's poetics. While according to Aristotle, characters must be represented in accordance to their status and must speak a language that reflects the rank they occupy in society (kings must speak like kings and servants like servants), in 1856, the daughter of a farmer can become the eponymous heroine of a novel and be represented by means of a language that would be fit for any other theoretically more noble subject. Not only that, but Flaubert's writing makes our gaze fall on things that would previously have been thought of as insignificant from a literary point of view. The novelist takes care to describe in minute detail objects that do not contribute to the action or the plot, but give writing its depth and thickness. Two points may be noted here, which help clarify the ways Flaubert's novel is particularly "adaptable" for filmmakers. First, Flaubert turns insignificant, everyday objects into subjects of writing and, as has been noted by many critics, this attention to detail gives a filmic quality to his prose, anticipating the invention of cinema by the Lumière brothers at the end of the nineteenth century.[3] Second, as Rancière puts it, "l'absolutisation du style [est] la formule littéraire du principe d'égalité démocratique" (Rancière 17). In other words, Flaubert, through his style and his subject matter, and despite his own political stance on it, foregrounds the democratization of art: Emma is trying to emulate the lifestyle that she has witnessed at La Vaubyessard and to make her own life into a work of art. While she fails and drives her husband to ruin, she embodies a certain "democratic appetite" in a context in which critics have traditionally established a cultural divide between what is regarded as high art and what is thought of as low art—"Hamlet versus Bugs Bunny; string quartets versus rap music," as John A. Fisher puts it in "High Art Versus Low Art" (527).

The questioning of the legitimacy and usefulness of distinguishing between high and low art is part of the discussion about the process of democratization to which literature is supposedly subjected when literary works are adapted for the big screen or television. Both thematically and stylistically, *Madame Bovary* somehow makes it possible for literature to travel into other media and thereby to reach new readerships, audiences, or "consumers" and thus to participate in challenging the very divisions and categories that were theorized in its name and in order to protect a certain notion of what "real" literature is or must be. However, literature in its modern sense, as it has been theorized through phenomenology, from Heidegger to Derrida, rests largely on the refutation of the idea that literature *must* fulfil some pre-existing criteria of definition, and lies rather in the very possibility of resisting any fixed definition. What literature *is* is first and foremost what it becomes. From that point of view, as I have argued elsewhere, the story of *Madame Bovary*, its trajectory and all the versions of it that we know, make visible the fact that adaptation—the possibility of adapting a literary work as much as the possibility for a literary work to be adapted—is constitutive of literature. Adaptation is literature's condition of possibility. Because of the particular way in which *Madame Bovary* focuses the question of literature on the question of style and aesthetics, including in relation to translation and adaptation, it becomes the means to articulate literary criticism in such a way that literary criticism is forced to engage with its own strategy and purpose. This is what Jonathan Culler formulates, having explained the specificity of Flaubert's approach to the novel as "an aesthetic object rather than a communicative act" (Culler 15), he asks: "why write this novel?" This question, Culler continues:

> points toward an absent answer, a kind of empty meaning which must serve as teleological determinant of our reading. That is to say, if critical discourse is designed to demonstrate the presence of a controlling purpose in all the parts and their interrelations, then the fact that the most sophisticated and "aesthetic" novels show a purposiveness without purpose cannot but affect our reading of them. (16)

However, adaptations and translations are also readings, even if they are of a different critical kind: adaptation always rests on the need to discriminate and to select what to retain and what to leave out of the adaptation, while translation consists of deciding which words to use in order to reproduce for Anglophone readers an effect similar to that made by Flaubert's text on Francophone ones. From that point of view, Culler's question is relevant to adaptation and translation as it is not only "why write this novel?" but also "how do we read it?" What adaptation and translation make more apparent is that the question of what we read is secondary to that of *how* we read because they exemplify and perform "strategies of reading and interpretation" (Culler 19). One of the questions central to Culler's approach to literature concerns the way in which literary criticism tries to impose a teleological perspective onto its object. In order to find meaning or make sense of the literary work, the critic attempts to organize characters, events, and objects into patterns, which in turn participate in a meaningful and coherent perspective or message. However, Culler argues, the critical gesture thus amounts to supplementing the novel with a meaning whose possibility it bears but lacks at the same time because the experience that the novel represents and offers is out of kilter with the meaning produced by the critic. Therefore, as Culler puts it: "The novel is an ironic form, born of the discrepancy between meaning and experience, whose source of value lies in the interest of exploring that gap and filling it, while knowing that any claim to have filled it derives from blindness" (Culler 24).

The blindness of filmic adaptations of *Madame Bovary* lies paradoxically in the artistry with which they attempt more or less successfully to organize and unify a number of mirroring effects, which, if they exist in the original text, need to be transposed from page to screen. The "good" adaptation will be one that emulates the mirroring effect, even if it is at the cost of a so-called "faithfulness." In the case of a novel, which problematizes reading, perhaps a "good" filmic adaptation ought to offer a problematization of watching, what it means to watch, what one should watch and how. One way of doing so without compromising the story line and committing an anachronism by making Emma a cinemagoer as opposed— or in addition—to a reader, consists of emphasizing the specular dimensions at work in Flaubert's novel. In order to make up for the impossibility for Emma, the reader, in Flaubert's book to become a "watcher" in the filmic adaptation (so as to parallel the mirroring effect that the novelist first established with his own medium), Chabrol sets up mirroring effects between different mirrors and windows in or through which Emma sees herself and/or is seen by others. Numerous readings have been offered analyzing the way in which, during the ball scene, Chabrol positions a mirror behind Emma in order to suggest that she gets carried away in her fantasy as she watches a couple of waltzers intently. This large mirror is echoed later during M. Lheureux's first visit and his attempt to tempt her with luxurious fabrics: we see Emma looking at herself in a mirror, which reflects the merchandise brought by the moneylender. The mirror signifies an alternative dream life for Emma. In contrast, windows are used by Chabrol to "frame" Emma, so as to evoke the flimsy and unfulfilling aspect of her life in Yonville. Quite significantly, what disappears from the film (as in Minnelli's) is the apparition of the peasants in the night outside once the window is broken by a servant to let some fresh air into the room. One reason for this is that it would have interrupted and compromised the unity and coherence of a sequence that is key to the storyline as well as to the protagonist's evolution, and it explains Emma's course of actions after what will remain in her memory like a magical parenthesis in her life. However, the play on mirrors culminates in Chabrol's film in the sequence of Emma's death. On her deathbed, Emma looks at herself in the mirror during her final moments. In this scene, whose exceptional length is used by Chabrol to show the full extent of Emma's suffering, the only thing that we do not actually see is what Emma sees in the mirror: her own reflection. Her smile suggests that she might see something else, but we will never know what. The mirror thus functions as a blind spot, which is also as a reference to the image and impression finally left by Emma in each viewer. This enables us to understand, metaphorically, how the mirroring effect of the film in relation to the text works insofar as the mirror is always at an angle and, therefore, always reflects both more and less than what any hypothetically "faithful" or "objective" mirror would.

Finally, in relation to the theme of the mirror, it is interesting to note that in Minnelli's version, following her return from the horse ride with Rodolphe, Emma looks at herself in the mirror, but does not say: "J'ai un amant! J'ai un amant!" As Donaldson-Evans observes, Minnelli here again complies with, and mirrors or reflects, the constraints imposed by censorship at the time he makes his film. This is also for us a good way of observing how adaptation always functions as a reflection of the very context in which it is created and performed. As Robert Stam suggests, "[e]very adaptation of *Madame Bovary* filters the novel through the grid of a national culture and through a national film industry, with its generic corollaries and so forth."[4] Not only that, but Hutcheon has shown how the story of *Madame Bovary* "translates [...] effectively across cultures," precisely because its story allows for specific cinematic cultures to be grafted onto it, as is the case with Ketan Mehta's adaptation in Hindi as *Maya Memsaab* (1992), which draws on the "illusions provoked by Bombay musicals" and "transcod[es] well Flaubert's own mix of the romantic and realist." (Hutcheon 151). Hutcheon also draws on the notion of "indigenization" used by Susan Stanford Friedman "to refer to this kind of intercultural encounter and accommodation," in order to explain how "[l]ocal particularities become transplanted to new ground, and something new and hybrid results" (Hutcheon 150).

Because it articulates a set of acute moral issues (around the theme of the adultery) with aesthetic concerns, *Madame Bovary* lends itself particularly well to reinterpretation and appropriation, so much so that the question as to which ideologies it may "serve" can only have an answer, as Donaldson-Evans puts it, that is "culture-bound and time-specific:"

> *Madame Bovary* can be used to decry the corruption of Western civilization (Mehta); to warn of the dangers of the inter-class marriage (Ray); to protest the backward-looking conservatism of modern-day Portugal (Oliveira), to evoke France's collaboration with Hitler in World War II (Schott-Shröbinger), to draw attention to the plight of women in a patriarchal society (Chabrol), to inspire reflection on the role of the artist (Minnelli), or simply, and most frequently, to warn of the dangers of allowing fiction and fantasy to gain pre-eminence over reality. (Donaldson-Evans 170)

Therefore, the contemporaneity of *Madame Bovary* lies in the many mirrors that it holds up across time and cultures as well as within individual contexts insofar as each adaptation is both a mirror and a window in which and through which Flaubert's text, but also a number of existing adaptations and translations, are reflected and make visible. While Emma's weakness and eventual downfall may be that she is forever "out of place" in a world she longs to leave, and out of time as Elissa Marder has shown, the novel bearing her name owes its endurance to the fact that it finds its place and time everywhere, again and again. One could argue that it does so by "adapting" rather than being adapted, so much so that we must question what is traditionally understood as the opposition between an original and its adaptations. What is potentially being adapted with each adaptation, is a series of readings and adaptations which all together constitute an ever growing intertextual corpus.[5] Depending on how one sees it, this represents both a wealth of possibilities for artists who can draw on existing interpretations in order to formulate their own and the danger of being overwhelmed by so many existing versions that one is unable to come up with a truly "new" and "original" interpretation. This is why, while on the one hand, Anne Fontaine could not envisage adapting Flaubert's novel and, therefore, decided to adapt an adaptation of it (Posy Simmonds' comic novel), on the other hand, Sophie Barthes very deliberately avoided watching existing filmic adaptations of the novel.

To conclude, it is the very question of cultural heritage, both as memory and as the anticipation of what has not been written yet, that Flaubert's first novel keeps triggering. The point is not so much that something, which used to belong to French literature now belongs to other literatures, too, but what Flaubert's text enables us to understand is that the very notion of belonging must be questioned. It is precisely because Flaubert's text never belonged exclusively to France or French culture that it became representative of what is often referred to as French literature because, however problematic this may sound from a postcolonial perspective, gestures of appropriation in the context of adaptation are, in a sense, always also gestures of restitution. By taking away and displacing the text into other languages and other media, adaptations and translations of it make room and create a space for "French literature" in a much more encompassing corpus, in relation to which it finds new resonances. It is how Flaubert's text owes as much to its adaptations as its various filmic versions and avatars owe to it.[6] If this is generally true of all texts, what makes this particularly acute in the case of *Madame Bovary* is the fact that, as Culler puts it:

> For Flaubert the artistic process was interminable and the work, by definition, imperfect; but the writer could not, for that, accept his limitations with a philosophical shrug without renouncing his artistic titles. Indeed, Flaubert seems very much at the source of a conception of the artist which is still with us. No doubt part of its attraction and reason for its persistence is the stress which falls on desire rather than accomplishment. (12)

The countless processes by which *Madame Bovary* continues to travel across cultures and media, confirms that desire is at the heart of

Flaubert's novel, not only thematically, but also structurally, as that which made Flaubert write in the very way he did. In turn, desire or what Barnes calls the pleasure of anticipation will endlessly shape again *our* reading—such and such critical, filmic, literary version of *Madame Bovary*—which in turn will become the reading of others.

Notes

1. A good example of a hypertext written from the hypotext *Madame Bovary* is Philippe Doumenc's *Contre-enquête sur la mort d'Emma Bovary*, in which two detectives investigate Emma's death as if it may not have been a suicide after all.

2. See McGrath, "*Madame Bovary* and *Gemma Bovery* Revive and Refract a Heroine."

3. See in particular Robert Stam commenting on "Flaubert's precise articulation of angle of vision" and how his "technique, true to the logic of the protocinematic, also anticipates a signature device of one of the cinema's most popular directors, Alfred Hitchcock, who often practices rotating point-of-view among various characters." (*Madame Bovary*, edited by Margaret Cohen, New York / London: W.W. Norton & Company, 2005: 335–6.)

4. Robert Stam, "*Madame Bovary* Goes to the Movies" in Flaubert, *Madame Bovary*, 2005: 546.

5. See, for instance, Donaldson-Evans's analysis of intertextuality between Minnelli's and Renoir's respective versions of the passage in which Emma and Rodolphe go horseback riding in the woods: "[…] what is most striking about this scene—aside from its conventional occulting of the erotic—is its intertextual allusion to Renoir." While Minnelli's camera "slowly tilts downward, first bringing two tethered horses into frame as they wait patiently for their riders, and then, continuing its downward journey, stopping at the ground, where a lady's hat and a riding crop lie abandoned." "In Renoir's adaptation, the camera had tilted upward in this scene, panning right through the trees in a low-angle shot" (85).

6. A parallel may be drawn with the question of the debt of the translator as raised by Derrida following Walter Benjamin.

Works Cited

Barnes, Julian. *Flaubert's Parrot*. London: Vintage, 2009.

_____. 'Writer's Writer and Writer's Writer's Writer.' *London Review of Books* 32.22 (18 Nov. 2010): 7–11. LRB Limited, 2015. Web. <http://www.lrb.co.uk/v32/n22/julian-barnes/writers-writer-and-writers-writers-writer>.

Benjamin, Walter. "The Task of the Translator." *Selected Writings, Vol. 1, 1913–1926*. Ed. Marcus Bullock & Michael W. Jennings. Cambridge/Massachusetts/London: Belknap Press of Harvard UP, 1997: 253–263.

Bluestone, George. "*Madame Bovary* in Book and Film." *The Tulane Drama Review* 1.3 (June 1957): 49–61.

Culler, Jonathan. *Flaubert: The Uses of Uncertainty*. London: Paul Elek, 1974.

Donaldson-Evans, Mary. *Madame Bovary at the Movies: Adaptation, Ideology, Context*. Amsterdam: Rodopi, 2009.

Doumenc, Philippe. *Contre-enquête sur la mort d'Emma Bovary*. Paris: Actes Sud, 2007.

Fisher, John A. "High Art versus Low Art." *Routledge Companion to Aesthetics*. 2nd ed. Ed. B. Gaut & D. Lopes. London: Routledge Press, 2005. 527–540.

Flaubert, Gustave. *Madame Bovary*. Trans. Lydia Davis. London: Penguin, 2010.

_____. *Madame Bovary*. Ed. Margaret Cohen. 2nd ed. New York/London: W.W. Norton & Company, 2005.

_____. *Œuvres Complètes* I. Édition établie et annotée par A. Thibaudet et R. Dumesnil. Paris: Gallimard, 1951.

Genette, Gérard. *Palimpsestes. La literature au second degré*. Paris: Seuil, 1982.

Griffiths, Kate & Andrew Watts. *Adapting Nineteenth-Century France: Literature in Film, Theatre, Television, Radio and Print*. Cardiff: U of Wales P, 2013.

Heath, Stephen. *Gustave Flaubert, Madame Bovary*. Cambridge: Cambridge UP, 1992.

Hutcheon, Linda. *A Theory of Adaptation*. New York: Routledge, 2006.

Laügt, Élodie. "Why Emma Bovary Had To Be Killed on Screen: From Flaubert to Chabrol via Rancière." *Forum for Modern Language Studies* (2013): 272–285.

Leonard, Suzanne. "The Americanization of Emma Bovary: From Feminist Icon to Desperate Housewife." *Signs* 38.3 (Spring 2013): 647–669.

Madame Bovary. Dir. Jean Renoir. Perf. Max Dearly, Valentine Tessier, and Pierre Renoir. Nouvelle Société des Films, 1934.

Madame Bovary. Dir. Vincente Minelli. Perf. Jennifer Jones, James Mason, Van Heflin, Louis Jourdan. Metro-Goldwyn-Mayer, 1949. Film

Madame Bovary. Dir. Claude Charbol. Perf. Isabelle Huppert, Jean-François Balmer, and Christophe Malavoy. Samuel Goldwyn Company, 1991. Film.

Madame Bovary. Dir. Sophie Barthes. Perf. Mia Wasikowska, Ezra Miller, Paul Giamatti. Aden Film, et al., 2014. Film.

Maya Memsaab. Dir. Ketan Mehta. Perf. Shahrukh Khan, Deepa Sahi, and Farooq Shaikh. 1992. Film.

McGrath, Charles. "*Madame Bovary* and *Gemma Bovery* Revive and Refract a Heroine." *The New York Times*, 21 May 2015.

Rancière, Jacques. *La Fable cinématographique*. Paris: Seuil, 2001.

_____. *La Politique de la littérature*. Paris: Galilée, 2007.

Simmonds, Posy. *Gemma Bovery*. London: Jonathan Cape, 2000.

Stam, Robert. 'Madame Bovary Goes to the Movies.' in *Madame Bovary*, Norton Critical. Ed. Margaret Cohen. New York: Norton, 2005: 535–548.

Stanford Friedman, Susan. *Mappings: Feminism and the Cultural Geographies of Encounter*. Princeton, NJ: Princeton UP, 1998.

Reading Flaubert's First and Second *Éducation sentimentale*

Leah Anderst

Gustave Flaubert's *Éducation sentimentale*, the 1869 novel chronicling France's 1848 revolution as well as the young adulthood of its protagonist, Frédéric Moreau, took its title from another novel penned by Flaubert twenty-four years earlier. This "first" *Éducation sentimentale*, completed in 1845, was published posthumously in serial form between November 1910 and February 1911 in the *Revue de Paris* and later in collected editions of Flaubert's juvenilia.[1] These novels are not two versions of the same work, as their titles might suggest, but by comparing their connections as well as their distinctions, we can trace the developments in Flaubert's style and recurring themes from their beginnings in the early novel to their manifestations in his later novel. Closely reading these two versions of *Éducation sentimentale* in conjunction, examining episodes of striking similarity, yet formal distinction, highlights the evolution of Flaubert's narrative voice and, in particular, what have become interconnected formal features of his mature works: impersonality, irony, and the use of *style indirect libre*.

Each of the two versions of *Éducation* presents Flaubert's reader with a pair of young men, friends as youths who together share dreams of living in Paris as artists, writers, or intellectuals. In both cases, one of the pair is more privileged than the other, with a family ready to support him in his studies, while the other languishes in a clerkship in the provinces. Readers of Flaubert are largely familiar with the later novel, which is widely available in French and English, but the first novel is less familiar. The *Éducation* of 1845 has been published as single editions as well as collected in the various "œuvres de jeunesse" published in the twentieth century. The 2001 Bibliothèque de la Pléiade publication, Œuvres de jeunesse with notes and critical commentary by Claudine Gothot-Mersch, provides heightened interest in this early novel as well as the other writings of Flaubert's juvenilia for readers of French. An English translation was completed by Douglas Garman in 1972 and published by the University of California Press with an introduction by Gerhard Gerhardi, but this edition is no longer available. As readers may not be familiar with the 1845 novel, a brief summary as well as a focused summary of the 1869 novel follows.

In the first *Éducation*, Henry and Jules are the two protagonists. The novel begins with Henry's move to Paris, where he will take up his studies and his residence with a private tutor. Henry's general lack of motivation for the law, his chosen field, and his boredom in Paris bring Émilie Renaud, the wife of his tutor, to his attention. The plot moves forward at a quick clip as Henry courts Émilie and the two begin a passionate love affair that finally brings them to abandon their lives in Paris for what they perceive to be the bountiful opportunities and freedoms in America. The couple sails for New York, where Henry hopes to make his fortune. Jules's existence for much of the novel is noted only in the letters he writes to Henry, bemoaning the tedium of his work and the lack of an artistic community in the provinces. Henry's return to France with Émilie after their failure in America brings about the couple's separation as well as Henry's eventual social and financial success. Henry completes his studies, learns to flatter and to climb the social ladder, and his future is thereby secured.

Flaubert largely abandons Henry to concentrate his attention on Jules. Jules is a budding writer, who, influenced by romantic readings, composes a play—inspired by the Spanish Middle Ages—that catches the attention of a theatre troupe traveling through the provinces. Jules falls in love with the troupe's principal actress, Lucinde, and he lends them money just before they skip town. Toward the end of the novel, Jules has an ominous encounter with a mangy, injured dog. The dog remains at Jules's heels, seeming to beckon him and reminding him of a dog he gave Lucinde as a gift. After this episode, the novel closes with a lengthy final chapter expounding Jules's newfound ideas about his artistic practices. Jules will turn his energy toward cultivating style: "Il entra donc de tout cœur dans cette grande étude du style" (Flaubert, ŒJ 1033). He will abandon his romantic inclinations to focus on the real world, "Le monde étant devenu pour lui si large à contempler, il vit qu'il n'y avait, quant à l'art, rien en dehors ses limites, ni réalité, ni possibilité d'être" (Flaubert, ŒJ 1038). The 1845 novel wraps up with a theatrical summary of the goings-on of each of the primary characters. "Allons – allons, vite!" Flaubert's narrator says, "que ce soit promptement fini. Rangeons en rond tous les personnages au fond de la scène. Les voici qui se tiennent par la main, prêts à dire leur dernier mot avant qu'ils ne rentrent dans la coulisse, dans l'oubli – avant que la toile ne tombe et que les quinquets soient éteints" (Flaubert, ŒJ 1075). Flaubert ends the novel with another self-reflective, theatrical line: "Ici, l'auteur passe son habit noir et salue la compagnie" (Flaubert, ŒJ 1080).

In the second *Éducation*, Frédéric Moreau and Charles Deslauriers take the places formerly occupied by Henry and Jules. The more privileged of the two, Frédéric leaves the provinces for Paris to study the law, while Charles takes up and suffers under his clerkship. Frédéric is an amalgam of Henry and Jules of the 1845 novel. He is at once Henry's privileged, but indifferent, law student pursuing women in Paris and Jules's aspiring romantic writer. Where both of the early characters come into "success," Henry with his social and professional life in Paris and Jules with his aesthetic discoveries and future plans, Frédéric's ambivalence vis-à-vis his various goals keeps him from similar success. Where many of his friends and associates evince passion for art or the revolution, Frédéric is perpetually tepid.

After the 1848 Revolution, Frédéric and Charles, like Henry and Jules, grow apart. Frédéric returns to his provincial home where he and Charles, reunited, ponder their childhood memories from a time well before the narrative began. One memory stands out: their first humiliating visit to the local brothel. Carrying the money, but buckling under nervousness, the young Frédéric flees the brothel just before he would have selected one out of the many girls smiling in front of him, and Charles, his pockets empty, can do nothing but follow. This novel's final words concern this memory: "Ils se la contèrent prolixement, chacun complétant les souvenirs de l'autre;

et, quand ils eurent fini: – C'est là ce que nous avons eu de meilleur! dit Frédéric. – Oui, peut-être bien? C'est là ce que nous avons eu de meilleur! dit Deslauriers" (Flaubert, ÉS 459).

As these sketches reveal, though there are certainly important differences, much is shared between these two novels. Of the critics who turn their attention to the early novel, however, many discount any connection beyond the shared title or claim that a comparison with the second only underscores the shortcomings of the first. For some, the early novel is simply an unpolished, inadequately finished, or only marginally useful record of Flaubert's developing aesthetic ideas and stylistic practices. A few fairly recent publications, however, bring this and other important early texts to a wider audience.

For readers of French the 2001 publication of Flaubert's Œuvres de jeunesse, volume one of the Œuvres completes, brings many of the early writings to light. Claudine Gothot-Mersch's notice following the text of the novel and her introduction to the edition provide valuable context for Flaubert's youthful writing and his literary influences, as well as new information based on her examination of Flaubert's manuscripts.

Gothot-Mersch explains Flaubert's biography during the period of his life surrounding composition of this first *Éducation*. Flaubert suffered his first epileptic fit during this period, and attempting to locate a break in the novel where Flaubert takes up his writing again following his recovery has remained a topic of critical commentary on the 1845 *Éducation*. Gothot-Mersch also offers textual criticism derived from her examination of the manuscript of this early novel. She describes the ease and spontaneity with which Flaubert writes and corrects this manuscript in comparison with those of his late period, "Ce qui frappe d'abord le lecteur habitué aux manuscrits des grands romans, c'est l'élan de l'écriture. Les corrections sont immédiates: Flaubert barre d'un trait épais le passage qu'il vient d'écrire et recommence avant de passer à la suite" (Gothot-Mersch 1511). Rather than Flaubert's often strenuous writing process, here "l'écriture est d'un aspect allègre" (1511). She points as well to Flaubert's reliance on and inspiration from important earlier novelists, such as Goethe, "Le sujet de *L'Éducation sentimentale* et sa structure doivent bien entendu quelque chose aux lectures de Flaubert. À Goethe d'abord, pour l'influence de *Werther* sur la création du personnage de Jules," and Balzac, "Le thème d'un jeune provincial monté à Paris renvoie d'abord au Rastignac du *Père Goriot* – qui vit lui aussi dans une pension – au Rubempré des *Illusions perdues* et de *Splendeurs et misères des courtisanes*" (1520, 1521).

In her discussion of Flaubert's style in this early novel, Gothot-Mersch acknowledges what many critics of this work have viewed as shortcomings. She describes the 1845 *Éducation* as "une œuvre bavarde," and "une œuvre où l'invention, généralement pauvre, procède trop souvent par parallèles et antithèses mécaniques" (Gothot-Mersch 1530). Still, Gothot-Mersch views this early novel as not only an important step away from Flaubert's earlier semi-autobiographical fictions and toward the writer's multi character, realist novels such as *Madame Bovary* and the 1869 *Éducation sentimentale*, but also as a key step in Flaubert's move to his late style,

> Du point de vue technique, la grande invention de *L'Éducation sentimentale*, c'est la scène flaubertienne, ce moment du récit où, l'échelle du temps s'étant modifiée, le lecteur assiste au déroulement d'un événement, présenté dans tous ses aspects à la fois, grâce à un savant découpage et à un entrelacement constant des registres traditionnels: narration, description, dialogue, analyse. (Gothot-Mersch 1530)

In Gothot-Mersch's estimation, the 1845 *Éducation* is an important move from Flaubert's earlier novels, *Mémoires d'un fou* and *Novembre*, to his masterpieces, *Madame Bovary* and the 1869 *Éducation*. Gothot-Mersch's analysis of Flaubert's style in this early novel is an important background for my comparison of the stylistic strategies of this novel with those of the 1869 novel, and I will return to her points throughout my discussion.

For readers of English, the 2004 *Cambridge Companion to Flaubert*, edited by Timothy Unwin, does much to remedy the lack of scholarly work in English dedicated to Flaubert's juvenilia in general and to the 1845 *Éducation* in particular. Unwin himself contributes a chapter entitled "Flaubert's Early Work," and there he provides an overview of the early writings with a particular focus on the "self-conscious mode of writing that will be characteristic of Flaubert" as it is seen in germ in many of the early texts (Unwin, "Flaubert's Early Works" 35). Importantly, Unwin shows that the seeds of Flaubert's mature works exist scattered across many of his youthful experiments. Themes and characters of the early *Éducation* feed into the later novel of the same title, but also into others of Flaubert's late works. Henry's father in the first *Éducation*, for example, speaks in clichés, and Unwin identifies this figure as a precursor to Homais, the pharmacist of *Madame Bovary*, and as a foreshadowing of the clichés and platitudes of the *Dictionnaire des idées reçues* (Unwin, "Flaubert's Early Works" 40–41).[2] Many of the other contributors to the *Cambridge Companion* usefully include the 1845 *Éducation* within larger discussions of Flaubert's place in French literary history, his style, his treatment of history, or the role of failure and stupidity (bêtise) in his novels.[3]

In the recently published volume, *Flaubert's First Novel: A Study of the 1845 Éducation sentimentale*, Alan Raitt focuses his attention solely on this early novel, seeking to demonstrate its particular importance.[4] "The reputation of the 1845 *Éducation sentimentale* has to some extent suffered from the inevitable comparison with the great 1869 novel of the same title," Raitt writes, "[b]ut, while it is far from being on the same plane as the novels of Flaubert's full maturity, it is a fascinating if problematical text, often misunderstood, and fully deserving attention in its own right" (2–3). Raitt's is the only book-length study focused on this early novel, and he dedicates chapters to Flaubert's earliest activities as a writer, to Flaubert's personal and sentimental life during the novel's composition, to the novel's structure, and to its important final chapter that spells out Jules's nascent aesthetic notions.

Near the end of the volume, Raitt includes a chapter exploring the relationship between Flaubert's early and late *Éducation*. He offers a summary of the two opposing critical views on this topic:

There are two diametrically opposed views about the relationship between the *Éducation sentimentale* of 1845 and the *Éducation sentimentale* of 1869. One was formulated by Maxime du Camp when the text of the work was still unpublished: 'Gustave avait écrit un roman: *l'Éducation sentimentale*, qui n'a de commun que le titre avec celui qu'il a publié en 1870.'... The other view is that rather more tentatively advanced by the title under which the novel appeared in the Garnier-Flammarion edition, *L'Éducation sentimentale première version*. This view seems to be supported by René Dumesnil who regards it as an 'ébauche' of the later novel. (Raitt 103)

Whereas Maxime du Camp sees nothing but the titles linking these two novels, Dumesnil views the first as an early version of the second that Flaubert would revisit later. Raitt prefers an alternative route: "So two unconnected works or two versions of the same novel? In fact, neither solution is fully tenable and the truth lies somewhere between the two" (105). Raitt traces out many of the particular pieces of evidence forwarded by each side and evaluates them, and he expresses his own view on the relationship between these two novels in this way: "there is no doubt that *L'Éducation* [of 1845] is a reservoir of themes, scenes and expressions of which the author, knowingly or not, will make extensive use in his later writings" (111). Raitt connects the *Éducation sentimentale* of 1845 with that of 1869, but he also, like Unwin, connects this early novel to *Madame Bovary*, demonstrating just as many similar episodes and themes there. By way of wrapping up, Raitt cites Pierre-Georges Castex's description of the connection between these two novels near the end of his chapter. "*L'éducation sentimentale* de Jules," Castex writes,

> c'est l'apprentissage de renoncement, mais ce renoncement n'est ni oublieux ni désespéré. Flaubert, de même, n'oubliera rien de sa jeunesse romantique, mais il laisse s'opérer en lui une décantation de ses souvenirs. De cette décantation et des nouveaux enseignements de l'expérience naîtra la seconde *Éducation sentimentale*. (112)

Castex equates Jules with Flaubert himself. Just as Jules realizes the potential of the real world as a subject for art, thereby renouncing romanticism, Flaubert, too, moves from his early romantic leanings to the realist fictions of his maturity. For Castex, then, the second *Éducation sentimentale* is not a later version of the first, but without the first, the second would not exist as we now have it.

My position is guided by Raitt's evaluation of the two opposing critical views. These works are not simply two versions of one text, one more successful than the other. They are distinct novels, but this does not preclude the strong presence of shared themes, characters, and episodes. As Castex writes in the passage quoted by Raitt, the *Éducation sentimentale* of 1869 "is born of" the experiences and lessons of the 1845 novel. There are shared family resemblances in many of Flaubert's works. The shared titles, the two young male protagonists, and the explicit theme of education and of growing up, however, draw these two novels very close to one another. Comparing parallel passages from the 1845 and the 1869 *Éducation* underscores the development of Flaubert's formal and thematic preoccupations and demonstrates, in particular, an important change in Flaubert's narrative voice. As Flaubert's writing evolves, his narrators and his characters grow increasingly farther apart. The relationship between Flaubert's early narrators and characters is marked by proximity. These figures often evince shared beliefs and perspectives in the early novels, in the 1845 *Éducation* especially. The parallel figures in the late masterpieces, however, are separated by wide gulfs. As he moves to his late novels, Flaubert's narrators attain greater objectivity, while his characters become ever more romantic, and the move between these figures from proximity to distance will have an important impact on the impersonality and the irony that is characteristic of Flaubert's work.

In a famous letter dated March 18, 1857, Flaubert discusses *Madame Bovary*, and his words point to one of the primary stylistic differences distinguishing the 1845 *Éducation* from his later novels: narrative impersonality,

> C'est une histoire *totalement inventée*; je n'y ai rien mis ni de mes sentiments ni de mon existence. L'illusion (s'il y en a une) vient au contraire de *l'impersonnalité* de l'œuvre. C'est un de mes principes qu'il ne faut pas *s'écrire*. L'artiste doit être dans son œuvre comme

Dieu dans la création, invisible et tout-puissant; qu'on le sente partout, mais qu'on ne le voie pas. (Flaubert, *Correspondance* 324)

Flaubert's style is famous for its "impersonality" for the invisibility of its narrator, and this impersonality distinguishes the first *Éducation* from the second. Flaubert's impersonality expresses itself most clearly in his descriptions and in the way he positions his narrator vis-à-vis his characters. In the late *Éducation*, Flaubert's nearly invisible narrative voice, a voice that describes scenes and situations in a disinterested manner, is presented as an alternative, at times even an opposing perspective to that of Frédéric. Frédéric's often fanciful ideas and perspectives cause him to see differently from the narrator of Flaubert's realist works. These two voices, then, are distinct, and the narrator stands apart from the character, keeping distance. The 1845 *Éducation*, however, reveals a narrator moving toward impersonality who is yet positioned very close to Henry's perspective. In the earlier novel, the perspectives of Henry and of the narrator often align. Flaubert has not yet learned to keep his distance, and the opening paragraphs of the two novels, reproduced below, illustrate this evolution in Flaubert's narrative voice.

Le héros de ce livre un matin d'octobre arriva à Paris avec un cœur de dix-huit ans et un diplôme de bachelier ès lettres.
Il fit son entrée dans cette capitale du monde civilisé par la porte Saint-Denis dont il put admirer la belle architecture. – Il vit dans les rues des voitures de fumier traînées par un cheval et un âne, des charrettes de boulanger tirées à bras d'homme, des laitières qui vendaient leur lait, des portières qui balayaient le ruisseau. Cela faisait beaucoup de bruit – notre homme, la tête à la portière de la diligence, regardait les passants et lisait les enseignes. (Flaubert, ŒJ 836)

Le 15 septembre 1840, vers six heures du matin, la Ville-de-Montereau, près de partir, fumait à gros tourbillons devant le quai Saint-Bernard.
Des gens arrivaient hors d'haleine; des barriques, des câbles, des corbeilles de linge gênaient la circulation; les matelots ne répondaient à personne; on se heurtait; les colis montaient entre les deux tambours, et le tapage s'absorbait dans le bruissement de la

vapeur, qui, s'échappant par des plaques de tôle, enveloppait tout d'une nuée blanchâtre, tandis que la cloche, à l'avant, tintait sans discontinuer.

Enfin le navire partit ; et les deux berges, peuplées de magasins, de chantiers et d'usines, filèrent comme deux larges rubans que l'on déroule.

Un jeune homme de dix-huit ans, à longs cheveux et qui tenait un album sous son bras, restait auprès du gouvernail, immobile. A travers le brouillard, il contemplait des clochers, des édifices dont il ne savait pas les noms; puis il embrassa, dans un dernier coup d'œil, l'île Saint-Louis, la Cité, Notre-Dame, et bientôt, Paris disparaissant, il poussa un grand soupir. (Flaubert, ÉS 19)

The 1845 *Éducation* opens with Henry's arrival in Paris, and this opening is dominated by description. Flaubert begins by setting the scene, by showing his readers the everyday world surrounding his character. Gothot-Mersch signals this novel's opening as a strong change in direction from his 1842 novella, *Novembre*, "Flaubert ne commence plus son récit par une méditation alliant le paysage d'automne et la mélancolie d'une âme, mais par l'installation à Paris et l'existence quotidienne d'un jeune bourgeois" (1529). Gothot-Mersch later notes of Flaubert's descriptions in this novel vis-à-vis his earlier works, "son talent d'observateur et sa capacité à rendre ce qu'il a vu sont en progrès manifeste. Le texte abonde en détails qui donnent au lecteur l'impression du réel" (1533). Already in this novel, and already in the opening paragraph, Flaubert moves strongly away from the romanticism of his youthful writing and toward the realism and the description that will characterize his later works.

The opening of the 1869 novel is likewise dominated by descriptions, but here the location, place, and time have gained even greater precision. Flaubert supplies the date, "Le 15 septembre 1840," the name of the quay, "Saint-Bernard," the name of the boat, "la Ville-de-Montereau," and the boat's time of departure, "vers six heures de matin" (ÉS 19). He anchors the storyline in precise and actual places and times. The second paragraph of the passage, with its string of short, swiftly moving phrases separated by semi-colons, describes the hurried activities of people boarding the riverboat,

"Des gens arrivaient hors d'haleine; des barriques, des câbles, des corbeilles de linge gênaient la circulation" (ÉS 19). Like "des voitures de fumier traînées par un cheval et un âne" of the 1845 novel, this long sentence of the later novel conveys a strong sense of the sights, sounds and movements of the scene (ŒJ 836). This penchant and facility for descriptions of the real world with all of its banal details, Flaubert carries from the 1845 to the 1869 *Éducation*. His later narrative voice will continue to rely on description, but it will become ever more fixed to the real world with its increased specificity and precision.

An important distinction between these two passages, a distinction tied to Flaubert's description, concerns the introduction of the two heroes and the perspective behind the descriptions. Whereas the reader of the 1845 novel knows that Henry sees those things described in the novel's opening passages, he sees them with "la tête à la portière," in the later novel, there is no indication who sees what the narrator describes. The reader doesn't know who sees that "des gens arrivaient" or who hears "le tapage s'absorbait dans le bruissement de la vapeur" (ŒJ 836, ÉS 19). Whereas the 1845 narrator tends to see through or with Henry's eyes, the 1869 narrator is a figure whose perspective is not tied to Frédéric. Flaubert's late narrators are known for their proto-cinematic characteristics, and the descriptive opening paragraph from the 1869 novel, with its impersonal "panning" connected to no character's perspective, acts as a disinterested "establishing shot," suggesting the larger *mise-en-scène* by focusing on details, such as baskets of laundry and piling baggage.

The opening of the 1845 *Éducation*, on the other hand, reveals a strong sense of Henry's subjective perspective, his satisfaction with his current situation as well as the objects and people around him that attract his attention. Henry is an eager spectator, "la tête à la portière de la diligence," and his attention is directed as much to the city's grand sights, the "belle architecture," as it is to the commonplace, "des charrettes de boulanger tirées à bras d'homme, des laitières qui vendaient leur lait" (ŒJ 836). An enthusiastic young man leaving his familial home, Henry takes in the visual and aural delights of the city, and Flaubert's narrator, tacitly sympathetic with the character, directs the reader according to Henry's perspective.

There is a closeness of perspective, a proximity between the vision of the narrator and of the protagonist in the 1845 *Éducation*. There is not an indication, for example, whether Henry or the narrator judges the architecture "belle." This evaluation could belong to one as much as to the other. Flaubert has not yet crafted the sharp distinction between his narrator and his characters that will become a hallmark of his late writing. Jonathan Culler calls attention to this particular line of the opening of the early *Éducation sentimentale* in *Flaubert: The uses of uncertainty*:

> "Dont il put admirer la belle architecture" is glaringly and disconcertingly ambiguous, especially since one feels that the choice between irony or praise is of no consequence... the whole scene is simply laid before the hero, who 'regardait les passants et lisait les enseignes' with no attempt at interpretation. (Culler 59)

Henry is an eager, yet essentially passive, observer of Paris. He and the narrator together take in the sights and sounds surrounding his arrival, and according to Culler, Flaubert's depiction refrains from "interpretation" of the hero's perceptions. Henry is not, as Frédéric later will be, subject to Flaubert's incisive irony. "There are here the beginnings of an ironic style," Culler continues, "but Flaubert has not yet mastered the complex dialectic of speech and silence nor the modes of anti-climax which will later distinguish his prose" (60).

Whereas the language and the style of 1845 novel tend to draw the narrator and Henry together, as they also will the narrator and Jules when the novel turns its focus to that character, highlighting the confluence of their perspectives, in the 1869 *Éducation*, the narrator's vision and perspective remain sharply distinguished from those of Frédéric. In many ways, Frédéric shares with Emma Bovary her romantic world view; these two characters' readings and misreadings of the world around them are informed by romantic literature. The impersonal narrative voice of Flaubert's later novels, on the other hand, "sees" the real world uninformed by such readings and notions; this narrative voice "sees" the world with all of its banal details.

In the opening paragraphs of the 1869 *Éducation*, the narrator describes the details typical of a riverboat departure with all of its hustle and bustle, while Frédéric's perspective does not accommodate such quotidian details as luggage and sailors. His focus lies instead on mythologized objects, whose presence dominates his desire for this capital city, "il contemplait des clochers, des édifices dont il ne savait pas les noms; puis il embrassa, dans un dernier coup d'œil, l'île Saint-Louis, la Cité, Notre-Dame, et bientôt, Paris disparaissant, il poussa un grand soupir" (ÉS 19). Whereas Henry *and* the 1845 narrator together "see" the banal and the grand sights of Paris, in these opening paragraphs of the 1869 novel, Flaubert conspicuously displays those things, those everyday details that Frédéric does not see. The 1869 narrator alone "sees" the sailors preparing for departure, while Frédéric keeps his vision above the fray, focused on clock towers and cathedrals. Flaubert sets up these two figures, Frédéric and the narrator, as contrasting visions that, in strong distinction from the earlier novel, do not intersect. This lack of proximity between Frédéric and the narrator plays an important role in others of Flaubert's late stylistic signatures: his use of irony and of *style indirect libre* as a source of irony.

Flaubert's changing use of irony from the 1845 to the 1869 novel is highlighted by a comparison of passages from the two corresponding scenes when Henry and Frédéric become conscious of their budding first loves. In addition to their similar educational paths, privileged, but indifferent, law students in Paris, the "sentimental" lives of Henry and Frédéric share a parallel focus. Their first and deepest loves are for older, married women, and the following two passages are the moments in the novels when Henry realizes his love for Émilie Renaud, Frédéric for Marie Arnoux:

> Et il se mit à l'aimer ; à aimer sa main, ses gants, ses yeux, même quand ils regardaient un autre, sa voix quand elle lui disait bonjour, les robes qu'elle portait, mais surtout celle qu'elle avait le matin, une façon de sarrau rose à larges manches et sans ceinture ; à aimer la

chaise où elle s'asseyait, tous les meubles de sa chambre, la maison entière, la rue où était cette maison. (ŒJ 827)

Jamais il n'avait vu cette splendeur de sa peau brune, la séduction de sa taille, ni cette finesse des doigts que la lumière traversait. Il considérait son panier à ouvrage avec ébahissement, comme une chose extraordinaire. Quels étaient son nom, sa demeure, sa vie, son passé? Il souhaitait connaître les meubles de sa chambre, toutes les robes qu'elle avait portées, les gens qu'elle fréquentait; et le désir de la possession physique même disparaissait sous une envie plus profonde, dans une curiosité douloureuse qui n'avait pas de limites. (ÉS 23)

The first passage, from the 1845 *Éducation*, focuses on Émilie's physical presence, the objects around her, and the spaces she inhabits. The description moves between her body, her clothes, and her furniture. Henry's love for Émilie has her physical presence at its centre, and it extends to encompass those little things around her that he has grown accustomed to seeing. Timothy Unwin discusses this particular passage in a chapter dedicated to the 1845 *Éducation* in *Art et infini*. Unwin writes: "Quand il se rend compte qu'il est tombé amoureux d'elle, il prête son attention à tout ce qui la concerne sauf à son caractère réel, et il se livre à une rêverie fétichiste qui annonce l'attitude de Frédéric vis-à-vis de Madame Arnoux" (161). Unwin draws a connection between the focus of these two heroes on their love interests; Henry and Frédéric fix on the possessions and the surroundings of their beloveds. Like the first, the second passage from the 1869 *Éducation* lists physical aspects of the beloved's person and then moves to objects connected to her that attract Frédéric. Henry is drawn to Émilie's gloves, to her dresses, and to her chairs, just as Frédéric gazes upon Marie's workbasket and imagines the chairs and rooms of her house and the people who surround her.

In this way, Flaubert's irony permeates both passages. As Unwin suggests, there is a distinctly fetishist quality in these characters' attraction to specific clothing and objects kept by the beloved. From the early to the late passage, though, there is a sharp increase in irony. Henry's attraction to a very specific morning outfit worn by Émilie, "une façon de sarreau rose à larges manches," is grounded in his experiences with his beloved. He has seen her wear this very robe. He has seen her room and the furniture that he fantasizes about as his affection for her increases. The passage from the 1869 *Éducation*, however, occurs during the novel's opening riverboat scene. This very passage marks the first time Frédéric has glimpsed Marie Arnoux; her name as well as the shape and style of her furniture is yet unknown to Frédéric. Whereas Henry loves precise things connected to Émilie that he has lived among, Frédéric knows nothing of Marie. After only this first glimpse of her, he wants to know and to love "toutes les robes qu'elle avait portées" (ŒJ 872, ÉS 23). In Frédéric, Flaubert creates a character who is much given to flights of fancy, a character whose thoughts, as depicted within the narration, leave him susceptible to idealized, impossible desires, and Flaubert marks these idealizations against the impersonal narrator's own objective vision.

Henry also idealizes Émilie, and he imagines a life between them influenced by romantic readings, but the difference is important. As Unwin notes of the 1845 novel, "l'ironie du romancier met en évidence la fausseté de l'attitude du personnage, mais Flaubert ne refusera pas pour autant de croire à la réalité des sentiments qu'éprouve Henry" (Unwin, *Art et infini* 161). The passage from the 1845 novel is not without irony, then, but this irony is minimal because Flaubert's narrator shares Henry's views on Émilie. Independently of Henry, the narrator evinces similarly romantic and fetishist readings of her. Flaubert's reader encounters Madame Renaud for the first time through the narrator's voice alone, and this figure, like Henry, highlights her physical characteristics, "Si sa gorge, qu'elle laissait volontiers voir, était peut-être un peu trop pleine, en revanche elle envoyait une si douce odeur quand on s'approche d'elle!" (ŒJ 845). Later, in a first-person intrusion, the narrator exclaims upon Émilie's eyes, reading them as a representation of amorous, passionate women in their thirties, "J'aime beaucoup ces grands yeux des femmes de trente ans – ces yeux longs – fermés – à grand sourcil noir… regards langoureux, andalous, maternels et lascifs, ardents comme des flambeaux" (ŒJ 853). Even when "speaking" independently of Henry, when not seeing through Henry's perspective, this often intrusive narrator reveals a similarly romantic bent and a parallel focus on the ways that Émilie conforms to a romantic ideal. Tied as the narrator and the character are, then, Henry is less a figure for irony than Frédéric will be in the 1869 novel. Whereas the narrator of the early novel is temperamentally close to Henry, the impersonal narrator of the 1869 *Éducation* is strongly distinguished from Frédéric, and this highlights the fantasy and the impossible romanticism of his reading of Marie Arnoux in this scene.

In addition to this particular irony, Flaubert's use of *style indirect libre* from the early to the late novel is impacted by the move to a narrative voice that shares little with the character. *Style indirect libre* is a mixing of the voices of a third-person narrator and a novel's character. Blended within a block of third-person narration, but lacking a phrase such as "he thought" or "he wondered," *style indirect libre* presents the thoughts of a character as if "spoken" by a narrator. Instances of *style indirect libre* in narrative fiction "tend to commit the narrator to attitudes of sympathy or irony. Precisely because they cast the language of a subjective mind into the grammar of objective narration, they amplify emotional notes, but also throw into ironic relief all false notes struck by a figural mind" (Cohn 117). Flaubert is known for using this mode regularly and to great ironic effect in his late novels, and the irony tied to *style indirect libre* in his late masterpieces is chiefly born of the distinction between the perspectives of the narrator and the character. Frédéric's thoughts represented in *style indirect libre*, appear as if "spoken" by an objective, impersonal narrator, and this clash of divergent perspectives within the same instance of narration in the later novel is a frequent source of irony.

Flaubert's use of *style indirect libre* is perhaps more frequent in the 1845 *Éducation* where instead of irony, it "commit[s] the narrator to... sympathy" for Henry and for Jules (Cohn 117). Because the perspective of Flaubert's early narrator often intersects with his characters', this early *style indirect libre* does not feature a strong clash of divergent voices and does not often result in an ironic presentation of the character. Discussing a few instances of *style indirect libre* in the Jules sections of the 1845 *Éducation*, Culler writes that the "*style indirect libre*" of this first novel "is in no way the vehicle of irony" (62). Culler makes the case that Jules's encounter with the strange dog, and his thoughts about that encounter, represented in *style indirect libre*, are "compelling" (62). That the narrator's perspective mixes with Jules's in these instances, then, results in sympathy rather than irony. This is likewise true for instances of *style indirect libre* that convey Henry's thoughts.

The two passages reproduced below occur at pivotal moments in the early and the late *Éducation*; they depict Henry and Frédéric waiting impatiently for their first assignations with Émilie and with Marie. Neither of the women arrives for the planned rendezvous, and during these moments of waiting, Flaubert makes extensive use of *style indirect libre* to convey Henry's and Frédéric's troubled thoughts,

> C'était bien un rendez-vous; il se promit de n'y pas manquer. Oh! que le temps lui sembla long jusqu'au lendemain!
>
> . . .
>
> Elle ne venait pas. Mais elle allait venir. Il se leva, il marcha de long en large, en tous sens, inquiet, le lorgnon braqué sur l'oeil, tâchant de la reconnaître de loin, s'attendant à voir son châle blanc apparaître tout à coup dans une allée. Comme elle tardait!" (ŒJ 876)

> Sans doute, elle avait un empêchement, et elle en souffrait aussi. Mais quelle joie tout à l'heure! – Car elle allait venir, cela était certain! «Elle me l'a bien promis!» Cependant, une angoisse intolérable le gagnait.
>
> Par un mouvement absurde, il rentra dans l'hôtel, comme si elle avait pu s'y trouver. A l'instant même, elle arrivait peut-être dans la rue. Il s'y jeta. Personne! Et il se remit à battre le trottoir. (ÉS 305)

From a technical standpoint, there is little to distinguish the use of *style indirect libre* in these two passages. Flaubert's move to *imparfait* from the *passé simple* serves as a signal for *style indirect*

---

libre in both novels, and in both, he mixes this mode with impersonal description. The first passage, including those sections marked by ellipses, however, includes no instances of direct internal discourse. Whereas Flaubert provides a quoted instance of Frédéric's first-person thoughts, "Elle me l'a bien promis!," in the 1845 novel, he provides only external indirect discourse and *style indirect libre*.

Somewhat surprisingly, then, both passages reveal sympathy for Henry and for Frédéric. Their thoughts are filled with anticipation, worry, and disappointment, and there is no indication that the two narrators here convey anything other than sympathy. Whether the narrator or the reader suspects that these two young men are self-deceived in these particular moments, whether we believe from the beginnings of these episodes that the women will not arrive, Flaubert crafts a scene that encourages identification with the suspense the characters suffer under. Henry and Frédéric swing between extremes of anticipation and disappointment, "Elle ne venait pas. Mais elle allait venir," "Mais quelle joie tout à l'heure! ... une angoisse intolérable le gagnait," and the very sincerity of their desires draws the narrator and the reader close to their perspectives (ŒJ 876, ÉS 305). In a move quite unusual for the impartiality of the late fictions, in fact, the narrator's perspective appears to align with Frédéric's in this passage.

There is still, however, irony in the second passage. This irony does not emerge from a stylistic difference in the use of *style indirect libre* from one novel to the next; the depictions of these two young men's minds are remarkably similar. The irony in the second novel arises from important contextual information, which is left out of this particular passage. While Frédéric waits for Marie Arnoux, the 1848 Revolution is exploding all around him, down the street and around the corner. Frédéric sees other young men tussling with the police in a struggle that he has himself claimed allegiance to. If he is to be committed to the revolutionary ideals that he has formerly attested to, Frédéric should join up with his comrades. Instead, he hides. He ducks behind corners and down alleys when the fighting comes very close to the spot where he and Madame Arnoux are to meet. He hides for fear of being seen by someone who would wonder why he isn't taking part. Flaubert gives little indication throughout the 1869 *Éducation* of his own views on the 1848 Revolution. The narrator, for instance, does not appear to align with one political perspective or another, but this narrator does underscore hypocrisy and bad faith. In this scene, Frédéric knowingly and with sufficient feelings of guilt to understand that he must hide, sets aside his suffering friends and a cause for which he formerly claimed to care deeply. Henry has no such cause or event unfolding in his life; his desire for Émilie is not a distraction from something else of seemingly greater import, so his anticipation and worry as he awaits his lover is not portrayed as a poor or a hypocritical choice by Flaubert's 1845 narrator.

In this particular passage of the 1869 *Éducation sentimentale*, Flaubert demonstrates his mastery in creating a deeply ambivalent character, but also an ambivalent reading experience. In a single instance of narration, Flaubert portrays Frédéric as deserving of sympathy because his hopes are about to be dashed and deserving of antipathy because by waiting for Marie Arnoux to arrive, by hiding so as not to be seen, he abandons his friends and their cause. Between the writing of these two novels, Flaubert has mastered this very deft combination of sympathy and irony, identification and criticism in his narration.

On January 16, 1852, seven years after completing the first *Éducation* and one year into his composition of *Madame Bovary*, Flaubert writes a letter to Louise Colet about his 1845 novel. He points to certain parts of the novel that he continues to appreciate, Henry and Émilie's trip to America in particular, and he points to other aspects that he considers failures. He explains that his writing has progressed, but he continues to desire more of himself as a stylist, "J'ai fait depuis des progrès en esthétique, ou du moins je me suis affermi dans l'assiette que j'ai prise de bonne heure. *Je sais comment il faut faire.* Oh mon Dieu! si j'écrivais le style dont j'ai l'idée, quel écrivain je serais!" (Flaubert, *Correspondance* 154, emphasis original,). A bit later, he suggests to her that "*l'Éducation* avait été un essai" (155). As Culler, Gothot-Mersch, Unwin, and Raitt have shown, in this *essai* are the seeds for Flaubert's important late novels. The 1845 *Éducation* offered the writer himself an education: an education in stylistic and thematic features that would crystalize in his later novels and in the 1869 *Éducation* in particular: impersonal description, third-person narration, and especially distances between narrators and characters.

Notes

1. Alan Raitt provides a detailed publication history in his introduction to *Flaubert's First Novel: A Study of the 1845 Éducation sentimentale* (Oxford: Peter Lang, 2010), p. 1.

2. In addition to his chapter in the *Cambridge Companion*, Timothy Unwin's *Art et infini: l'œuvre de jeunesse de Gustave Flaubert* (Rodopi: Amsterdam, 1991) draws many parallels between the 1845 novel and *Madame Bovary*.

3. Particularly useful in this regard are chapters by Michael Tilby, Anne Green, Laurence M. Porter, Alison Finch, and Lawrence R. Schehr.

4. Though this study was published in 2010, Raitt passed away in 2006, and the material of his study was inspired by and completed following the 2001 Bibliothèque de la Pléiade publication of the Œuvres de jeunesse.

Works Cited

Cohn, Dorrit. *Transparant Minds: Narrative Modes of Presenting Consciousness in Fiction*. Princeton, NJ: Princeton UP, 1978.

Culler, Jonathan. *Flaubert: The Uses of Uncertainty*. London: Elek Books, Ltd., 1974.

Demorest, Jean-Jacques. "Flaubert's First *Sentimental Education*." *The American Society Legion of Honor Magazine* 38 (1967): 97–110.

Flaubert, Gustave. *Correspondence*. Paris: Gallimard, 1998.

_____. *L'Éducation sentimentale*. Paris: Gallimard, 1965.

_____. *The First Sentimental Education*. Trans. Douglas Garman. Berkeley: U of California P, 1972.

_____. *Madame Bovary*. Trans. Geoffrey Wall. London: Penguin Books, 2002.

_____. Œuvres de jeunesse. Eds. Claudine Gothot-Mersch & Guy Sagnes. Paris: Gallimard, 2001.

_____. *Sentimental Education*. Trans. Robert Baldick. London: Penguin Books, 2004.

Raitt, Alan. *Flaubert's First Novel: A Study of the 1845 Éducation sentimentale*. Oxford: Peter Lang, 2010.

Unwin, Timothy. *Art et infini: l'œuvre de jeunesse de Gustave Flaubert*. Amsterdam: Rodopi, 1991.

_____. "Flaubert's Early Works." *Cambridge Companion to Flaubert*. Ed. Timothy Unwin. Cambridge: Cambridge UP, 2004.

Textual Memory: *L'Éducation sentimentale*____

Éric Le Calvez

Flaubert's *L'Éducation sentimentale*[1] displays numerous effects of repetition and parallelism,[2] a structural device, which is a finality resulting from the writer's intentions to *combine the plan* while writing the narrative to make it real and, for the reader, an issue when reading the text. Indeed, Flaubert explains the failure of the novel with the public in these terms, ten years after its publication, in a letter to Edma Roger des Genettes: "C'est trop vrai et, esthétiquement parlant, il y manque *la fausseté de la perspective*. À force d'avoir combiné le plan, le plan disparaît. Toute œuvre doit avoir un point, un sommet, *faire la pyramide*, ou bien la lumière doit frapper sur un point de la boule. Or rien de tout cela dans la vie" (October 8, 1879).

Recurrence and circulation of details from one context to another create frequent instances of superimposition as scenes and moments often echo one another. Memory (and, of course, its inevitable counterpart, loss of memory) is a part of this process. The memory of the character, of course (in particular that of Frédéric Moreau, on whom most of the scenes are focalized); the memory of the narrator, who interrupts the flow of the narrative to look back to the past; but perhaps, above all, the memory of the text itself, which, from a narratological standpoint, takes on an analeptic form, that is to say "any evocation after the fact of an event that took place earlier than the point in the story where we are at any given moment"[3] and, therefore, imposes a certain effort on the part of the reader's memory. For instance, in the scene at the Alhambra, when Delmar (still named Delmas then) sings *Le Frère de l'Albanaise*, Frédéric recollects another moment (although one cannot understand why it is that specific moment):

> Les paroles rappelèrent à Frédéric celles que chantait l'homme en haillons, entre les tambours du bateau. Ses yeux s'attachaient involontairement sur le bas de la robe étalée devant lui. Après chaque

couplet, il y avait une longue pause—et le souffle du vent dans les arbres ressemblait au bruit des ondes. (131)

The reader must remember that this is an echo of the first chapter, where "l'homme en haillons" sings "une romance orientale" (49), but then the harpist is not located between the two "tambours," which appear on the first page ("les colis montaient entre les deux tambours," 43) and reappear right before Frédéric enters the first class area ("le capitaine, sur la passerelle, marchait d'un tambour à l'autre," 47). The reader also understands that the comparison links "le souffle du vent," which belongs to the present with the "bruit des ondes" which belongs to the past, that is, the Seine, mentioned and described several times in the first chapter. What about Frédéric's glance, however: "Ses yeux s'attachaient involontairement sur le bas de la robe étalée devant lui"? The temporal level where the detail of the dress is located is unclear because Flaubert uses the character's vision ("Ses yeux s'attachaient") instead of his memory, which makes the image quite ambiguous: is this Miss Vatnaz's dress at the Alhambra (she is standing close to Frédéric) or Madame Arnoux's, described when she first appears ("Sa robe de mousseline claire, tachetée de petits pois, se répandait à plis nombreux," 47)? The text seems to confuse two temporal levels and plays with the reader's memory.

In *L'Éducation sentimentale*, space and time are two essential devices and so, analepses and descriptions are frequently intertwined, following a specific type of association when the narrative "retraces its own path" (Genette 54). It will be useful to consider in parallel the two scenes in which Frédéric walks through the streets of Paris at night; the first shows his return from his first dinner at the Arnoux's (60), and the second, his return from the Alhambra (76). Each scene contains a description of the space surrounding the character:

Les rues étaient désertes. Quelquefois une charrette lourde passait, en ébranlant les pavés. Les maisons se succédaient avec leurs façades grises, leurs fenêtres closes; et il songeait dédaigneusement à tous ces êtres humains couchés derrière ces murs, qui existaient sans la voir, et dont pas un même ne se doutait qu'elle vécût! Il n'avait plus conscience du milieu, de l'espace, de rien; et, battant le sol du talon, en frappant avec sa canne les volets des boutiques, il allait toujours devant lui, au hasard, éperdu, entraîné. Un air humide l'enveloppa; il se reconnut au bord des quais.

Les réverbères brillaient en deux lignes droites, indéfiniment, et de longues flammes rouges vacillaient dans la profondeur de l'eau. Elle était de couleur ardoise, tandis que le ciel, plus clair, semblait soutenu par les grandes masses d'ombre qui se levaient de chaque côté du fleuve. Des édifices, que l'on n'apercevait pas, faisaient des redoublements d'obscurité. Un brouillard lumineux flottait au-delà, sur les toits; tous les bruits se fondaient en un seul bourdonnement; un vent léger soufflait.

Quand un piéton s'avançait, il tâchait de distinguer son visage. De temps à autre, un rayon de lumière lui passait entre les jambes, décrivait au ras du pavé un immense quart de cercle; et un homme surgissait, dans l'ombre, avec sa hotte et sa lanterne. Le vent, en de certains endroits, secouait le tuyau de tôle d'une cheminée; des sons lointains s'élevaient, se mêlant au bourdonnement de sa tête, et il croyait entendre, dans les airs, la vague ritournelle des contredanses. Le mouvement de sa marche entretenait cette ivresse; il se trouva sur le pont de la Concorde.

Alors, il se ressouvint de ce soir de l'autre hiver,—où, sortant de chez elle, pour la première fois, il lui avait fallu s'arrêter, tant son cœur battait vite sous l'étreinte de ses espérances. Toutes étaient mortes, maintenant!

Des nues sombres couraient sur la face de la lune. Il la contempla, en rêvant à la grandeur des espaces, à la misère de la vie, au néant de tout. Le jour parut; ses dents claquaient; et, à moitié endormi, mouillé par le brouillard et tout plein de larmes, il se demanda pourquoi n'en pas finir? Rien qu'un mouvement à faire! Le

Il s'était arrêté au milieu du Pont-Neuf, et, tête nue, poitrine ouverte, il aspirait l'air. (103)

poids de son front l'entraînait, il voyait son cadavre flottant sur l'eau; Frédéric se pencha. Le parapet était un peu large, et ce fut par lassitude qu'il n'essaya pas de le franchir. (135–36)

The two descriptions of the streets act as a link between these two antithetic contexts. In the first, Frédéric is euphoric and "aspirait l'air" (103; see also the end of the description: "un vent léger soufflait"); in the second context, which is dysphoric, the defeat of the character is metonymically translated into the wind, which "en de certains endroits, secouait le tuyau de tôle d'une cheminée" (135). The reappearance of the buzzing ("bourdonnement") precedes in each context the mention of the bridge, whose reappearance—although there are two different bridges: Pont-Neuf (103), Pont de la Concorde (135)—legitimizes or even implies (as shown by the adverb *alors*) an explanation of these textual similarities: "Alors il se ressouvint de ce soir de l'autre hiver" (with no date: it is the reader's task to remember the scene in question). The analepsis is thus motivated by difference, its function is mainly deceptive (the lack of progression of the narrative pointing to Frédéric's failure, also suggested by the use of pronominal verbs in the two contexts: "il se reconnut" and "il se trouva," alluding to his passivity). The reference brings together two somewhat remote scenes, while revealing the differences that set them in opposition (see also "brouillard lumineux" vs. "nues sombres").[4]

The description of the Champs-Élysées, at the end of the episode at the races (Part II, chapter 4), is built upon the same pattern. Here again, space implies the recall with the same adverb ("*Alors* Frédéric se rappela"):

Les crinières étaient près des crinières, les lanternes près des lanternes; les étriers d'acier, les gourmettes d'argent, les boucles de cuivre, jetaient çà et là des points lumineux entre les culottes courtes, les gants blancs et les fourrures qui retombaient sur le blason des portières. Il se sentait comme perdu dans un monde lointain. Ses yeux erraient sur les têtes féminines; et de vagues ressemblances amenaient à sa mémoire Mme Arnoux. Il se la figurait, au milieu des autres, dans un de ces petits coupés, pareils au coupé de Mme Dambreuse. – Mais le soleil se couchait, et le vent froid soulevait des tourbillons de poussière. Les cochers baissaient le menton dans leurs cravates, les roues se mettaient à tourner plus vite, le macadam grinçait et tous les équipages descendaient au grand trot la longue avenue, en se frôlant, se dépassant, s'écartant les uns des autres, puis, sur la place de la Concorde, se dispersaient. Derrière les Tuileries, le ciel prenait la teinte des ardoises. Les arbres du jardin formaient deux masses énormes, violacées par le sommet. Les becs de gaz s'allumaient; et la Seine, verdâtre dans toute son étendue, se déchirait en moires d'argent contre les piles des ponts. (70–71)

Puis tout se remettait en mouvement; les cochers lâchaient les rênes, abaissaient leurs fouets; les chevaux, animés, secouant leur gourmette, jetaient de l'écume autour d'eux; et les croupes et les harnais humides fumaient, dans la vapeur d'eau que le soleil couchant traversait. Passant sous l'Arc de triomphe, il allongeait à hauteur d'homme une lumière rousseâtre, qui faisait étinceler les moyeux des roues, les poignées des portières, le bout des timons, les anneaux des sellettes, et, sur les deux côtés de la grande avenue, – pareille à un fleuve où ondulaient des crinières, des vêtements, des têtes humaines, – les arbres tout reluisants de pluie se dressaient, comme deux murailles vertes. Le bleu du ciel, au-dessus, reparaissant à de certaines places, avait des douceurs de satin.

Alors Frédéric se rappela les jours déjà loin où il enviait l'inexprimable bonheur de se trouver dans une de ces voitures, à côté d'une de ces femmes. Il le possédait, ce bonheur-là, et n'en était pas plus joyeux. (293–94)

As in the previous example, the text merges distinct moments in Frédéric's life. The first are in the iterative mood ("Les jours de soleil, il continuait sa promenade jusqu'au bout des Champs-Élysées," 70), the second in the singulative (it is a specific scene), but they are associated with the same location: Champs-Élysées. This points to Frédéric's lack of progress: even if he is now sitting in one of the coaches, whereas before he was merely a witness of their *défilé*, his initiation has been fruitless, and textual memory reveals once again the immobilism of the narrative. Indeed, motifs and details from the previous description of the Champs-Élysées reappear (coaches, sunset, trees, sky, movement), but they are transformed: the sky takes on the color of the slates (an unpleasant hue), when Frédéric thinks that his ideal is unreachable (70), but is as soft as satin (294) when he believes—for a brief moment—that he has reached it. The descriptions exchange their qualities: previously the Seine was greenish (71), whereas here, the trees are transformed through the comparison into two green walls along the avenue, whose watery aspect recalls that of the Seine: "pareille à un fleuve"; before, the trees in the Tuileries were "deux masses énormes, violacées par le sommet." More strangely still, the influence of this analepsis bypasses the very limits of the scene. The shimmerings which describe the Seine in the first context ("la Seine [...] se déchirait en moires d'argent contre les piles des ponts," 71)[5] reappear a few paragraphs after the episode at the races, in the description of the boulevards seen by Frédéric from the Café Anglais: "Par les deux fenêtres ouvertes, on apercevait du monde aux croisées des autres maisons, vis-à-vis. De larges moires frissonnaient sur l'asphalte qui séchait, et un magnolia posé au bord du balcon embaumait l'appartement" (295); the verbs are also opposed ("se déchirait" vs. "frissonnaient"), the smell is euphoric ("embaumait"), and the details have a positive effect on the character: "Ce parfum et cette fraîcheur détendirent ses nerfs."

The circularity implied by analepses apparently plays a role similar to that of involuntary memory in the Proustian narrative, where "the comparison between two situations that are similar and also different often motivates recalls."[6] The memory itself is sometimes introduced by an arbitrary, but strategic signal, as in the episode of the ball at the Dambreuses where the name "Roque" evokes the past for Frédéric: "À ce nom, Frédéric revit la petite Louise, sa maison, sa chambre; et il se rappela des nuits pareilles, où il restait près de sa fenêtre, écoutant les rouliers qui passaient" (238), which refers to this sentence in the first episode of Nogent: "Il se levait très tard, et regardait par sa fenêtre les attelages de rouliers qui passaient" (154).

In all of these cases, since the reference is provided by the text, the readability is maximal. However, in numerous passages, *L'Éducation sentimentale* is far more obscure, as for the analepsis that links Rosanette with Madame Arnoux during her walk with Frédéric in the streets of Paris. In Frédéric's mind, Rosanette's presence is almost annulled (as the double negation suggests: "ne s'apercevait plus," "n'y songeait pas"): "Ils allaient côte à côte, elle appuyée sur son bras, et les volants de sa robe lui battaient contre les jambes. Alors il se rappela un crépuscule d'hiver, où, sur le même trottoir, Mme Arnoux marchait ainsi à son côté; et ce souvenir l'absorba tellement, qu'il ne s'apercevait plus de Rosanette et n'y songeait pas" (227). Here again, the text lacks the precision that is expected ("un crépuscule d'hiver") as it remembers its location: "sur le même trottoir." However, the name of the street is absent, so that the precision is, in fact, illusory: the reader cannot identify the scene. Nevertheless, this passage is most certainly a reflection of the short walk of Frédéric with Madame Arnoux in winter (which will be later mentioned again by yet another recall right after the Auteuil episode: "il lui rappela qu'une fois ils étaient sortis ensemble, par un crépuscule d'hiver, un temps de brouillard. Tout cela était bien loin, maintenant!," 371):[7]

On n'y voyait plus; le temps était froid, et un lourd brouillard, estompant la façade des maisons, puait dans l'air. Frédéric le humait avec délices; car il sentait à travers la ouate du vêtement la forme de son bras; et sa main, prise dans un gant chamois à deux boutons, sa petite main qu'il aurait voulu couvrir de baisers, s'appuyait sur sa manche. À cause du pavé glissant, ils oscillaient un peu; il lui semblait qu'ils étaient tous deux bercés par le vent, au milieu d'un nuage. (125)

The text displays a few signs that allude to a possible link between these two moments, which are actually opposed (only time—winter—and space—sidewalk—are common to both), although Frédéric's memory sets them in parallel (and once again his modes of recollection are unclear): awful weather in the first context ("froid," "puait"), beautiful weather in the second ("Il faisait un beau temps, âpre et splendide," 226), while the "lourd brouillard" has become light "vapeurs grises." Moreover, the detail *pavé glissant* is a dysphoric stereotype, which finds here its counterpart: "des équipages défilaient au grand trot sur le pavé sec" (227).

Many times in *L'Éducation sentimentale*, meaning is obscured and recalls play a part in this process, in different ways. An analepsis may refer to a sequence that is missing in the narrative. For instance, in the scene of Madame Arnoux's visit to Frédéric, the narrator remembers previous visits that she paid him with her husband, although they have never been recounted (here the narrator's memory is superior to that of the text): "Elle était venue plusieurs fois chez Frédéric, mais toujours avec Arnoux" (268). In the same way, the comparison that appears in the description of Paris viewed by Frédéric has lost its point of reference: "ses yeux [...] se dirigeaient toujours vers le quai aux Ormes, sur un massif de vieux arbres, pareils aux tilleuls du port de Montereau" (121), as there are no lime trees shown at Montereau when Frédéric arrives in chapter one (51). It is worth noting the specific aspect of this detail: the text displays no temporal rupture so there is no analepsis *per se*. In other words, it is only by interpreting the comparison as mnemonic—a memory of Frédéric, which the text does not designate as such—because the description is focalized on the character, that it can be granted its analeptic status due to the underlying presence of Madame Arnoux in his mind ("C'était par derrière, de ce côté-là, que devait être la maison de Mme Arnoux," at the end of the description), even more so, as her absence from Paris causes intense boredom: "Alors commencèrent trois mois d'ennui. Comme il n'avait aucun travail, son désœuvrement renforçait sa tristesse" (121).

In a different way, the analepsis found in the scene where Frédéric seduces Madame Dambreuse also obscures meaning (with the adverb *alors* again):

> Mme Dambreuse ferma les yeux, et il fut surpris par la facilité de sa victoire. Les grands arbres du jardin qui frissonnaient mollement s'arrêtèrent. Des nuages immobiles rayaient le ciel de longues bandes rouges, et il y eut comme une suspension universelle des choses. Alors, des soirs semblables, avec des silences pareils, revinrent dans son esprit, confusément. Où était-ce ?... (481–82)

Here the confusion ("revinrent dans son esprit, confusément") prevents the designation of the moments that are compared ("des soirs," "des silences"). Frédéric has lost his memory, and, as the analepsis is deactivated, the text does not allow any reference to previous scenes. Furthermore, there are no similar moments seen before in the narrative; this is in parallel an ironic way to erase the importance of the past.

The Fontainebleau episode also plays with memory, and with the reader, in several ways. First, ironically: while Frédéric and Rosanette attempt to escape history happening in Paris (i.e., the June days), history comes to the forefront of the narrative and merely leads to "la fugacité des dynasties, l'éternelle misère de tout" (430). Then, Frédéric's memories about the past appear on several occasions during the visit to the castle: "il semblait venir un écho des hallalis poussés dans les trompes d'ivoire, et des ballets mythologiques, assemblant sous le feuillage des princesses et des seigneurs travestis en nymphes et en sylvains" (429), "Il songeait à tous les personnages qui avaient hanté ces murs, Charles-Quint, les Valois, Henri IV, Pierre le Grand, Jean-Jacques Rousseau et 'les belles pleureuses des premières loges,' Voltaire, Napoléon, Pie VII, Louis-Philippe" (430), whereas his fantasies are counterbalanced by Rosanette, who says: "Ça rappelle des souvenirs!," a cliché forcing the reader to use intertextual memory, as it is found in *Pyrénées-Corse* ("à Montlhéry, la tour ne m'a point rappelé de souvenirs.

Expression des plus charmantes surtout comme il en arrive dans la bouche de ceux qui ne savent rien et qui l'adoptent par passion historique"[8]) and in the 1845 version of *L'Éducation sentimentale* ("un marchand de suif de sa connaissance [...] déclara qu'on aimait à se promener en ces lieux parce que ça rappelait des souvenirs, déclama aussitôt une douzaine de vers de Mme Desbordes-Valmore, écrivit ensuite son nom sur la muraille, et s'en alla enfin, l'âme pleine de poésie disait-il"[9]). Later in the episode, Rosanette uses her memory to tell about her childhood to Frédéric, in particular how she was prostituted by her mother ("Enfin un monsieur était venu, un homme gras, la figure couleur de buis, des façons de dévot, habillé de noir. Sa mère et lui eurent ensemble une conversation, si bien que, trois jours après... Rosanette s'arrêta," 437; see also 438) while Flaubert uses here memories of his friend Suzanne Lagier![10] This recollection stimulates Frédéric's memory as he now asks Rosanette how she met Arnoux. Here appears (in Genettian terms) a completing analepsis (or *return*), whose function consists of filling in "after the event, an earlier gap in the narrative (the narrative is thus organized by temporary omissions and more or less belated reparations, according to a narrative logic that is partially independent of the passing of time)" (Genette, 51): the reference is found at the end of chapter three, when Frédéric is at the Palais-Royal theater. The distance between the initial moment and its echo is here so great[11] that it would require some effort from the reader (as it does for Rosanette!) to find the scene in question. Moreover, if the two contexts are considered in parallel, some oddities become obvious:

Puis une jeune fille blonde, les paupières un peu rouges comme si elle venait de pleurer, s'assit entre eux. Arnoux resta dès lors à demi penché sur son épaule, en lui tenant des discours qu'elle écoutait sans répondre. Frédéric s'ingéniait à découvrir la condition de ces femmes, modestement habillées de robes sombres, à cols plats rabattus. (73)

Il lui demanda, seulement, comment elle avait fait la connaissance d'Arnoux.
— 'Par la Vatnaz.'
— 'N'était-ce pas toi que j'ai vue, une fois, au Palais-Royal, avec eux deux ?'
Il cita la date précise. Rosanette fit un effort.
— 'Oui, c'est vrai!... Je n'étais pas gaie dans ce temps-là!' (439)

At this point, Frédéric seems to have more memory than the text. The sentence "Je n'étais pas gaie dans ce temps-là" is symmetrical to this detail in her portrait: "les paupières un peu rouges comme si elle venait de pleurer"; however, the scene at the Palais-Royal is not dated ("Un soir") —although Frédéric at Fontainebleau cites its exact date (which the text omits)—and only a reconstitution from sparse chronological indications allows the reader to determine that it takes place during the summer of 1841 (seven years before, in the chronology of the novel). Furthermore, at the Palais-Royal, Rosanette is blonde, whereas in the Fontainebleau episode, she is a brunette ("ses bandeaux châtains qui bouffaient," 435). Here variations of focalization interfere with the acuteness of memory and hence with the precision of the analepsis, and it is very unlikely that the reader could remember the scene in question.[12]

The last two chapters of Part III (6 and 7) are also full of recollections and analeptic notations, especially because they have the function to summarize, for the reader, some aspects of the novel and to bring conclusions or solutions to facts that have not yet been solved (such as Arnoux's debt; Madame Arnoux gives the fifteen-thousand francs back to Frédéric, the sum "dont les terrains de Belleville devaient répondre" [542], referring to Part II, chapter 3). Symmetrical to chapters one and two, these two chapters both contain two short scenes, one between Frédéric and Madame Arnoux, the other between Frédéric and Deslauriers.

In chapter six, analeptic notations take on diverse aspects. Some explain a previous gap in the narrative, as when Frédéric tells Madame Arnoux that after the couple's bankruptcy he went to their place; she knew it: "Elle l'avait aperçu dans la cour, et s'était cachée" (542), which refers to this passage:

> Rue Paradis, le portier jura que M. Arnoux était absent depuis la veille; quant à Madame, il n'osait rien dire; et Frédéric, ayant monté l'escalier comme une flèche, colla son oreille contre la serrure. Enfin, on ouvrit. Madame était partie avec Monsieur. La bonne ignorait quand ils reviendraient; ses gages étaient payés, elle-même s'en allait.
> Tout à coup un craquement se fit entendre.
> — 'Mais il y a quelqu'un?'
> — 'Oh! Non, Monsieur! C'est le vent.' (524–25)

The reader finally understands the previous allusions ("il n'osait rien dire," "un craquement"). Then, when Madame Arnoux looks at furniture and objects "avidement, pour les emporter dans sa mémoire" (542), the detail of Rosanette's painting appears ("Le portrait de la Maréchale était à demi caché par un rideau"), and Madame Arnoux says: "Je connais cette femme, il me semble?" Frédéric replies with a lie: "'Impossible! [...] C'est une vieille peinture italienne'." Madame Arnoux at this point forgets that she knows of the painting ("La femme dont vous avez le portrait, votre maîtresse!," 470), which further refers to several moments in the narrative. When Frédéric buys it, the text contains an analepsis: "Le soir même, le tableau fut apporté. Il lui parut plus abominable encore que la première fois. Les demi-teintes et les ombres s'étaient plombées sous les retouches trop nombreuses, et elles semblaient obscurcies par rapport aux lumières, qui, demeurées brillantes çà et là, détonnaient dans l'ensemble" (362). The moment to which the text refers here appeared about twenty pages before:

> En sortant du cabinet de lecture, il aperçut du monde devant la boutique d'un marchand de tableaux. On regardait un portrait de

femme, avec cette ligne écrite au bas en lettres noires: "Mlle Rose-Annette Bron, appartenant à M. Frédéric Moreau, de Nogent."

C'était bien elle,—ou à peu près,—vue de face, les seins découverts, les cheveux dénoués, et tenant dans ses mains une bourse de velours rouge, tandis que, par-derrière, un paon avançait son bec sur son épaule, en couvrant la muraille de ses grandes plumes en éventail. (324–25)

At this point, the reader must remember the passage in Part II, chapter 2, where the portrait is described in the conditional mood (from Pellerin's point of view) in order to fully comprehend the painter's failure (225; one hundred pages before).[13]

The analeptic reference may, of course, contain diverse degrees of precision. For Frédéric's and Madame Arnoux's final recollections, one paragraph is entirely based on memories:

Ils se racontèrent leurs anciens jours, les dîners du temps de *L'Art industriel*, les manies d'Arnoux, sa façon de tirer les pointes de son faux-col, d'écraser du cosmétique sur ses moustaches, d'autres choses plus intimes et plus profondes. Quel ravissement il avait eu la première fois, en l'entendant chanter! Comme elle était belle, le jour de sa fête, à Saint-Cloud! Il lui rappela le petit jardin d'Auteuil, des soirs au théâtre, une rencontre sur le boulevard, d'anciens domestiques, sa négresse.
Elle s'étonnait de sa mémoire. (543)

The text is somewhat heterogeneous: "les dîners du temps de *L'Art industriel*" refers to Part I (they begin in chapter four), "les manies d'Arnoux" is quite vague (as is "d'autres choses plus intimes et plus profondes"); "sa façon de tirer les pointes de son faux-col" is not present in the narrative, but "sa façon […] d'écraser du cosmétique sur ses moustaches" is mentioned in chapter four—although it is not described (87–88); Madame Arnoux is viewed singing during Frédéric's first dinner at the Arnoux's (102). The evocation of Saint-Cloud (141) and that of the garden at Auteuil (368) do not display any detail; no evenings at the theater with Frédéric and the Arnoux couple have been shown in the novel; "sa négresse" is present from chapter one, but disappears after chapter three (70), as if the narrator were forgetting about her. As to "une rencontre sur le boulevard," it is unsure whether it refers to the sole encounter mentioned between Madame Arnoux and Frédéric in the streets of Paris: "Le lendemain, comme il se rendait chez Deslauriers, au détour de la rue Vivienne et du boulevard, Mme Arnoux se montra devant lui, face à face" (353), although Flaubert uses the term "boulevard." Even if Madame Arnoux is surprised by Frédéric's memory, the text remains very condensed and does not elaborate memories, as if it had lost its own memory.[14]

On the other hand, the final chapter is the one that contains the analepsis with the broadest scope: Frédéric and Deslauriers talk about their visit to the brothel of the Turque. This external analepsis covers more than one page and is extremely precise, with numerous details:

> [...] beaucoup de personnes la croyaient une musulmane, une Turque, ce qui ajoutait à la poésie de son établissement, situé au bord de l'eau, derrière le rempart; même en plein été, il y avait de l'ombre autour de sa maison, reconnaissable à un bocal de poissons rouges près d'un pot de réséda sur une fenêtre. Des demoiselles, en camisole blanche, avec du fard aux pommettes et de longues boucles d'oreilles, frappaient aux carreaux quand on passait, et, le soir, sur le pas de la porte, chantonnaient doucement d'une voix rauque. (550)

The text seems to recover a memory it had lost before, as it is now explaining two mere allusions in chapter two. First, when the narrator says why Madame Moreau did not like Deslauriers ("elle crut savoir qu'il avait conduit son fils dans des lieux déshonnêtes," 59) and then, at the end of the chapter:

> Cependant à vingt toises des ponts, sur la rive gauche, une lumière brillait dans la lucarne d'une maison basse.
> Deslauriers l'aperçut. Alors, il dit emphatiquement, tout en retirant son chapeau:
> — 'Vénus, reine des cieux, serviteur! Mais la Pénurie est la mère de la Sagesse. Nous a-t-on assez calomniés pour ça, miséricorde!'

Cette allusion à une aventure commune les mit en joie. Ils riaient très haut dans les rues. (63)

The text is here so opaque that the reader cannot understand the "allusion"; only the last scene of the novel gives the solution to this mystery (a mystery that the reader has obviously long forgotten). Furthermore, the final analepsis has a singular effect: as the two characters declare these moments their best ones ("C'est là ce que nous avons eu de meilleur," 551)—although it is questionable how a failure can be defined as best moments in a lifetime—the entire diegesis is suddenly erased, as what was best occurred during the vacation of 1837, three years before the beginning of the story.[15]

In his study on Proustian analepses, Genette notes that the most persistent function of recalls in the *Recherche* is to "modify the meaning of past occurrences after the event, either by making significant what was not so originally, or by refuting a first interpretation and replacing it with a new one" (Genette 56); this technique is one of the most effective methods for circulating meaning. In *L'Éducation sentimentale*, analepses are deceptive and merged with constant reappearance and changes of states of mind, of places that are no longer unique. Their repetition reveals the unlikelihood of any notion of apprenticeship or reconstruction of meaning, contrary to Proustian analepses (see Genette 58). Memory is merged with the structural complexity of the novel; it is both a theme and a technique, and its appearance (or disappearance) has a tendency to make the narrative opaque. This is also one of the reasons why, when the reader looks for a specific passage, he or she usually cannot find its page. Paradoxically, analepses partake of the devices that obscure the novel, as if Flaubert had untied the threads that compose the fabric of his text.

Notes

1. All references are to the Garnier-Flammarion revised edition by Stéphanie Dord-Crouslé (Paris: Flammarion, "GF," 2013).

2. On which many comments have been made; see for instance Krystyna Falicka ("L'architecture de *L'Éducation sentimentale*," *Romanica*

Wratislaviensia, VII, 156, 1972, 31–46); Jean-Pierre Duquette (*Flaubert ou l'architecture du vide*. Montréal: Presses Universitaires de Montréal, 1972); and Jeanne Bem (*Clés pour L'Éducation sentimentale*. Études Littéraires Françaises. Tübingen: Gunter Narr Verlag, 1981).

3.   Gérard Genette, *Narrative Discourse*. 1972. Trans. Jane E. Lewin. Ithaca: Cornell UP, 1980. 40. Genette makes a distinction between *external* analepses, which deal with events occurring earlier than the temporal point of departure of the first narrative, and *internal* analepses, which deal with events occurring later than the point of departure of the narrative (49).

4.   And this intratextual echo is further complicated by an intertextual one, as the narrator of *Novembre* wishes to commit suicide and mentions the "Pont-Neuf" (euphoric context in *L'Éducation sentimentale*): "Un jour, à Paris, je me suis arrêté longtemps sur le Pont-Neuf [...]. Combien de gens avaient passé à la place où je me tenais alors, courant la tête levée à leurs amours ou à leurs affaires, et qui y étaient revenus, un jour, marchant à petits pas, palpitant à l'approche de mourir! Ils se sont approchés du parapet, ils ont monté dessus, ils ont sauté," *Novembre*, in Œuvres complètes, Vol. 1 (Claudine Gothot-Mersch and Guy Sagnes eds.). Bibliothèque de la Pléiade. Paris: Gallimard, 2001, 778–79. Note the presence of the *parapet* which in *L'Éducation sentimentale* prevents Frédéric from committing suicide.

5.   The way the text plays with memory (that of the reader, too) should be emphasized: a little earlier on the same page, "Une négresse, qu'il croisa un jour dans les Tuileries tenant une petite fille par la main, lui rappela la négresse de Mme Arnoux" (she appeared in chapter one, 48) whereas the women that Frédéric now watches at the Champs-Élysées "amenaient à sa mémoire Mme Arnoux"; Frédéric imagines her in "un de ces petits coupés, pareils au coupé de Mme Dambreuse," which was described at the beginning of the chapter (66), and the Tuileries gardens reappear.

6.   Genette, 55. See also, from a different standpoint, Léo Bersani, "Déguisements du moi et art fragmentaire," in *Recherche de Proust* (Gérard Genette & Tzvetan Todorov, eds.). Points. Paris: Seuil, 1980. 20–22.

7. The same pattern appears in the scene of Frédéric's visit to the Dambreuses in Part II, chapter 3 (where the association *space/time/focalization* can be noticed again): "tout ce bien-être luxueux établissait dans la pensée de Frédéric un contraste avec un autre déjeuner chez Arnoux" (269–70). The passage mentioned is not recognizable. The reader may remember one scene at the Arnoux's and set the two contexts in parallel, as the luxurious comfort at the Dambreuses is opposed to the untidiness of Arnoux's apartment, which was found about twenty pages earlier (252). However, the Dambreuse scene mentions "un autre déjeuner chez Arnoux" and the context is obviously that of a lunch ("Le lendemain, à onze heures, il se présenta chez M. Dambreuse. On le reçut dans la salle à manger. Le banquier déjeunait en face de sa femme," 269; see also the "hors-d'œuvre" in the description), whereas in the previous scene at the Arnoux's "C'était l'heure du premier déjeuner," which implies a breakfast (see the details: "bols de café au lait," "caleçon," "tartine"). Therefore, the analepsis does not seem to function properly and the reader remains confused about the reference.

8. *Pyrénées-Corse*, in Œuvres complètes, Vol. 1 (Claudine Gothot-Mersch & Guy Sagnes, eds.). Bibliothèque de la Pléiade. Paris: Gallimard, 2001. 648.

9. *Ibid.*, 1032.

10. "Un enfant (16 ans) attend dans un boudoir la perte de son pucelage—souper servi—ne mange que des confitures et s'endort sur des gravures lubriques" (S. Lag.) *Carnets de travail* (Pierre-Marc de Biasi, ed.) Paris: Balland, 1988. 284.

11. Making the narrative *skilful*, as Roland Barthes would put it: "the narrative technique is impressionistic: it breaks up the signifier into particles of verbal matter which make sense only by coalescing: it plays with the distribution of a discontinuity [...]; the greater the syntagmatic distance between two data, the more skilful the narrative; the performance consists in manipulating a certain degree of impressionism: the touch must be light, as though it weren't worth remembering, and yet, appearing again later in another guise, it must already be a memory," *S/Z*. 1970. Trans. Richard Miller. New York: Hill and Wang, 1974. 22–23.

12. It is worth noting that when Rosanette reappears in the story (Part II, chapter 1), no analepsis associates her with the previous scene: the text lacks memory as Frédéric does not recognize her. On the other

hand, the enigma concerning Miss Vatnaz, who is with Rosanette at the Palais-Royal, is almost immediately resolved with a recall in chapter four: "C'était la femme entrevue, l'été dernier, au Palais-Royal" (87).

13. The painting is also mentioned in Part II, chapter 3: "Pellerin l'avait engagé à venir voir le portrait; il l'éconduisait toujours" (253), in Part II, chapter 4, in the scene where Pellerin comes to Frédéric's to try to sell him the painting (301–2), and during the dinner at the Dambreuses in Part III, chapter 2: "Un jour que le père Roque et sa fille l'attendaient chez lui, ils avaient vu le portrait de la Maréchale. Le bonhomme l'avait même pris pour 'un tableau gothique'" (456; see also 462). A similar pattern is followed by the *calf's head* network associated with Compain (who alludes to it several times, mysteriously). Deslauriers gives the solution in Part III, Chapter 7 (548); the reader must therefore once again remember the past (see 412, 470, 513).

14. Even more so when Madame Arnoux tells Frédéric that she found out that he was in love with her "un soir que vous m'avez baisé le poignet entre le gant et la manchette" (544); a fake analepsis, since in the narrative this gesture applies to Rosanette, not to Madame Arnoux: "Et, lui tenant toujours le poignet, il appuya dessus ses lèvres, entre le gant et la manchette" (286).

15. On other mnemonic devices, see Ippolito's analysis of the *line subtext* ("C'est peut-être le défaut de ligne droite," 549) in the novel, *Narrative Memory in Flaubert's Works*. "Currents in Comparative Romance Languages and Literatures." New York: Peter Lang, 2001, 188–201.

Works Cited

Barthes, Roland. *S/Z*. 1970. Trans. Richard Miller. New York: Hill & Wang, 1974.

Bem, Jeanne. *Clés pour L'Éducation sentimentale*. Études Littéraires Françaises. Tübingen: Gunter Narr Verlag, 1981.

Bersani, Léo. "Déguisements du moi et art fragmentaire." *Recherche de Proust*. Ed. Gérard Genette & Tzvetan Todorov. Paris: Seuil, 1980. 13–33.

Duquette, Jean-Pierre. *Flaubert ou l'architecture du vide*. Montréal: PU de Montréal, 1972.

Falicka, Krystyna. "L'architecture de *L'Éducation sentimentale*," *Romanica Wratislaviensia*, VII, 156, 1972. 31–46.

Flaubert, Gustave. *L'Éducation sentimentale*. Ed. Stéphanie Dord-Crouslé. GF. Paris: Flammarion, 2013.

_____. *Œuvres complètes*. Vol. 1. Œuvres de jeunesse. Eds. Claudine Gothot-Mersch & Guy Sagnes. Bibliothèque de la Pléiade. Paris: Gallimard, 2001.

_____. *Carnets de travail*. Ed. Pierre-Marc de Biasi. Paris: Balland, 1988.

Genette, Gérard. *Narrative Discourse*. 1972. Trans. Jane E. Lewin. Ithaca, NY: Cornell UP, 1980.

Ippolito, Christophe. *Narrative Memory in Flaubert's Works*. "Currents in Comparative Romance Languages and Literatures." New York: Peter Lang, 2001.

Seduction by Story in Flaubert and Conrad_____

Mark Conroy

> There is a story, always ahead of you. Barely existing. Only gradually
> do you attach yourself to it and feel it. You discover the carapace that
> will contain and test your character. You find in this way the path of
> your life.
>
> (Michael Ondaatje, *The Cat's Table*)

Among the many delightful features of Julian Barnes' famous novel
Flaubert's Parrot are three versions of life chronology for the author
who is its subject. In addition to one, arguably the most salient,
consisting only of quotations from Gustave Flaubert himself, there
are two more conventional chronologies with successive dates and
the significant events to go with them. A covert principle of selection
governs each chronology, however. The first picks out all high
points—or, at worst, optimistic "spin" on the less-than-inspiring
moments—and ends as follows: "1880—Full of honour, widely
loved, and still working hard to the end, Gustave Flaubert dies at
Croisset" (Barnes 20). The second seems considerably darker. For
example, in the first chronology, even his epileptic seizure proves
"beneficial in the long run," encouraging him to drop his pursuit
of the law and turn to literature; whereas in contrast, the second
chronology speaks of the "shattering first attack of epilepsy," evoking
"others... to follow," and lamenting: "Without having entered the
world, Gustave now retires from it." This pessimistic account sums
up the arc of Flaubert's life as follows: "Impoverished, lonely and
exhausted, Gustave Flaubert dies" (Barnes 18–24). Barnes' point is
probably that most people's lives are various and random enough
that this very fact allows us, invites us really, to shape those lives
according to a certain emotional need, seducing us to construe
events with, as they say, an end in view. The happy end can, in
effect, reverse-engineer the events chosen and interpreted to lead up

to it, and so can the shabby one. Either ending typically has enough ammunition to inform a satisfying, if partial, story line.

This insight is all too apt for a book about Flaubert, who himself seldom forgot the mind's ability to fashion the raw material of experience into a factitious, but reassuring, narrative shape. For Flaubert, as for some strains of psychological theory, the myth-making faculty is often wrong, but seldom in doubt. Ego psychology has taught us that individuals take their identities, their personal myths, from their reference groups and then tailor them. Erik Erikson in particular tells us that the story a member of the community tells himself must come from others in order to "reconcile his *conception of himself* and his *community's recognition* of him" (225; emphasis Erikson's). And just as Immanuel Kant tells us that experience isn't really experience without the forms we supply to order it, so Flaubert is famous for telling the story of how people take in the stories they are given by others, and then give themselves those stories to try to live. Of course in itself, this interest is hardly unique to Flaubert's novels. One could argue, as some have, that it goes all the way back at least to *Don Quixote*, that book to which *Madame Bovary* and its heroine are so often compared. So what is especially distinctive about Flaubert's interest in this phenomenon? And how does this make him such a useful point of influence for Joseph Conrad?

For we do know, thanks in part to Yves Hervouet, that the French novelist influenced Conrad quite a bit. The specialty of that scholarship is chiefly stylistic, gleaning eerie echoes of Flaubertian prose in Conrad's fiction. But Hervouet does also supply thematic connections, as in his analysis of *Lord Jim,* which he argues owes for its overarching themes of romantic self-dramatization and personal myth to Emma Bovary's futile pursuit of the dreams implanted in her by the reading of her convent girlhood. It may be telling, for our purposes anyway, that Hervouet also observes a possible rhyme between the character of Jim in Conrad's novel and the figure of Frédéric Moreau in Flaubert's *L'Éducation sentimentale*: "Jim's dream of greatness, although it destroys him, gives him a certain stature, and in this he is close to Frédéric whose dream, as [Paul] Kirchner has noted, gives distinction to his otherwise mediocre life"

(Hervouet 70). Just as Emma's dreams of love were nurtured by what she read, so Jim's dreams of glory took their inspiration from the "light holiday literature" by which he'd been seduced. Hervouet notes how Jim's early career in Patusan is one he speaks of as something from a storybook; and further he likens Jim's execution by the Patusan islanders to Emma's suicide at the conclusion of Flaubert's novel (Hervouet 64–65, 68–69). The narcissistic tendency in both characters receives its symbolic expression in the many instances where Jim and Emma are presented in their favorite position: high up above everyone else (Hervouet 65). There is even some remembrance of Emma's convent upbringing and its attendant idealism in Jim's boyhood residence in his father's parsonage. Without being too literal-minded about it, it is still quite sensible to see *Lord Jim* as a book that would not be recognizable to us were all the seeming parallels to Flaubert's novel removed.

But does this influence extend to the theme of story and seduction? Maybe it would be best just to say that Conrad and Flaubert share a common interest in how the stories we take in provide the models by which we live, or at least the alibis for the lives we end up living. It might be too much to go the next step and claim that Conrad himself was in fact seduced by Flaubert's presentation of seduction by story to the point where he unconsciously reproduced its effects in his own creations as well. It is true that Conrad, toward the end of his life, goes out of his way to nullify the suggestion that *Bovary* had much role to play at all in the development of his themes. He writes to Hugh Walpole in June 1918: "You say that I have been under the formative influence of *Madame Bovary.* In fact, I read it only after finishing *A. F. [Almayer's Folly],* as I did all the other works of Flaubert, and anyhow, my Flaubert is the Flaubert of *St. Antoine* and *Ed[ucation] : Sent[imentale]*: and that only from the point of view of the rendering of concrete things and visual impressions… I don't think I learned anything from him" (Hervouet 12).

With such a thoroughgoing and implausible feint, who could imagine Flaubert as anything other than an overweening presence in the text of Conrad? In any event, the case for the proposition that *Bovary* constitutes some precedent for *Lord Jim,* not merely in point of visual impressions, but also with regard to thematic and psychological resonance, is very close to self-evident. And insofar as it needs further proof, Hervouet can be said to supply most of it already. The only thing to add to his analysis, which looks not only at *Bovary* and *L'Éducation,* but also at Flaubert's wayward, biblical spectacular *Salammbô,* is that Jim, unlike his forerunner figure, does not succumb to the disillusionment occasioned when his story—his "conception of himself"—is threatened by the "fire" of life's vicissitudes. Despite the faint echo of her suicide and his honorable amends, I think Jim exhibits greater stubbornness—or, if you will, stronger reserves of denial—than does Emma. His "proud, unflinching glance" as he is killed is quite different from Emma Bovary's embittered final laugh, to make the most dramatic contrast. Perhaps the fact that Emma's dream relied on other people—men, to be specific—allowed her to relinquish them without destroying her sense of self (Flaubert shows that even in her extremity she blames the outside world for her troubles); but the result of life without an ideal, even a banal one, was still too much to support. Jim's fantasy, however, relied ultimately on his own self-worth; and no matter what the verdict of reality on that fantasy, Jim always felt he could retrieve it by taking his punishment. He does so after the *Jeddah* incident and when his tenure on Patusan comes to grief as well. There is also the difference that, in Jim's case, the death adheres to a ritual, allowing it a mythic aspect, while Emma's beautiful death fails to go as planned.

Although *Lord Jim* takes a larger, colonial canvas for its tale, unlike what *Madame Bovary*'s provincial setting affords, both novels place their stress upon individual psychology: the dreams in each case work their effects first and foremost on the dreamers, even if in Jim's case there are also secondary effects (big ones!) on many others in addition. Put otherwise, neither book is primarily about collective dreams, except indirectly. What is striking in this respect about Conrad's major book of the middle phase, his *Nostromo,* is how completely the personal myths of the characters and the nascent political story of Sulaco itself are bound up, to the point where it is often hard, until the third section anyway, to tell them apart. Jim's

---

heroism is acted out aboard ship and on a remote island, but the origins are simple to detect. At least the delivery system for those dreams of heroism is straightforward. But the major figures in *Nostromo* are another matter. Their dreams, because the future of the part of the world they inhabit is itself so in doubt, are part and parcel of the collective dream, or rather the competing visions, of Sulaco.

When we get to the possible thematic relevance for Conrad of *L'Éducation sentimentale*, Hervouet is careful to acknowledge it by one evident marker: Everything about each work seems to recall the other one. Hervouet notes how "both works, which are permeated by the sense of failure conveyed in the collapse of all dreams and the general degradation of all ideals, embody not only the same rejection of the notion of Progress, but also the same disillusionment with life, the same overpowering feeling of the 'cruel futility of things' (*N,* p. 364)" (Hervouet 89). The sheer inclusiveness of the statement seems to carry all before it. Yet when we get to specifics, there aren't many here. Rather than invent some more specifics, one thing we can do is to explore further these larger thematic connections, thereby giving greater definition and articulation to how the story of susceptibility to narrative, to myth, has itself been transferred, as by contagion, from one work to the other.

The thematic and symbolic lines that run between *Madame Bovary* and *Lord Jim* are more straightforward, and certainly more generally recognized, than those between *L'Éducation sentimentale* and *Nostromo*. If one were to tell a similar story of influence for these latter two texts, though, what would one say? It's possible that Conrad's profound respect for Flaubert's work did not necessarily translate into a specific set of clear and distinct patterns of symbol, character or preoccupation: Joyce's *Ulysses* has millions of admirers and very few epigones. But one tentative move can be made in this direction by observing, with inevitable brevity, the way the theme of *L'Éducation sentimentale* complicates the myth of the seductive story, a fiction of self-identity that roots itself as early as, say, Emma's convent reading.

Whereas in *Madame Bovary* the chief locus of the story is the person of the heroine, hence the title, in the latter novel the title is more general—and no doubt ironic at that. Flaubert's stated goal in the book was to write the "psychological *[morale]* history of the people of my generation," as we know; and thus at least one register of the power of story in this work is explicitly collective. There's no question that the stories that grip Emma and help to determine her actions in life are also in a way collective, or commonly shared, entities. Indeed, the power of certain mythologies is said to reside in their commonplace quality: that the archetypes are so deeply held precisely because they are, in a way, not one's own so much as everyone's, finally impersonal. But in *Madame Bovary,* the heroine is defined above all by her abortive modernity; that is, as a character whose individuality must be asserted, whose non-conformity must be exercised. To do this she must see herself as resisting and overcoming the received existence of her provincial town—a resistance so complete that, were she to achieve it, she would have to surrender her previous identity. This might be one meaning of the famous sentiment the novel attributes to her: that after reading her stories, she both wanted to die and also wanted to live in Paris. The tragedy of Emma, the one that as much as anything triggers the more evident tragedy of her suicide, is that in trying to break out of the commonplaces of her provincial existence, she merely exchanges them for another set of commonplaces, which leads to her bitter reflection at one point that she had discovered in adultery all the banalities of marriage. It is her inability to transcend the banal as much as her money woes and the humiliations attendant on the end of her affairs that lead to her decision to die. The impersonal, even when it comes in the garb of a storybook role, is the greatest enemy to Emma in this scenario. Her seduction is not at the hands of her suitors, still less of her husband Charles, so much as at the hands of her reading.

By contrast, what animates the characters—almost all of the chief ones—in the later novel of Flaubert is a quite conscious relationship to collective myth. They are, after all, living in the city Emma only dreams of inhabiting; and this city is defined by the denizens of *L'Éducation sentimentale* in at least a couple of salient ways. First, and essential to the story of the novel's chief character Frédéric

Moreau, is its identity as the place of romantic love; and second, and of signal interest to Moreau's ongoing friend and rival Deslauriers, is the way Paris has acquired the status of a locus (perhaps *the* locus) for republican self-assertion, the place where people without status can gain access to political power. The "myth" of Paris is a conscious part of the lives of the characters who move about Paris and how the fortunes of that myth change in the course of the century is a distinct theme of the novel itself as well. One register of romantic love for the Paris myth is, at least on the surface, intensely personal, even subjective. Yet as in the case of Emma Bovary, Frédéric's dream of love is, in most ways, fairly conventional. Even the two recurring loves of his adult life, vivacious Rosanette and the more demure (and married) Marie Arnoux, contrast each other in his mind roughly the way that whores and virgins traditionally have. (This is why we know that when he takes Rosanette to the apartment whose bedroom he has prepared for Mme. Arnoux and says, "Il y avait trop longtemps que je te désirais," he must be thinking of Mme. Arnoux. Rosanette is practically defined as what doesn't have to be waited for [Flaubert 111].)

The same thing is true in reverse of Deslauriers. His dream of Paris, like the progressivist dream of so many post-revolutionary French citizens, concerns the Paris where History gets enacted. He waxes nostalgic at one point about a Paris he has personally never known, one where "On vivait dans ce temps-là, on pouvait s'affirmer, prouver sa force! De simples avocats commandaient à des généraux, des va-nu-pieds battaient les rois, tandis qu'à present…" Such a once and future utopia (Deslauriers adds here, "l'avenir est gros!," though it seems obligatory) is an always pregnant possibility in the Paris that furnished the stage for the inaugural modern political moment. And Deslauriers believes in it (Flaubert 49). But, and this is the crucial modification, this is chiefly because he believes in himself; in his own career, his own potential for power. Just as Frédéric's desire for a personal story of romantic love partakes of a commonplace psychology and thus is self-defeating, no one woman being able to play both virgin and whore at the same time; so Deslauriers' collectivist vision is in its ultimate instance really a belief in *la carrière ouverte au talent,* i.e., his. It is true that both of these characters prove equally maladroit in entering into the other's dreams: Deslauriers tries to seduce Mme. Arnoux with grotesquely disastrous results, and Moreau's brief foray into the political arena as the hand-picked candidate of his mistress's husband doesn't go well. But in the end they have scarcely better success realizing their own personal dreams either.

By the concluding two chapters that form the novel's epilogue, it is clear that Frédéric's dreams of love have been well and truly dashed, but he returns to see Mme. Arnoux for a last interview. It is not in any way satisfactory: She all but openly offers herself to him, and whether because of her age or the fact that his obsession with her was finally not really about sex anyway, he turns aside the offer. (She gives him instead a lock of her hair, which is white.) But the final chapter is a revisiting of his old friend Deslauriers, as they look back fondly on their lives from the vantage point of people who have not achieved what they had wanted to. Frédéric and Deslauriers tell each other the story of their youthful excursion to a whorehouse in Nogent. What is interesting here is that the story is compounded of Frédéric's memories, Deslauriers' and seemingly those of the townspeople of Nogent who witnessed them running out of there:

Ils se la contèrent prolixement, chacun complétant les souvenirs de l'autre; et, quand ils eurent fini:
— C'est là ce que nous avons eu de meilleur! dit Frédéric.
— Oui, peut-être bien? C'est là ce que nous avons eu de meilleur! dit Deslauriers. (Flaubert 163)

Most of the commentary on this closing chapter focuses on the overweening irony of the story's content. For a start, this isn't even the memory of a sexual initiation, only of two boys fleeing the site of possible sentimental education. So the "happiest time" is defined not just by innocence, but by the refusal of experience. But if we emphasize the form of the final story as much as past commentators have the content, another truth starts of emerge. What the story affirms is the artisanal cooperation between the

Frédéric and Deslauriers of the present. Most of the stories that have governed people's lives in both of these novels have been "off the rack" kitsch of one sort or another. For the double-faceted myth of Paris that went unmentioned in this regard is that of the city of art and commerce.

Of course most major European cities could be put under a similar rubric. But the Paris of *L'Éducation sentimentale* is almost defined by the relation between art and commerce, not surprisingly, since this was a topic Flaubert had been concerned with since his youth (when he wrote an essay entitled *"Les Arts et le Commerce"* (Flaubert 184–86). These great stories, the grand narratives of Paris, bedeck themselves with ornaments provided by the machine of the market; and the goods that provide its fetishes are worked by craftsmen such as the elves in M. Arnoux's Art Industriel, for example. The casket that belongs to Mme. Arnoux and makes its way eventually to Mme. Dambreuse, the rich but vulgar woman Frédéric ends up seeing, is Flaubert's most sustained illustration of the way a commodity becomes part of one person's myth. But again, what is enabled with one hand is destroyed with the other because, when Mme. Arnoux's goods are sold at auction, Mme. Dambreuse buys it and, in Moreau's eyes, profanes it in that act. In a way, Frédéric and Deslauriers' closing dialogue reverses this dynamic, taking back their story from its community circulation and fashioning from it their own (albeit no doubt delusional) meaning and moral. In other words, they're not in Paris anymore.

If L'Éducation sentimentale is finally as much about Paris itself as its inhabitants, about the myth of Paris; then by analogy, *Nostromo* (1904) is more about the province and then state of Sulaco than it is about even its title character. Beyond that the striking thing about the setting of Conrad's novel is the way it inverts the relationship between mythology and place that obtains in Flaubert's world. The Paris Flaubert gives us has already in place at least a couple of strong mythological roles, as the site of political emancipation and as the city of love. But both of these myths are received ideas of Paris and so have the quality of a fixed store of value. The various characters who hustle from one career to another, one identity to the next, as if constantly placing their own reputations on a sort of *bourse*, do so against the gold standard of Paris itself, the myth of Paris. Again, the epilogue where Frédéric and Deslauriers concoct their own personal myth indicates that they've gone off the *bourse:* their personal myths are homemade and not put into relation to the French master narrative that is Paris—rather than the provinces, such as Nogent (Conroy 72–73).

In *Nostromo*, the artisanal process is the heart of myth-making because the very setting is still so much in process. Sulaco's "story" seduces all the characters in the novel, not because it is a ready-made absolute value, but because everyone imagines he can play a part, a hero's part of course, in forging the story. Sulaco does have a myth of foundations of sorts, from the days of Costaguanan federalism, but in the present of the novel, the myth of Sulaco is still nascent, a name in search of a reality. Such a fictional basis for history is probably what causes Christopher GoGwilt to declare, "Of all his writing, *Nostromo* perhaps best illustrates the Conradian entanglement of political and novelistic representation" (193). The sound and fury of political strife that has confused so many readers down through the years only emphasizes the up-for-grabs quality of this piece of real estate, and its susceptibility to charlatans and lawgivers alike. It may be for this reason that the "imagined community" that is Sulaco and the personal myths of the various main characters are so intertwined in this text.

The three central figures in *Nostromo,* Charles Gould, Martin Decoud, and Gian' Battista (called "Nostromo" by Conrad's one recurrent storyteller, the redoubtable Captain Mitchell)—all of these characters come to construe their personal stories as implicated in the fate of Sulaco's grand, or grander, narrative. As in *L'Éducation*, each character plays a role that has been dictated, or anyway broadly suggested, by some barely offstage public opinion. Conrad's mastery of what the narrative theorists sometimes call "focalization" becomes especially acute in his rendering of this force of public opinion. There is, in general, as much *style indirect libre* in this book as there is in Flaubert's work; but especially in adopting a kind of collective point of view on the main characters, subtly but insistently. So many of the actions in this novel and, above all, most of the important characters are framed by this collective voice.

The three major characters each enact a threefold process of seduction by story, each phase logically, if not temporally, succeeding the last. The first phase is that where gossip or rumor, the *doxa* of the community in short, furnishes to the individual a role to play or a myth to enact. Charles Gould is the dictator in waiting, the man of few words all backed by the power of the silver mine who can still the parliamentary squabbling of "pronunciamentos and reforms." The story of his growing into dictatorship is also Sulaco's collective story. (Sulaco, like its "king," comes to live out the story that it is given by others.) Gian'Battista is the man who is always defined as the hero, both by his employers and by the crowd, who saves the day and the premier; whose "prestige is his fortune" in the wry but just words of Dr. Monygham (Conrad 268). Decoud is a bargain-basement Lamartine or Victor Hugo, the man of letters who also engages, or dabbles, in politics in order to further the vaguely progressive aims of enlightenment liberalism. It may be of interest that the latter two men, by virtue of their romantic connections, have taken republican father figures: Giorgio Viola, an old Garibaldi hand, for Nostromo; and Don José Avellanos, the author of *Fifty Years of Misrule* and supporter of parliamentarism, for Decoud.

If the characters are in the first instance given, by their surrogate fathers and/or the ambient public, stories to live out by others, then the second phase of this process is the answering gesture by which the individual assimilates the myth and comes into ownership of the role. In Flaubert's novel, the same dynamic, what Jean-Paul Sartre calls "being for others," enacts itself above all in Frédéric, who is forever posing, even in the absence of an audience. Here the most complete beneficiary, and victim, of his assimilation of myth is surely the title character. (Decoud, writer that he is, prefers to play his roles at one remove, leaving him at a particular loss when the audience vanishes.) Until he discovers the virtues of secrecy late in the novel, Gian' Battista is forever playing a conscious role in the community. Gould, though his English modesty forbids any public avowal, clearly believes that, in furthering the mine, he can bring paternalistic security to the region itself, thus making good his father's failure in this regard. In other words, he really does come to regard himself, in the most modest possible way to be sure, as king of Sulaco.

So the first phase is the story supplied by the public to an individual: the garment is tailored. And there is the second phase where the individual puts the garment on. But there is the third, and most dangerous, phase to this story seduction: when the individual acts in concert with this role. Gould, perhaps because his role is (as in monarchy) inherited, has the least problem with this phase, at least on the surface. (That is, he survives.) Whether his actions actually result in what he thinks they will is another matter: his wife Emilia Gould clearly has her own thoughts on this, as does Dr. Monygham. But Decoud, who drowns himself, and Nostromo, who becomes a thief, both come to grief in good part because they try at first to live out, or live up to, their roles *vis-à-vis* Sulaco. If these two are both seduced by a story, their fates suggest that, all the same, they somehow lost the plot. Frédéric and Deslauriers relinquish their Parisian identities, returning to the provincial lives they started out embodying. The main characters in Conrad's novel cannot return anywhere once their Sulaco stories—that is, the garments they have been given by that social world—end up betraying them. They stay, and their fates serve to inform the story that Sulaco itself acquires. Still, Conrad's dramatization of the way someone takes on, and for better and worse lives out, a story he's been given by the collective entity recalls *L'Éducation sentimentale* quite strongly. The individuals have been seduced by stories and, in various ways, abandoned by them as well. Even this abandonment, though, becomes the basis for a narrative or myth of gringo failure. This myth is first enunciated in the novel's opening chapter, with its tale of gringos lost on the Azuera peninsula, and it is reprised toward the end by Dr. Monygham, who as a tragic, or anyway pathetic, figure is the appropriate one to convey it: his personal myth, it turns out, is also one of failure.

Hence, as I read *Nostromo,* even the failure of story becomes a sort of myth the text puts forward. The inevitability of story is not a theme generally read into Conrad, or for that matter Flaubert. I suppose we are more comfortable, as skeptical *biens pensants,* with Conrad and Flaubert solely as demystifiers, as people who see through other people's myths rather than as fashioning their own. Very well; but if the novelist has relied on anything down through the years, it is that any myth is better than none, even when a failure or a tragedy is its basis. We need only ponder Decoud's fate as he slips into the 'indifference of things' to realize that there's only one thing worse than being taken in by a bad story, and that is not to be in any story at all.

Works Cited

Barnes, Julian. *Flaubert's Parrot.* New York: McGraw-Hill, 1984.

Conrad, Joseph. *Nostromo: A Tale of the Seaboard.* Harmondsworth, UK: Penguin, 1963.

Conroy, Mark. *Modernism and Authority: Strategies of Legitimation in Flaubert and Conrad.* Baltimore, MD: Johns Hopkins UP, 1985.

Erikson, Erik H. "The Problem of Ego Identity." *Adolescent Identities: A Collection of Readings.* Ed. Deborah L. Browning. New York: Analytic Press, 2008: 223–40.

Flaubert, Gustave. *L'Éducation sentimentale.* Œuvres complètes, 2nd ed. Bernard Masson. Paris: Seuil, 1964.

GoGwilt, Christopher. *Invention of the West: Joseph Conrad and the Double-Mapping of Europe and Empire.* Stanford, CA: Stanford UN, 1995.

Hervouet, Yves. *The French Face of Joseph Conrad.* Cambridge: Cambridge UN, 1990.

Ondaatje, Michael. *The Cat's Table.* New York: Alfred A. Knopf, 2011.

Schizophrenia, Revolution, and *Trois contes*————

Kathryn Oliver Mills

In January of 1852, in a noteworthy and well-known letter to his intimate friend Louise Colet, Gustave Flaubert wrote:

> Il y a en moi, littérairement parlant, deux bonshommes distincts: un qui est épris de *gueulades*, de lyrisme, de grands vols d'aigle, de toutes les sonorités de la phrase et des sommets de l'idée; un autre qui fouille et creuse le vrai tant qu'il peut, qui aime à accuser le petit fait aussi puissamment que le grand, qui voudrait vous faire sentir presque *matériellement* les choses qu'il reproduit; celui-là aime à rire et se plaît dans les animalités de l'homme. (*Correspondance* 2: 30)

That schizophrenic tension between romanticism and realism defined Flaubert's œuvre as much as his psyche: in September of 1868, Flaubert wrote to Ernest Chesneau that "La manière dont l'Absolu et le contingent doivent être mêlés dans une œuvre d'art me semble indiquée nettement page 62 [sic]. Je pense comme vous... Bref, on n'est idéal qu'à la condition d'être réel, et on n'est vrai qu'à force de généraliser" (*Correspondance* 3: 807).

In Flaubert's own estimation, his earlier works did not achieve the desired balance between the real and the ideal:

> *L'Education sentimentale* a été, à mon insu, un effort de fusion entre ces deux tendances de mon esprit...J'ai échoué...Une qualité n'est jamais un défaut, il n'y a pas d'excès. Mais si cette qualité en mange une autre, est-elle toujours une qualité?...Les causes sont montrées, les résultats aussi; mais l'enchaînement de la cause à l'effet ne l'est point. Voilà le vice du livre, et comment il ment à son titre. (*Correspondance* 2: 30)

The early version of *La Tentation de saint Antoine* (1849) failed, too, this time with "éperduments de style...Je n'y ai oublié qu'une chose, c'est le fil" (*Correspondance* 2: 31). And *Madame Bovary* (1856,

---

1857) does not harmonize Flaubert's two "bonshommes" either, presenting realism in its ugly extreme, while representing only a false version of idealism: "On me croit épris du réel, tandisque je l'exècre. Car c'est en haine du réalisme que j'ai entrepris ce roman. Mais je n'en déteste pas moins la fausse idéalité dont nous sommes bernés par le temps qui court" (*Correspondance* 2: 643). Flaubert's novels of the 1860s do not achieve his personal and literary ideal.

In April of 1874, twenty-two years after his revealing letter to Colet, Flaubert's good friend George Sand took him to task for the same lacunae and imbalances he had already noticed himself. Further, she challenged him to join his gift for representing the real with his "facultés d'intuition," to merge the "réel" with the "poétique:"

> Je crains…que ce soit encore du trop vrai, du trop bien observé et du trop bien rendu. Tu as ces qualités-là au premier chef, et tu en as d'autres, des facultés d'intuition, de grande vision, de vraie puissance qui sont bien autrement supérieures. Tu as…travaillé tantôt avec les unes, tantôt avec les autres, étonnant le public par ce contraste extraordinaire. Il s'agirait de mêler le réel et le poétique, le vrai et le fictif. Est-ce que l'art complet n'est pas le mélange de ces deux ordres de manifestation? (Flaubert, *Correspondance* 4: 786)

Flaubert started writing "La Légende de saint Julien l'Hospitalier" shortly after Sand's exhortation. And, although the novelist qualified the first of the *Trois contes* with many disclaimers—"Ce n'est rien du tout, et je n'y attache aucune importance" (Flaubert, *Correspondance* 4: 972)—and his work self-admittedly did not always rise to the challenge of his literary ideals, in his three tales, Flaubert came at his literary ideal for modernity once again. In the process, he achieved a highly innovative reconciliation of his "deux bonshommes," one that I will explore on the level of language as theme and as form.

In *Madame Bovary* and *L'Education Sentimentale*, the protagonists rely on verbiage to give meaning to their lives. Emma "cherchait à savoir ce que l'on entendait au juste dans la vie par les mots de 'félicité,' de 'passion,' et 'd'ivresse,' qui lui avaient paru si beaux dans les livres" (69). When Frédéric finally makes a declaration of love to Mme Arnoux at the end of *L'Education Sentimentale,* his love is a matter of words: "...et les délices de la chair étaient continues pour moi dans votre nom que je me répétais, en tâchant de le baiser sur mes lèvres" (619). In neither case is this verbal meaning true to the real circumstances of their lives, nor is it lasting. Emma's love life literally bankrupts her. In the end, Frédéric's declaration not only does not correspond to his true feelings, it also obscures them: "Frédéric, se grisant par ses paroles, arrivait à croire ce qu'il disait" (619).

In contrast to these self-consciously wordy beings, Félicité of "Un Cœur simple" can hardly talk. She can't argue her case against the unjustified accusation of theft; she doesn't say a word to her would-be lover throughout courtship and abandonment; she can't locate her nephew, Victor, on the map; she can't read the letter announcing Victor's death; she can't understand the catechism; and the meaning of her existence is reduced to three clichéd phrases that she exchanges with a parrot standing in for the Holy Ghost. Some of these events are outside her power to modulate—Victor's death, for example—but on many occasions, Félicité seems unable to rectify her situation because of her limited linguistic ability. Marc Bertrand has argued that "pour dérisoire qu'il soit," Félicité evolves in her grasp of language and that her internalization of that limited "parole" denotes her ultimate triumph (Bertrand 196). In my view, it is specifically the limited character of Félicité's words that allows her to go beyond them; transcendent poetry arises from the prose of her prosaic and difficult existence.

Examination of Félicité's courting scene, where she seems utterly powerless, reveals a series of physical reactions that form a code of effective and non-verbal resistance. Against the lover's flow of indistinct words Félicité makes tacit responses that—in contrast to the suitor's words—have actual effects. Théodore offers to drive her home and then assaults her; "Elle eut peur et se mit à crier" (Flaubert, *Trois contes* 13) and so he is forced to flee. Félicité's would-be lover meets her again and makes his excuses, "Elle ne sut que répondre et avait envie de s'enfuir" (13). He then launches into a speech intended to seduce, and she defends herself modestly and inarticulately: "Ah dit-elle, and "Elle baissa la tête." She lets him know that "c'était mal de se moquer." "Elle disparut dans l'ombre." And "elle hésitait à le croire" (13–14). Though Félicité is hurt by Théodore, she is not damaged by him: the end result of Félicité's responses to Théodore's words is that "la raison et l'instinct l'empêchèrent de faillir" (14). Félicité's physical language, motivated by qualities such as instinct, honor, and reason, protects her and triumphs over the seducer's standard patter, a patter that reveals verbal language's potential meaninglessness as it semi-dissolves into ineffectual clichés.

Félicité's relations with M. Bourais, the Church, and Loulou further illustrate that her language is not always a spoken one, and that its non-verbal quality makes it all the richer. Flaubert describes a striking contrast between verbal and non-verbal means of communication in the encounter between Bourais, who represents education and power (notably over Mme Aubain's finances), and Félicité, whose "entire literary education" came from "l'explication des gravures de Bourais" (Flaubert, *Trois contes* 17). M. Bourais tries to explain the whereabouts of Félicité's sailor nephew, Victor, by using a map; Félicité thinks she'll see Victor's portrait on the map itself, "tant son intelligence était bornée" (33). But the reader is left to wonder whether Bourais'—or Emma's—abstractions are any more real or desirable than Félicité's pictures: M. Bourais babbles about latitudes and longitudes in the same spirit in which Emma sought the real in a map of Paris and thus, as Wing notes, "allegorizes the separation between figures of desire and its referents" (Wing 54). In contrast, Félicité—"à cause des cigares"—has fertile pictures of Victor circulating "parmi les nègres, dans un nuage de tabac" (Flaubert, *Trois contes* 33). And Félicité's imagination gives her empathy for Victor, and thus has a direct impact on her experience: "Les jours de soleil elle se tourmentait de la soif; quand il faisait de l'orage, elle craignait pour lui la foudre" (31). Furthermore, the deaths and disgraces of Emma and M. Bourais can be linked to their mental and verbal abstraction. Emma reads too many books and projects herself into a mode of life that reality cannot sustain; Bourais falsifies the books, steals, and is dishonored. In any case,

Bourais' supposed enlightenment, and Emma's would-be superiority, ultimately leave them no better off than a poor, beaten servant-girl. For Félicité, on the other hand, the real and the imaginary—the real and the lyrical—interact, bringing Flaubert's two "bonshommes" together as one.[1]

Félicité's non-verbal mode of apprehension is further illustrated by her religious experience. On the one hand, Félicité is an illiterate whose education has, indeed, been restricted to Bourais' "gravures," and even what she understood of Virginie's catechism is limited: "Quant aux dogmes, elle n'y comprenait rien" (Flaubert, *Trois contes* 26). Once again, though, the power of Félicité's imagination makes religion real to her and to Flaubert's readers in a way that Bourais' sophisticated language does not. Listening to Virginie's lessons, "Elle croyait voir le paradis, le déluge, la tour de Babylon, des villes en flames…"; "Puis elle pleura en écoutant la Passion. Pourquoi l'avaient-ils crucifié, lui qui chérissait les enfants…" (25). In contrast with words alone, these vivid images have a direct impact on Félicité's life. Unlike Emma in her religious phase, Félicité's appreciation of the divine makes her reach out to others selflessly. She so loves Virginie that she puts herself in the child's place: "… avec l'imagination que donnent les vraies tendresses, il lui sembla qu'elle était elle-même cet enfant…" (27). This capacity for love extends to others ("elle aima plus tendrement les agneaux par amour de l'Agneau"), and it translates to action ("Elle soigna les cholériques. Elle protégeait les Polonais…Le Père Colmiche…allongeait les mains dès qu'il la voyait s'éloigner" [41–2]). Moreover, Félicité's compassion bears fruit in other people. When Mme Simonne takes care of Félicité as she lies dying, Mme Simonne reasons that "un jour il lui faudrait passer par là" (56), offering a glimmer of hope that the light of kindness will be passed on after Félicité's death.

Félicité's relations with her parrot, Loulou, are a final, paradigmatic indication of the significance within Félicité's silence and of the transcendence arising from within her limited circumstances. Because of her deafness, in the end Loulou is all that Félicité can hear: "Le petit cercle des ses idées se rétrécit encore; et le carillon des cloches, le mugissement des boeufs, n'existaient plus. Tous les êtres fonctionnaient avec le silence des fantômes. Un seul bruit arrivait maintenant à ses oreilles, la voix du perroquet" (Flaubert, *Trois contes* 46). But Loulou, like the Bible stories, makes the servant girl's faith in the unseen real: "Ils s'associèrent dans sa pensée, le perroquet se trouvant sanctifié par ce rapport avec le Saint Esprit, qui devenait plus vivant à ses yeux et plus intelligible" (50). Unlike Emma, then, Félicité does not contemplate the meaning of such words as "félicité," "passion," or "ivresse" (36), nor does she speak in overblown romantic jargon. The language Félicité and Loulou speak with each other is of an extremely limited nature: Loulou recycles mechanically learned phrases, and Félicité responds "par des mots sans suite" (46). But Félicité's heart "s'épanchait" in her disjointed words, and Loulou helps her understand the mystery of the Holy Ghost, a mystery that sustains her in her many acts of kindness.

And so the interaction between Félicité and Loulou demonstrates that ordinary words and sentiments can touch on the sacred. Indeed, the fine line Flaubert traces between the ridiculous and the sublime, the real and the ideal, in this "conte" is encapsulated in the word denoting her pet. Analyzing the name "Loulou," Eugenio Donato has brilliantly demonstrated that—like Félicité's language—it is both nonsensical and transcendent. On the one hand, the moniker is a meaningless repetition of two syllables. On the other hand, Flaubert's nickname for his beloved niece was Loulou. Thus Flaubert inserts the divergence between babbling and *logos* both in the interaction and within the name of a principal character in "Un Cœur simple" (Donato 108).

Together with Félicité's total lack of pretension, the coexistence and tension between the real and the ideal in Félicité's relations with her bird give her language greater depth. Jonathan Culler has elaborated on this dynamic: "The stupidity which refuses to comprehend objects in accordance with received modes of understanding but prefers to seek freedom and enrichment in reverie, the irony which explores alternative views both as polemical activity and as a way of enlarging horizons," are both attempts to arrive at the sacred, through "arbitrary meanings not by man but by God" (Culler 232). Following Culler's analysis, it is the paradoxical union of opposites that redeems Félicité's situation. If Félicité's room looked only like a chapel, her world would be purely ordinary and sentimental, and if it resembled only a bazaar, her life would be purely grotesque. However, the improbable coexistence of the real and the ideal allows for the possibility of transcendence. Likewise, Félicité's grasp of language is both grotesquely limited and highly imaginative, allowing her to surpass traditional verbal structures and modes of understanding.[2] Félicité's unconscious subversion of conventional categories of experience—physical and linguistic—redeems her flawed existence. And it is Flaubert's successful marriage of the "choses" rendered "matériellement" to the "vols d'aigle" that ultimately allows him to transcend language in "La Légende de saint Julien l'hospitalier" and "Hérodias" as well as in "Un Cœur simple."

The image of "crépuscule" permeates "La Légende de saint Julien l'hospitalier," setting that "conte" in a mixed and liminal state with parallels to the tensions of "Un Cœur simple." It is "crépuscule" when Julien takes a first shot at his mother (Flaubert, *Trois contes* 76); the rooms of Julien's castle are filled with "crépuscule" (81); he kills his parents in morning's "crépuscule," "les vitraux garnis de plomb obscurcissaient la pâleur de l'aube" (89). The French word "crépuscule" connotes an ambiguity on two levels: not only does it signify the indeterminate period between night and day, but it can also be used to signify either end of the day, "dawn" or "dusk." Flaubert was well aware of this term's ambidexterity—as we shall see at the end of this discussion, he used it to define his own literary position between eras as well as to describe the atmosphere surrounding Saint Julien. Like Flaubert and Félicité, the hero of "La Légende" straddles opposing identities and experiences which are betrayed by words.

Julien's hybrid fate is sealed in language at his birth. According to one prophetic utterance, Julien will be a warrior; according to another, he will be a saint. A third declaration, the stag's curse on Julien, confirms Julien's dual destiny by putting the first two prophecies together: Julien will somewhat perplexingly be holy as well as criminal.

The specific nature of these linguistic structures develops the role Flaubert ascribes to words in *Trois contes*. First, these prophecies are set under the charm of three, and they are indeed magical: whatever challenges their contradictions pose to meaning, they are all true and fulfilled in fact. Furthermore, and most significantly, the prophecies—like the language of Félicité—represent unconventional forms of verbal communication. The hermit announcing to the mother that Julien will be a saint speaks "sans desserrer les lèvres" [without opening his lips] (Flaubert, *Trois contes* 62), a physical impossibility. The second prophecy is also delivered in an unusual fashion, this time with a touch of the ridiculous: a beggar "bégaya d'un air inspiré ces mots sans suite" to the king (63) and then falls over into the grass. Finally, the third inspired prediction regarding Julien's fate defies expectations for speech by coming from a non-verbal source, a normally dumb animal (74). In "La Légende," language is at once contradictory, paradoxically true, and magical. Like "Un Cœur simple," "La Légende" transgresses the boundaries of traditional forms of verbal communication.

Indeed, like "Un Cœur simple" in this respect as well, "La Légende" ultimately goes beyond verbal symbols to locate meaning in visual signs. The physical world signifies at the tale's outset, in this way developing Matthey's thesis of a "concrétisation du sens" (Matthey 19), and illustrating the constructive dynamic between what other critics have characterized as oppositional dualities. Félicité's life displayed a play between the ordinary and the sublime. Analogously, in Julien's life, the physical world does not oppose the conceptual sphere; the two arise from and inform one another. An early description of the castle's grounds describes "basilic" and "héliotrope," plants which have significance as "cruauté" and "inspiration divine," and notes how "des combinaisons de fleurs dessinaient des chiffres" (Flaubert, *Trois contes* 59). Then, as the story develops, banal images or events recur, creating patterns with a significance greater than the narrative's plot. The phrase "le ciel était rouge comme une nappe de sang" (73), for example, introduces a color that threads through the legend. When Julien kills his parents, "le reflet écarlate du vitrail éclairait ses tâches rouges et en jetait de plus nombreuses dans tout l'appartement" (90). When Julien is at the hermitage "le soleil, tous les soirs, étalait du sang dans les nuages" (93). This last description links red with windows, laying the foundation for a final reference to the meaning of color and of patterns. The story concludes with the stained glass window depicting Julien's "légende": here, fragments of color come together literally to encapsulate story (words) in image (100). Indeed, the word "légende" can represent both a narrative ("Le récit de la vie d'un saint destiné à être lu") and the inscription of a picture ("Tout texte qui accompagne une image et lui donne un sens") (*Le Petit Robert* 1080). Thus Flaubert's verbal and visual modes of expression in this tale are rendered explicit in the story's very title. Indeed, the text's last line establishes that the entire "conte" is the verbal gloss of a stained-glass window: "Et voilà l'histoire de saint Julien l'Hospitalier, telle à peu près qu'on la trouve, sur un vitrail d'église, dans mon pays." This "légende" in two senses of the word (as narrative and as inscription) anchors the story's words to a non-verbal, visual image. Symbolic meaning is "transferred" to things, "forgotten" there, and then symbol and thing are retrieved together as sacred: as Cécile Matthey defined, it, a legend "désymbolise pour réinscrire le légendaire dans une logique de l'adhésion religieuse" (Matthey 22).

The significance of eyes in "La Légende" underlines the importance of vision in this tale as much as the centrality of visual images. The stag's eyes are "flamboyants" when he pronounces his fatal prophecy (Flaubert, *Trois contes* 63). Julien marries his wife because she impresses him with "ses grands yeux [qui] brillaient comme deux lampes douces" (80). After he kills his father, Julien sees a "prunelle éteinte qui le brûla comme du feu" (90); his parents' faces convey the presence of mystery, of a "secret éternel" (90). And the description of the leper's eyes most closely resembles the stag's: "et ses yeux tout à coup prirent une clarté des étoiles" (100).

Beyond underlining the significance of vision, Flaubert's manner of exploiting the imagery of eyes in this "conte" shows that the sacred arises from a special ordering of ordinary experience in "La Légende" as in "Un Cœur simple." In *Trois contes*, signs do not blur together, as Rosanette and Mme Arnoux do in *L'Éducation sentimentale*. In "Un Coeur simple," "La Légende," and also "Hérodias," images remain distinct and they recur in patterns intimating unstated meaning. The language of "La Légende," and of the other tales, is magical and it is effective because it draws its significance from the material world it represents rather than from ideals that have no bearing on reality. *Trois contes* establishes a working rather than a warring relationship between its dualities, and in this way, it comes close to the ideal Flaubert had for modern art. Flaubert's seemingly contradictory tendencies are on the way to being reconciled; as Baudelaire wrote about art in 1863, "la dualité de l'art est une conséquence fatale de la dualité de l'homme."

Like "La Légende de saint Julien," "Hérodias" is organized around the power of words. On the level of plot, John is a threat to Antipas, the ruler, because of his prophecies, in particular the one that recurs throughout the novel: "Pour qu'il croisse il faut que je diminue"; thus words may pose what is perceived to be a military threat, one that drives the story's narrative. Furthermore, the climactic moment of the tale comes about because Antipas is bound by his word to grant Salomé's wish, the head of Iaokanaan. And while "Un Coeur simple" and "La Légende" merely intimate resolutions, John's prophecy as well as his death boldly announce the imminent arrival of Christ, who is the "Word made flesh." The story told in "Hérodias" represents the ultimate union of the "éternel" with the "transitoire."

Flaubert develops the nature of language's dominance thematically in this "conte" as well. Words have many manifestations in "Hérodias." They function as a prop for the Pharisees and Sadducees, who greet Antipas in tiaras laden with "des bandelettes de parchemin, où des écritures étaient tracées" (Flaubert, *Trois contes* 118); similarly, the Romans arrive "serrant sous leurs aisselles des tablettes de bois" (119). Words can also proliferate in the forms of different languages, as when the translator repeats John's imprecations "d'un ton impassible" in another tongue:

he "redisait, dans la langue des Romains, toutes les injures que Iaokanaan rugissait dans la sienne. Le Tetrarque et Hérodias étaient forcés de les subir" (128). Most strikingly, words become incarnate throughout this final tale and not just in its underlying storyline about a God made man. While Félicité used recycled phrases as a springboard to the world of the imagination, and "Un Cœur simple" as well as "La Légende" rely on the visual and allusive properties of words to intimate significance, in "Hérodias" words consistently embody meaning directly. Phanuel reads the sky to foresee the death of an important man—"ces marques d'une colère immortelle effrayaient sa pensée" (131). Salomé pushes Antipas into killing Iaokanaan with a dance defined as physical expression. "Ses bras arrondis appelaient quelqu'un, qui s'enfuyait toujours... ses attitudes exprimaient des soupirs" (145). Eyes, the source of vision, speak as well: "Par l'ouverture de leurs cils, les prunelles mortes et les prunelles éteintes semblaient se dire quelque chose" (149). These words of "Hérodias" are not only found in physical life (the landscape, the dance) and death (the dead eyes); they also produce life and death. At the beginning of the story, Mannaeï curses, believing "que les mots avaient un pouvoir objectif" (106). Indeed, John's death results from the word Antipas gave to Salomé, and John's cries are those of "une femme qui enfante"—a "carnalisation du sens" indeed.

Flaubert illustrates two possible and opposing responses to the powerful words of this final and climactic "conte." Incomprehension or rejection is one possibility. Phinées refuses to translate John's prophecies, and most people who hear either don't understand them or reject them. Comprehension is a second possibility, and it does occur for at least one person at the end of the story. Seeing Iaokanaan's head, "L'Essénien comprenait maintenant ces paroles: Pour qu'il croisse, il faut que je diminue" (Flaubert, *Trois contes* 150). It is significant that comprehension—reading the world correctly—is directly related to contact with the physical world. Material reality has importance in its own right in "Hérodias." Having conveyed the meaning of John's words and his beheading, the head's status as dead weight is emphasized by the difficulty the load causes its bearers: "comme elle était très lourde, ils la portaient alternativement" (150). However, "la traduction de l'esprit de la lettre dans une entité corporelle" acquires a sacred dimension in these tales (Matthey 21). As Flaubert underlines the earthly nature of human understanding with the heaviness of the tale's final image, he also reminds us that sacred meaning flickers in the physical world. Conversely, embodied words—John's head is the fulfillment of the prophecy regarding his diminution—signify; disembodied words— as in the case of M. Bourais' erudition, or the empty words of Emma and Frédéric—do not.

Writing about Flaubert's early novels, Eugenio Donato observed that, "If there is a nostalgia in Flaubert, it is the nostalgia not for a lost object, but rather, as we saw earlier, for a language and mode of representation that might achieve an original and linguistically mediated relation to its objects" (Donato 52). In this last work, Flaubert achieved a linguistic reconciliation between the real and the ideal that warred in his psyche, and that failed to occur in his earlier works. The language of *Trois contes* somewhat paradoxically did so by going beyond language. As Flaubert wrote: "En fait de métaphysique surtout, la plume ne va pas loin, car la force plastique défaille toujours à rendre ce qui n'est pas très net dans l'esprit" (Flaubert, *Correspondance* 2: 179). The pen, however, must be pushed as far as it will go. Language must break out of conventional literary, linguistic structures. The language of Félicité, Julien, and Hérodias did this. And by combining prose with poetry, the form itself of Flaubert's language did as well.

The paragraph describing Flaubert's "deux bonshommes" has a formal as well as a thematic component. "Lyrisme" and "toutes les sonorités de la phrase" appear right alongside "les grands vols d'aigle." And if Flaubert designates a form of poetry to express his flights of idealism, prose is logically the formal counterpart for his realist persona because it is a form that traditionally "fouille et creuse le vrai tant qu'il peut, qui aime à accuser le petit fait aussi puissamment que le grand, qui voudrait vous faire sentir presque *matériellement* les choses qu'il reproduit" (Flaubert, *Correspondance* 2: 30). As Flaubert gauges his literary success by his ability to "fuse" his two "bonshommes," moreover, he defines his goal for form as a union of poetry with prose. Further on in 1852, he writes to Colet, "Je crois pourtant qu'on peut lui donner la consistance du vers. Une bonne phrase de prose doit être comme un bon vers, *inchangeable*, aussi rythmée, aussi soudée" (Flaubert, *Correspondance* 2: 135). And, like Baudelaire, Flaubert perceives the combination of prose with poetry as the best way to extract significance from modern life. Flaubert wrote of "Vouloir donner à la prose le rhythme du vers (en la laissant prose et très prose) et écrire la vie ordinaire comme on écrit l'histoire ou l'épopée (sans dénaturer le sujet) est peut-être une absurdité…Mais c'est peut-être aussi une grande tentative et très originale!" (Flaubert, *Correspondance* 2: 287).

Flaubert achieves this union of poetry with prose in *Trois contes*. The accent on emotions and the imagination in "Un Cœur simple," the importance of recurrent signs in "La Légende," the Divine power of the Word invoked by "Hérodias," and the importance of imagery and symbols throughout, all engage the language of poetry. Other aspects of *Trois contes*—the lyric rhythm of its prose, with its frequent groups of three; the tight *enchaînements* between chapters; the space created between the lines for Félicité's emotions; the relatively short length of the tales, as compared to Flaubert's very lengthy early novels—only emphasize the link between lyricism and Flaubert's last published work. And yet, this lyricism is set into paragraphs of prose. Thus the form as well as the themes of *Trois contes* manifests Flaubert's schizophrenia and brings Flaubert's two "bonshommes" together on the level of its form.

In our day, form-breaking experimentation is nothing new. In Flaubert's time, however, combining prose with poetry, which had been defined as verse since Aristotle, was radical. The poems composing Baudelaire's *Le Spleen de Paris* were the first lyrical works in prose to be officially entitled "poems," and they first started appearing in the mid to late 1850s. Flaubert notion of "une bonne phrase de prose…comme un bon vers" still represented a drastic break not too much later. And the formal revolution effected by Baudelaire's prose poetry and *Trois contes* were direct responses to their period.

In 1875, Flaubert was acutely aware that the old strategies for both art and religion no longer worked in a modern era. His indictments of romantic novels, language, and modes of sentiment in *Madame Bovary* and *L'Education sentimentale* indicate that— according to Flaubert—romanticism is dysfunctional as a literary mode in nineteenth-century France and that mid-nineteenth-century society, clinging to inappropriate models in fiction as in life, was false. So, when George Sand issued Flaubert her challenge to unify the real and the ideal in his work, he agreed heartily and linked the common goal directly to the imperative of a new era. However, he did not yet see how he could possibly achieve it. Answering Sand's objection that he lacks "une vue bien arrêtée et bien étendue sur la vie," Flaubert wrote back:

> Vous avez mille fois raison! Mais le moyen qu'il en soit autrement? Je vous le demande. Vous n'éclairerez pas mes ténèbres avec de la Métaphysique, ni les miennes ni celles des autres. Les mots Religion ou Catholicisme d'une part, Progrès, Fraternité, Démocratie de l'autre, ne répondent plus aux exigences spirituelles du moment. Le dogme tout nouveau de l'Egalité que prône le Radicalisme, est démenti expérimentalement par la Physiologie et par l'Histoire. Je ne vois pas le moyen d'établir, aujourd'hui, un Principe nouveau, pas plus que de respecter les anciens. Donc je cherche, sans la trouver, cette Idée d'où doit dépendre tout le reste. (Flaubert, *Correspondance* 4: 1001)

Critics hold that Flaubert never found a language that could adequately represent the modern era; indeed, they perceive his articulate expression of that goal's impossibility as his greatest achievement. Jonathan Culler noted that in Flaubert's early novels, language is used to thwart meaning. Nathaniel Wing wrote of the "complex disruption of sense" in the age of empire (Wing 117), explaining that the drastic socioeconomic and political changes taking place in mid-nineteenth-century France were such that words, as political slogans, as poems, or as novels, failed to reflect society accurately. Peter Brooks showed how Flaubert subverts the form of the novel by demonstrating that Balzac's conventions no longer work (Brooks 178). In *Madame Bovary on Trial,* LaCapra argued that the prosecution of both *Les Fleurs du mal* and *Madame Bovary* in 1857 amounted to the Second Empire's recognition that both Baudelaire and Flaubert had lost faith in the society and literature of the 1850s and 1860s. Critics agree overwhelmingly that in the end the failures of Emma and Frédéric illustrate the inauthenticity of literary structures in Flaubert's work.

That conclusion, though, is almost universally based on the novels Flaubert wrote in the 1850s and 1860s, and does not take into full account the transitional nature of the period in which Flaubert wrote and lived. It is true that at the time of his correspondence with Sand, Flaubert was seeking, but could not find, an underlying principle that would sustain "tout le reste," the whole of modern life. Traditional religion on the one hand, and revolutionary ideology on the other, do not respond to the "moment." Flaubert's early works very articulately convey that the traditional form of the novel was no longer capable of conveying the truths of actual life. "Les mots...ne répondent plus aux exigences spirituelles du moment."

However, this seminal author used the word "crépsucule" to describe the time of historical transition in which he found himself as he struggled with "l'avenir de l'art," and as I mentioned earlier in connection with "La Légende de saint Julien de l'Hospitalier," "crépuscule" means both "dusk" and "dawn." *Madame Bovary, L'Education sentimentale, Salammbo,* and *La Tentation de saint Antoine* were written during the dusk of one period. *Trois contes,* Flaubert's last published work, was composed at the break of dawn in another era, and like Baudelaire in "À Arsène Houssaye," Flaubert knew that the problem of modernity was one of expression. In *Trois contes,* Flaubert found a "principe nouveau" that breaks traditional forms to get beyond the inadequacy of words. With the poetry, prose, and themes of his three tales, he not only forged a new literary form that responded to his personal contradictions and his period's "spiritual demands," he also gave expression to the "moment" of modernity. The rest is history.

Notes

1. Timothy Unwin, too, notices that, in contrast with *Madame Bovary*, where Flaubert's irony accentuates the "décalage entre la réalité objective et le monde intérieur de son héroïne" (46), the "monde intérieur" and a "réalité objective" coexist in *Trois contes.*

2. Ann Murphy also develops the sacred of Félicité's discourse in "The Order of Speech in Flaubert's *Trois contes.*" Her focus, though, is on the function of repetition: "In 'Un Cœur simple,'" therefore, speech is the intersection of repetition/imitation and then continuation in a transcendent mode" (405).

Works Cited

Bertrand, Marc. "Parole et silence dans les *Trois Contes* de Flaubert." *Stanford French Review* 1 (1977): 199–203.

Brooks, Peter. *Reading for the Plot: Design and Intention in Narrative.* New York: Vintage Books, 1984.

Culler, Jonathan. *The Uses of Uncertainty.* Ithaca: Cornell UP, 1985, 2006.

Donato, Eugenio. *The Script of Decadence.* Oxford: Oxford UP, 1993.

Flaubert, Gustave. *Correspondance.* 5 vols. Ed. Jean Bruneau. Paris: Gallimard, 1973–2007.

_____. *L'Éducation sentimentale.* Ed. Pierre Marc de Biaisi. Paris: Librairie Générale Française, 2002.

_____. *Madame Bovary.* Ed. Jacques Suffel. Paris: Garnier Flammarion, 1966.

_____. *Trois contes.* Paris: Gallimard, 2003.

LaCapra, Dominick. *Madame Bovary on Trial.* Ithaca: Cornell UP, 1982, 1986.

Matthey, Cécile. *L'écriture hospitalière de l'espace de la croyance dans les Trois contes de Flaubert.* Amsterdam, New York: Rodopi, 2008.

Murphy, Ann. "The Order of Speech in Flaubert's *Trois contes.*" *The French Review* 65.3 (Feb 1992): 402–14.

Unwin, Timothy. *Flaubert et Baudelaire: Affinités spirituelles et esthétiques.* Paris: Nizet, 1982.

Wing, Nathaniel. *The Limits of Narrative.* Cambridge, UK: Cambridge UP, 1986.

"Un cœur simple:" An Uneventful Narrative_____

Michael Sayeau

Roland Barthes's seminal essay "The Reality Effect" begins by citing a seemingly random detail from Flaubert's story "Un cœur simple:" "an old piano supported, under a barometer, a pyramidal heap of boxes and cartons" (Barthes 141). What is notable to Barthes about this apparently utterly ordinary bit of descriptive detail is the difficulty that it and others like it present to literary critics. By trade and nature, critics attempt to find the meaning of various elements of literary works and the ways that the various elements work together to form a whole. The problem, however, with moments of issueless description (issueless in the sense that these details will not reappear to serve some use later in the story) is that it is difficult to extract a meaning or purpose from them. Would the story have been any different at all, save for being a few words shorter, had Flaubert chosen not to include the piano, the barometer, and the heap of boxes at all?

As he continues, it is the barometer in particular that draws his attention. The other two details, he explains, could be redeemed to significance by seeing them as signs construed to impart contextual information to the reader:

> if, in Flaubert's description, it is just possible to see in the notation of the piano an indication of its owner's bourgeois standing and in that of the cartons a sign of disorder and a kind of lapse in status likely to connote the atmosphere of the Aubain household, no purpose seems to justify reference to the barometer, an object neither incongruous nor significant, and therefore not participating, at first glance, in the order of the *notable*. (Barthes 141–2)

The barometer does not, in Barthes's analysis, bear any narrative or contextual meaning at all. It is simply "there:" it doesn't push the plot forward, it doesn't reveal anything interesting about the characters or the milieu, it is simply a bit of extraneous furnishing that is mentioned by Flaubert.

Barthes, by the end of the essay, generates a theory of how such moments of what he calls "insignificant notation" operate in narratives.

> Flaubert's barometer, Michelet's little door finally say nothing but this: *we are the real*: it is the category of "the real" (and not its contingent contents) which is then signified; in other words, the very absence of the signified, to the advantage of the referent alone, becomes the very signifier of realism: the *reality effect* is produced, the basis of that unavowed verisimilitude which forms the aesthetic of all the standard works for modernity. (Barthes 148)

Through a complex process, in other words, these details can be said to bear a kind of significance through their very failure to bear any significance. They mean something because of their very absence of meaning. Realistic-ness, or even realism in general, is a rhetoric, what he calls a "referential illusion" (Barthes 142). It is a case of going through the motions of narrative meaning-making while failing to do any such thing, if only momentarily.

Barthes could have picked his example from any text—all works of prose fiction contain examples of such "insignificant notation." We even generate "reality effects" when we tell each other stories in our ordinary lives. "There I was, minding my own business, waiting for the bus, noticing how fluffy and white the clouds were today, when it happened...." But it is no coincidence that he chose his primary example of this effect from Flaubert's "A Simple Heart." For it is not just the represented objects in the work that resist alignment with the norms of narrative construction of meaning. Rather, almost every aspect of the story—from the nature of the protagonist and other characters, the use of the symbolism involved in the tale, the connection between the various episodes, and so on. But above all else, it is the plot (or, we might say, lack thereof, at least in any conventional sense) that runs against the grain of the generic mandates of prose fiction.

Generally speaking, we expect *something to happen* in the stories and novels that we read. The sort of "something" that happens of course varies from work to work, from genre to genre. The key moment of psychological revelation that comes at the climax of a novel studied in a university classroom is very different kind of event than that which punctuates someone's steamy beach-read. But no matter the sophistication of the work in question, readers have certain presumptions when they open a work of fiction: that the characters are worthy of attention; that what will be described will be, however complexly, eventful; that the sequence of events described will show some development of whatever kind; and that, taken cumulatively, some sort of meaning, however subtle and complex, will emerge from the reading of the work. But it is exactly these presumptions that "Un cœur simple" violates. It can be read as an incredibly subtle experiment in constructing a sort of anti-fiction, a fiction whose temperature is set at degree zero. In it, we find a character of no importance (at least conventionally speaking) to whom nothing fictionally significant happens (again, conventionally speaking) and whose life, which the work traces out more or less in full, fails to show any (once more, conventional) real development or change from start to finish. Never is this more clear, as I will show below, as when the story does register "something happening"—at its conclusion (with Félicité's terminal vision of her parrot ascending to heaven), but also elsewhere in the text. If with *Madame Bovary*, Flaubert constructed a novel about a woman whose very aspiration to live a novelistic life led her, despite herself, to live a novelistic life, "Un cœur simple" centers on another woman who has no inclination—nor real potential—for ascending to appropriateness for fiction.

A summary of what happens (or doesn't) in the story would be appropriate at this point. Félicité has worked for fifty years for Madame Aubain in Pont-l'Évêque. Some backstory is presented. Orphaned young, she finds work very young at a sequence of farms. At one point, there is an issueless (and unconsummated) semi-romance with a young man that ends anti-climactically. (More on this later.) In the wake of this, she leaves her position and finds work with the woman who would be her mistress for the rest of the latter's life. She takes loving care of Madame Aubain's children, Paul and Virginie, and suffers a loss when her own nephew, Victor, dies abroad. Virginie too succumbs to illness at school, which breaks both her and her mistress's heart. Finally, she comes to possess a parrot named Loulou, who in turn dies. Félicité has him stuffed and continues to treasure him. Eventually, Madame Aubain dies, but Félicité lives on in her room, penniless and increasingly deaf. Finally, at the conclusion of the work, Félicité herself dies—but at her moment of her death has a vision "in the opening heavens" of "a gigantic parrot hovering above her head" (Flaubert, *Three Tales* 56).

There were biographical factors at play in the development of "Un cœur simple"—most notably, Flaubert seems to have drawn upon his childhood nursemaid, Julie, who was still in the family's service when he composed the story, as a model for Félicité (Wall 338). But the artistic origin of the story, according to Flaubert himself, is to be found in an epistolary conversation with the novelist George Sand. Responding in a letter of January 1876 to the public's dislike of Flaubert's *Sentimental Education*, Sand blames the failure on Flaubert's cynical (and impersonal) portrayal of foul characters—and the absence of good and heroic personages in his work:

> There should have been a short preface, or, here and there, an expression of judgment, even if only a well-chosen adjective to condemn a wrong, to characterize a defect, to emphasize an aspiration. All the characters in this book are weak and come to nothing except those with evil instincts; that is what you are reproached with, because people don't understand that you wanted to depict precisely a deplorable society, which encourages those bad instincts and destroys noble aspirations. (Steegmuller 228)

As she continues, the problem with such a writerly stance is that it confuses the reader ethically:

> Your story is inevitably a conversation between you and the reader. If you show him evil coldly, without ever showing him good, he's angry. He wonders whether he is the villain or you. What you wanted

to do, however, was rouse him and maintain his interest; and you will never concede if you are not roused yourself, or if you conceal your emotion so effectively that he thinks you are indifferent. (Steegmuller 229)

Clearly, this admonition made an impression on Flaubert, an impression that—at least according to his response to Sand in his own letters—inspired the composition of "A Simple Heart." As he wrote to her in May 1876:

You will see from my *Story of a Simple Heart* (in which you will recognize your own direct influence) that I am not as stubborn as you believe. I think you will like the moral tendency, or rather the underlying humanity, of this little work. (Steegmuller 234)

But despite Flaubert's insistence here about the "underlying humanity" of the work, Enid Starkie (among others) has argued that, on a deeper level, it is more similar to his earlier works than his descriptions of it in his letters suggest. As she wrote *in Flaubert: The Making of the Master*:

Even in *Un Cœur Simple*, a tale written to please George Sand and to be consoling; even here the good, simple servant girl, Félicité the heroine, in spite of all her goodness, is gradually stripped of everything until, at the end, she is left with only a moth-eaten stuffed parrot to represent the Holy Ghost. The fact that she does not realize her plight does not alter the matter, and the tale is basically as pessimistic as anything that he ever wrote. (Starkie 339–40)

I will have more to say about whether "Un cœur simple" is, in my view, an optimistic or pessimistic (or optimistically pessimistic, or vice versa) work at the end of this piece. But what is most important to see from the start about the story, as I mentioned above, is the way that it handles plot, the passage of time, and in particular, the complex rhythm of eventfulness and uneventfulness that shapes its movement. The issue of temporality—especially temporalities inappropriate to the usual pacing of a piece of fiction—is brought to the fore even in the very first sentence. "For half a century the women of Pont-l'Evêque envied Mme Aubain her houseservant Félicité" (Flaubert, *Three Tales* 17). Fifty years, here intensified into half-a-hundred, is a very long time for any fictional protagonist to have not only a fixed position in life, but also a consistent evaluation in the eyes of society. Unless something dramatic is about to happen, "half a century" into her tenure, which as it turns out is more or less not the case, Flaubert has pushed us from the start into a very unpromising narrative situation.

Further, just as soon as we have received the first descriptions of our protagonist, the narrator mentions the pre-history of the woman who would become her mistress, Madame Aubain. Early in life, the narrator reports, she "had married a young fellow who was good-looking but badly-off, who died at the beginning of 1809, leaving her with two small children and a pile of debts" (Flaubert, *Three Tales* 17). This is an altogether more promising start to a story, or even the framework of a short story or novella in and of itself. But here we are introduced to it in passing, only to turn back to Félicité and her non-eventful life.

This quick turn toward and then back away from Madame Aubain's short, but tumultuous, marriage is a characteristic feint on Flaubert's part in this story, where he incessantly inserts abstracts, summaries, or briefs of other, more properly fictional scenarios throughout "A Simple Heart." Early on, as Félicité and the family that employs her trudge towards a recuperative beach holiday at Trouville, they pass through Toucques, where the man who is driving them tells a telegraphically cryptic story about one of the inhabitants of the town.

> [I]n the middle of Toucques, as they were passing underneath some windows set in a mass of nasturtiums, [Liébard] shrugged his shoulders and said:
> "There's a Madame Lehoussais lives here. Now instead of taking a young man, she…"
> Félicité did not hear the rest, for the horses had broken into a trot and the donkey was galloping along. (Flaubert, *Three Tales* 25–6)

Félicité—and thus the reader, due to the cloaking veil of free indirect discourse—never hears the end of the tale. We already know something of this story (as I will discuss below, in a very bathetic sense Madame Lehoussais is Félicité's romantic rival), and we might sense that it has the makings of a conventionally "better," or at least more appropriate, narrative than the one we are reading. But it is introduced into "Un cœur simple" only to disappear again.

Even the illustrated geography book that Monsieur Bourais, who manages Madame Aubain's properties, brings to the latter's son Paul seems to be more an atlas of melodramatic story-kernels than anything else. Its pictures "represented scenes in different parts of the world, such as cannibals wearing feather head-dresses, a monkey carrying off a young lady, Bedouins in the desert, a whale being harpooned, and so on" (Flaubert, *Three Tales* 23). And likewise, the biblical stories that Félicité hears when she accompanies Virginie to her catechism classes at church stand in dramatic contrast to the banal existence that is the focus of Flaubert's story.

> The priest began with a brief outline of sacred history. Listening to him, Félicité saw in imagination the Garden of Eden, the Tower of Babel, cities burning, peoples dying, and idols being overthrown [...] Then she wept as she listened to the story of the Passion. (Flaubert, *Three Tales* 29)

Further, Flaubert plays games with the weighting of various episodes—spending many words on relatively issueless episodes. Perhaps the best example of this is the first extended anecdote, which is found at the beginning of the second section of the story. None of the readily available English translations of the first line of this vignette quite do justice to the resonances of it in French: "Elle avait eu, comme une autre, son histoire d'amour" (Flaubert, *Œuvres* 2: 592). Literally: *She had had, like others, her love story.* Right from the first, that which is ostensibly the most personal—one's first great romance—becomes here utterly generic. Imagine, for instance, one of the great literary romances beginning in such a fashion: *This is the romance of Romeo and Juliet—a love story like so many other love stories.*

But further, it is when we discover what this "love story" was actually composed of that we get a sense of Flaubert's anti-evental intentions are with Félicité. The story begins with Félicité having been taken along by her employers to a country fête in a nearby town, where a rakish young man, Théodore, asks her to dance. He plies her with sweets and with drink, offers to accompany her home, and then, while on the way, attempts to have his way with her, which she resists by screaming, which drives him away. Some love story! But it doesn't even end here. On "[a]nother night" (Flaubert, *Three Tales* 19), she encounters him on the road, and he excuses himself for his previous actions by blaming them on drink. He makes vaguely insinuating references to marriage and then kisses her only again to disappear. When she agrees to meet him again, "at the bottom of a farm-yard, behind a wall, under a solitary tree" (20), he seems to make another sexual attempt on her, which is refused, and so (naturally) he proposes marriage. We never hear if Félicité accepts (she is inclined not to believe him on the matter), but he subsequently informs her that he is in a bit of trouble in relation to military service that he has not performed. On their next appointed meeting time, a friend appears in his place to inform her that "she would not see Théodore again," as in order to "make sure of avoiding conscription, he had married a very rich old woman, Mme Lehoussais of Toucques." Félicité is devastated—and thus ends her one and only "histoire d'amour."

In the rendition of Félicité's "love story," then, Flaubert has done a curious thing. It is not so much that "nothing happens" during this episode, but rather that what happens takes a shape vaguely approximating the sort of arc that we associate with a literary romance—an encounter with a mysterious stranger; reluctance on the part of the female, which eventually gives way to the energies expended by the suitor on his courtship of her; and the prospect of a marriage—while simultaneously heavily and ironically undercutting the eventfulness of the vignette. Everything that happens happens too quickly, too cynically, and too transparently—Félicité's one brush with romantic love comes and goes in the course of two-and-a-half pages.

Likewise, the trip to Trouville is rendered in great detail—great detail about seaside activities that are repeated daily "in the afternoons," "almost always," and "sometimes" (Flaubert, *Three Tales* 27). The descriptions stand in contrast to the uneventfulness of the trip. Even seemingly important things that do happen on it reduce themselves down, as if automatically, to anti-climactic endings. For instance, Félicité encounters a long lost sister and her children—seemingly the very stuff of melodrama—only to have the reunion turn sour when the family starts to take advantage of her kind-hearted generosity and Mme Aubain decides that they will all would return home, in part from her discomfort about "the familiar way in which the nephew spoke to Paul" (28). Further, upon their return, Paul is sent away to school. Félicité finds compensation in a new "distraction," as she would begin to accompany Virginie to her catechism classes. That daily trips to for such lessons—in other words, repetitive trips to occasions grounded in the rote repetition of language—are registered as a "distraction" speaks volumes about the temporal rhythms of Félicité's life.

Eventually, one by one, like Théodore at the start, the figures that populate Félicité's life disappear or die. Paul has gone to school; Virginie eventually is sent away as well, only to die of pneumonia; and a nephew, Victor, sets sail for the Americas only to die of yellow fever. Time settles into an even more terminally repetitive pattern than before:

> Then the years slipped by, each one like the last, with nothing to vary the rhythm of the great festivals: Easter, the Assumption, All Saints' Day. Domestic events marked dates that later served as points of reference. Thus in 1825 a couple of glaziers whitewashed the hall; in 1827 a piece of the roof fell into the courtyard and nearly killed a man; and in the summer of 1828 it was Madame's turn to provide the bread for consecration. (Flaubert, *Three Tales* 41)

At this point in the story, given all that I have shown above about the uneventfulness of the proceedings and the ironic downdrafts that blow through them, one might begin to wonder what Flaubert's goal was in composing such a narrative. Was he simply fixated to the perverse presentation of boredom where a "story" was meant to be? To this point, "Un cœur simple" displays symptoms of a rare and virulent disorder—a pathological addiction to commonness, mundanity, and stupidity for their own sake. Friedrich Nietzsche himself may have been the first to diagnosis Flaubert's "sickness" in *Beyond Good and Evil*:

> The psychologists of France—and where else are any psychologists left today?—still have not exhausted their bitter and manifold delight in the *bêtise bourgeoise*, just as if—enough, this betrays something. Flaubert, for example, that solid citizen of Rouen, in the end no longer saw, heard, or tasted any more: this was his kind of self-torture and subtler cruelty. (Nietzsche 146–7)

Nietzsche's Flaubert works a perverse enjoyment of bourgeois *bêtise* (stupidity)—and while Félicité is a servant of the bourgeoisie rather than a full member of the class, her story, to the point we have reached in my reading, might seem like a manifestation of a sort of ascetic masochism (or perhaps sadism, from the reader's perspective—or from Félicité's for that matter!)

But then, suddenly, something happens—a very strange sort of "something" indeed. The most important thing that happens in Félicité's life, at least as far as Flaubert's narrative organization of it is concerned, is the arrival of a parrot, Loulou, which her mistress receives as a gift, but which immediately falls under her care. The bird is a burst of color in a monochrome life, both literally and figuratively; he is all the more interesting because he comes from America, "and that word reminded her of Victor" (Flaubert, *Three Tales* 44), the nephew that died abroad. She teaches it to talk, or at least believes she does—"How odd, she thought, that Loulou should be so stubborn, refusing to talk whenever anybody looked at him!" (44)—and it possesses the only voice that Félicité can hear after she has gone deaf. In short, Loulou becomes everything to this servant-woman. After her series of anticlimactic misadventures with males—the only ever pseudo-romantic or pseudo-maternal dealings with Théodore, Paul, and Victor—Loulou is the first male in Félicité's life who doesn't disappoint her or tragically disappear, even if it takes some taxidermic help to make it so. As the narrator tells us at one point, "In her isolation, Loulou was almost a son or a lover to her" (47).

Eventually, as is wont to happen with parrots, Loulou dies, and Félicité has him stuffed—and at it is only with the advent of its taxidermic afterlife that Félicité's affection becomes fully enflamed. He ascends to the level of a religious icon, the transcendental referent of Félicité's affections and imagination. At once exotic and banal, materially graspable and ineffably idealized, Loulou enters into a relation of metonymic substitution with other auratically-charged objects. At one point, the maidservant purchases a print representing the baptism of Christ, in which the rendering of the Holy Ghost reminds her of her deceased pet.

> She bought the print and hung it in the place of the Comte d'Artois, so that she could include them both in a single glance. They were linked together in her mind, the parrot being sanctified by this connexion with the Holy Ghost, which itself acquired new life and meaning in her eyes. God the father could not have chosen a dove as a means of expressing Himself, since doves cannot talk, but rather one of Loulou's ancestors. And although Félicité used to say her prayers with her eyes on the picture, from time to time she would turn slightly toward the bird (Flaubert, *Three Tales* 50).

The wonderful image of Félicité occasionally turning her eyes from the devotional portrait toward Loulou during her prayers echoes other instances when she displayed a tendency to compound the religious and the real.

But what is most important in the tale of Félicité and her parrot comes at the very end of "A Simple Heart." The last paragraph of the work, which concludes a montage sequence playing Félicité's death against the Corpus Christi celebration of the local parish, enacts a final blurring of the distinction between religious idealism and the exotic banality of the everyday, which is the fault line of her life. As the incense of the church procession reaches the room in which she lies, Félicité is released into a final epiphany of parrot-as-divinity:

A blue cloud of incense was wafted up into Félicité's room. She opened her nostrils wide and breathed it in with a mystical, sensuous fervour. Then she closed her eyes. Her heart-beats grew slower and slower, each a little fainter and gentler, like a fountain running dry, an echo fading away. And as she breathed her last, she thought she could see, in the opening heavens, a gigantic parrot hovering above her head (Flaubert, *Three Tales* 56).

Somehow this conclusion, for all its absurdity, escapes from the totalizing grip of Flaubertian satiric irony and instead inspires a welling-up of feeling to which the reader of his works might not be accustomed. How do we explain this change in affect, in the entire tonal substructure of this work?

One clue is unusual verbal structure of the final clause—a structure, at least, that is unusual for Flaubert. In French, it reads: "et, quand elle exhala son dernier souffle, elle crut voir, dans les cieux entrouverts, un perroquet gigantesque, planant au-dessus de sa tête" (Flaubert, *Œuvres* 2: 622). In his standard rendering of the delusions of his characters, irony is established by the very *blankness* of the description of the phantasm. The free indirect mode enacts the false factuality of the situation, the sense of "reality" that the subject, mired as it is in received ideas and *bêtise*, refuses to look into deeply. In other words, if the same conclusion could be translated to one of the earlier works—say, *Madame Bovary* or *Sentimental Education*—the verbal structure of the final clause might have read, "elle vit, dans les cieux entrouverts, un perroquet gigantesque" ("she saw, in the opening heavens, a giant parrot"), alternately, "*il y avait*, dans les cieux entrouverts, un perroquet gigantesque" (*there was*, in the opening heavens, a giant parrot").

The slight distance established by the construction "crut voir"—"believed herself to see"—in which the discourse backs away, ever so slightly, *from style indirect libre* identification with the character, opens up a space where something new, something unexpected, can emerge. Strangely enough, then, in light of Flaubert's œuvre as a whole, this statement that she *believed* herself to see the parrot marks a breakdown in the satiric machinery of his narrative technique and conceptualization of the subject. Her ability to believe, *her faith*, rather than her *bêtise*-ridden self-delusion, comes to the fore. The ironic exposure of the contents of human belief gives way to the very gesture of believing itself. Whether or not we snicker at the baroque ludicrousness of Félicité's final moments of consciousness, what does it matter to her—she *believed* in it, and this was her end. It is a case of *bovarysme* that, in effect, wins the game—wins by maintaining itself right through to the conclusion. True to the religious atmospherics that suffuse the story, Félicité's tale is to, for instance, Emma Bovary's tragedy of everydayness what Christ's death and resurrection is to the classical tragedy—it is a triumph of faith over pathos and catharsis.

But does this reversal of the critical energy of Flaubert's prose really mark a moment of the victory of and against the everyday? "Un cœur simple" is a compelling and tolerant parable of human attachment to the things of the world, but one that, like the story of Christ's resurrection, relies on a serious case of *deus ex machina* to escape from the gravitation of the vicious circle that it rejects. And the machinery in question works by deflating in advance Félicité's character, by the establishment of a person so simple and good, so devoid of Emma Bovary's longing for erotic fireworks or Frédéric Moreau's ambiguous pursuit of the ideal, that the critical eye (of the writer and the reader both) simply has no purchase upon her. As Jonathan Culler puts it in *Flaubert: The Uses of Uncertainty*,

> It is as though the text were engaged in probing and testing, trying on ironies to see if there is anything to be deflated, attempting to ensure the sloughing off of the purely sentimental by subjecting it to a cold and detached treatment, but doing so only in order that the purity of whatever successfully resists this treatment might be guaranteed. The mechanism here is closely analogous to what Empson calls "pseudo-parody to disarm criticism." (210)

Rather than an eventful break from all of the uneventfulness that has come before the story, this ending represents something more complex, something stranger, than simply the sort of climactic revelation that we are accustomed to finding at the end of a piece of fiction. The subtle positioning of the Flaubertian narrator in relation to Félicité's vision—in all of its simultaneously real pathos and bathetic absurdity—stands as a continuation of the logic of the story, but a continuation in a different key. It has the feel of a gesture dripping in authorial bad faith—a forced happy ending—while at the same time, given what we know about Flaubert and his caustic relation to his own characters, the badness of the faith comes to seem like unprecedented goodness on the part of the author. A character and a situation that would seem to be devoid of literary potential is, in the end, charged with a sort of utopian energy that comes, miraculously, without abandoning his self-assigned mandate to record the "simple life" of a "simple heart."

Works Cited

Culler, Jonathan. *Flaubert: The Uses of Uncertainty.* Revised edition. Ithaca, NY: Cornell UP, 1985.

Flaubert, Gustave. *Œuvres*. Paris: Pléiade, 1951.

_____. *Three Tales*. Trans. Robert Baldick. London: Penguin, 1961.

Nietzsche, Friedrich. *Beyond Good and Evil*. Trans. Walter Kaufmann. New York: Vintage, 1989.

Starkie, Enid. *Flaubert: The Making of the Master*. Harmondsworth, UK: Penguin, 1971.

Steegmuller, Francis, ed. & trans. *The Letters of Gustave Flaubert 1857–1880*. London: Faber & Faber, 1982.

Wall, Geoffrey. *Flaubert: A Life*. London: Faber & Faber, 2001.

Flaubert and the Art of Caricature

Michael Tilby

—Tu exagères! dit Pécuchet (Flaubert)

The purpose of this essay will be twofold. Firstly, it will offer a more nuanced discussion of Flaubert's response to nineteenth-century French caricature than has been available hitherto, and secondly, it will suggest that Flaubert's mature fictional narratives set in contemporary France embody an exploitation of the logic and practice of caricature that reveals its importance for him as writer to extend well beyond explicit allusion. The necessary restriction of my corpus will, therefore, exclude such potentially interesting avenues of exploration as that suggested by the caricature of Louis-Philippe and his ministers, which Daumier entitled "La Tentation du nouveau St. Antoine" or "The Temptation of the New St Anthony" (*Le Charivari*, 1 January 1835) and which indicates that the subject later given literary form by Flaubert could readily be harnessed to the needs of political caricature.

By and large, Flaubert had scant liking or respect for the work of the visual artists who were his contemporaries. Prominent among the exceptions, however, were the caricaturists, notably Daumier, Gavarni, Monnier, Traviès, Grandville, and Cham. It was a preference he shared with Ernest Chesneau, whose work *Les Nations rivales dans l'art* he discussed thoughtfully in a letter to the author shortly after its appearance (Flaubert, *Correspondance* 3: 806–08). Chesneau had singled out Gavarni and Daumier as representatives of "nos vrais peintres de mœurs" or "our true painters of manners" (4). From his early appreciation of Philipon's weekly *La Caricature* (as revealed by allusions in his correspondence to "Louis Fils-Lippe" (Flaubert, *Correspondance* 1: 8) and Traviès's hunchback, Mayeux (1: 7) to his reference to Mayeux in a letter of 1868 to Princess Mathilde (3: 757) and his request to Edmond de Goncourt in 1873 for the date of the issue of *La Presse* in which Gavarni had been accused of immorality (4: 680), Flaubert's fascination with caricature remained steadfast. Zola maintained that as part of his documentation for *L'Education sentimentale* he studied the caricatures in an entire run of *Le Charivari*.

It would have been surprising if Flaubert had not found himself attracted to visual caricature, whether they be examples that alluded to specific political events or those of a more generic nature. Common to both was a critical assessment of human behavior, whether individual or *en masse*. He would have appreciated what Henry James, with reference to a caricature of three old crones, termed Daumier's "representation of confidential imbecility" (137). He may well have been familiar with Annibale Carracci's insistence that the caricaturist's task was "exactly the same as the classical artist's" (Gombrich & Kris 11). He would likewise have been responsive to the intellectual challenge presented by caricature's allusive nature.

Flaubert's familiarity with individual caricaturists themselves nevertheless varied. No evidence exists of his having known Daumier personally. On the other hand, he knew Gavarni at least from the fortnightly Magny dinners that the Goncourt brothers had initiated in 1862 in an attempt to relieve the artist's depression. Most Flaubert scholars are inclined to believe that he also knew Henry Monnier and possibly even before the latter wrote proposing that he play the role of Homais in a stage version of *Madame Bovary* of his own confection. Yet there is not a single piece of incontrovertible evidence that the two men ever met. Prudence dictates the conclusion that, for all the enjoyment Flaubert undoubtedly derived from imitating Monnier, any personal acquaintance stopped short of close friendship. This is not contradicted by his revelation to the journalist Alfred Baudry, in a letter of February 10, [1858] concerning Monnier's approach: "Ah! une nouvelle qui vous fera rire. Je suis l'ami intime d'Henry Monnier. *Il m'adore*" 'This will make you laugh. I'm Henry Monnier's close friend. *He thinks I'm wonderful*' (Flaubert, *Correspondance* 2: 798). The tone hardly encourages the announcement to be taken at face value.

Yet while there is, as will be seen, clear evidence of Flaubert's appreciation of contemporary French caricature and of such legendary creations as Robert Macaire and Joseph Prudhomme, it is striking how little given he was to analysis of the art of caricature and how unconcerned he was to articulate what differentiated the artists in terms of their practise, techniques, or underlying intentions. He was clearly more interested in what their art had in common, with the generic characteristics of a form that nonetheless depended for success on instant recognition of the individual artist's trademark.

Daumier, with his caustic wit and his denunciation of the violence to which Louis-Philippe's governments had recourse, might seem the most likely caricaturist to strike a chord with Flaubert. Indeed, it should not be assumed that he was not. Yet Daumier's name as such goes unmentioned by Flaubert, at least in his correspondence. Occasional reference in his writings is to be found to Robert Macaire, whom in a letter he hailed as "le plus grand symbole de l'époque et comme le mot de notre âge" 'the foremost symbol of the times and, as it were, the idiom of our age' (Flaubert, *Correspondance* 1: 227). Even so, it was not exclusively Daumier's caricatures that he had in mind, but the entire Macaire phenomenon and, above all, the figure's origins in the theatre. In the course of his travels in 1845, he was delighted to happen on the eponymous inn of the melodrama (*L'Auberge des Adrets*) in which the rogue had first been introduced to Parisian audiences. In a letter to Zola, it was again this play he recalled, in connection with the elections of 1877. Even his apparent allusion in the same year to a Daumier caricature of 1834, which depicted ministers picking each other's pockets, would appear to be a reference to the stage play, the recently revised version of which provided elements for the *légende*. In *L'Education sentimentale*, it is clearly the actor Frédérick Lemaître's pose that the loud-mouthed Hussonnet is said to assume when Frédéric first encounters him, though Deslauriers's coded message with regard to the impending insurrection ("the pear is ripe") is a patent reference to the most infamous image of Louis-Philippe of all, which was associated primarily, though not exclusively, with Daumier.

Among Flaubert's references to caricaturists by name, it is Monnier and Gavarni who receive the principal honors, though in the case of the former, the references are mainly to Monsieur Prudhomme. No assessment of Monnier's art is offered. The mentions of Prudhomme raise questions similar to those posed by the references to Robert Macaire or to Louis-Philippe as pear, since he was not Monnier's exclusive property. Nor did he belong solely to the realm of visual caricature, having first been introduced in several theatrical *scènes* by Monnier and featured subsequently in stage plays in which the author cast himself in the principal role. Prudhomme was appropriated both by other writers and, in an extensive series of caricatures, by Daumier. A youthful dialogue of Flaubert's featuring himself and his female porter was conceived in obvious imitation of a scene by Monnier the writer. The same is true of Chapter 23 of *La Première Education sentimentale*, where Henry's father is an unmistakable Prudhomme. Flaubert almost certainly had Monnier's writings partly in mind when he maintained in a letter to Maupassant that "Monnier n'est pas plus vrai que Racine" or "Monnier is no truer than Racine" (*Correspondance* 5: 154). The majority of his references to Prudhomme are to the latter's *words*. As a correspondent, he enjoyed adopting phraseology reminiscent of Monnier's self-congratulatory figure before signalling with a parenthetical "style Prudhomme" or similar that he knew what he was doing. With George Sand and Turgenev, this became a habit in the manner of a game, with the Russian writer clearly feeling obliged to imitate him. A parallel with Prudhomme is used to deride to correspondents the politics of Thiers (3: 717) and the "so-called philosophy" of Victor Hugo (3: 236). In *Madame Bovary*, it is through their trite utterances that Homais and the Prefect separately bring Prudhomme to mind, though as has been noted (Porter & Gray 58), both the former and Bourais (in "Un cœur simple") share with Monnier's Prudhomme, "professeur d'écritures" (in a play of 1831 in which Monnier played four parts in addition to that of Prudhomme) neat handwriting, an indication of their intellectual nullity. (An association with copying is emphasized by the profession of Bouvard and Pécuchet.) In *L'Education sentimentale*, Hussonnet,

---

in "caricature mode," attempts to entertain his colleagues with a *Prudhomme sur une barricade* (348).

The closest Flaubert comes to appreciation of a caricaturist's visual art is with reference to Gavarni, "the wittiest, the most literary and must acutely profane of all chartered mockers with the pencil" (James 119), though, significantly, it is again the *word* that is the focus of his attention when he alleged in a letter to George Sand that he would sacrifice all Gavarni's *légendes* for certain expressions created by such "master authors" as Hugo or Montesquieu (Flaubert, *Correspondance* 4: 1001). It was nonetheless the inducement of an unpublished caricature by Gavarni in each number of the *Revue musicale* that tempted his sister Caroline to renew her subscription and led him to write encouraging her to do so (1: 201). The letter to Edmond de Goncourt to which reference has been made reveals his particular attraction to Gavarni's depiction of masked balls during Carnival. His request for details of the item in which the artist was charged with immorality stressed his "need" for the information.

Present in Flaubert's novels, nonetheless, are a number of more or less specific examples of visual caricature. The genre is particularly prominent in *L'Education sentimentale* (which includes in its cast a fictional caricaturist by the name of Sombaz) and in Flaubert's notes for that novel. These include, in addition to references to certain identifiable political caricatures from 1848, the transcription of an entire Gavarni légende, and a Gavarni series-title ("Fourberies de femmes" or "Female knavery"), together with a short list of figures featured in Gavarni's masked-ball caricatures. Literal transcription of this list obscures the fact that it reproduces Gavarni's actual titles. The "foreign general" and the "islander (from wherever)" appeared in *Le Charivari* on January 24 and 31, 1841, and the "cacique" on February 21. As for "les débardeurs," this was a title Gavarni gave to a series of caricatures, though the plural serves also as a reminder of the innumerable such figures he drew in this period, including those that formed the basis for Maurice Alhoy's *Physiologie du débardeur* (1842), an example of a popular series that Cisy is surprised not to find represented on Frédéric's table. These were not dockers as such, but Carnival revellers of either sex who wore a superior version of the docker's work outfit at popular balls, where, incidentally, the Robert-Macaire and the *chahut* (alluded to in *La Première Education sentimentale* [283]) were danced, both being early versions of the cancan. At Rosanette's ball, the revellers' costumes are based on Gavarni caricatures that are not restricted to those featured in the author's jottings. They include the postilion (more specifically the "postillon de Longjumeau," the eponymous pin-up of Adolphe Adam's *opéra comique* of 1835), Pierrot, the Turk, the fishwife, and the *domino* (Frédéric's choice of costume). Although the Carnival *débardeurs* were often cross-dressing women, the throng at Rosanette's ball included men no longer in the first flush of youth who are said to be "en costumes de roulier, de débardeur ou de matelot," that is, "wearing wagoners', dockers', or sailors' costumes" (Flaubert, *L'Education sentimentale* 117). One of the author's drafts nonetheless includes "une débardeuse (Gavarni)." A *lorette* identified only as "La Débardeuse" is a prominent presence at the ball, her body appearing disjointed like a clown's (127). Although Flaubert does not necessarily retain the features that define Gavarni's images as caricatures, a definite sense of a madcap occasion is communicated. On two occasions, he also depicts Rosanette responding to caricatures. Thus, her attention is captured by caricatures in a shop window of Louis-Philippe as pastry-cook, tumbler, dog, and leech (298). (An earlier version of this list included the king as blindman and cesspool emptier [*vidangeur*].) These drawings have received little attention, but more or less specific originals exist for all, barring possibly the dog and probably the discarded *vidangeur*. Daumier had portrayed the Citizen-King losing his balance on a tightrope in *Le Charivari* on August 31, 1833 ("Mr. Chose, premier saltimbanque d'Europe" or "Mr. Thingamebob, premier tumbler of Europe"), and drew him, though not unambiguously, in "Les Sangsues" or "The Leeches" (*Le Charivari*, April 9, 1835). He also featured Louis-Philippe's former Interior Minister, the Comte de Montalivet as "Mr. Montaugibet en pâtissier gâte-sauce" or "Mr. Montaugibet as gormless [slow-witted] pastry-cook" (*Le Charivari*, February 3, 1833); the concoction on the salver has the shape of a giant pear, though there also existed an anonymous caricature artfully entitled "Leroi [sic] pâtissier." Later in the novel, a moment of intense emotion is broken by an exchange provoked by Frédéric's perusal of a copy of *L'Illustration* and consisting of Rosanette's simple "Oui" to the banal question: "Ces caricatures de Cham sont très drôles, n'est-ce pas?" or "They're very funny, these Cham caricatures aren't they?" (Flaubert, *L'Education sentimentale* 359).

Also summarized in the same chapter is a conversation at the Dambreuse mansion that includes the statement "On faisait des plaisanteries sur la queue phalanstérienne" or "They cracked jokes about the phalansterian tail" (Flaubert, *L'Education sentimentale* 366). Michael Wetherill relates this to a caricature in which Cham (who goes unmentioned in Flaubert's correspondence) depicts Fourier's disciple Victor Considerant possessed of a tail the tip of which is endowed with an eye symbolizing the sixth sense that represented for Fourier the stage of human perfection (*Le Charivari*, November 15, 1849). This leaves out of account not only the fact that the *queue phalanstérienne* appears in other caricatures by Cham situating Considerant in his ideological battle with Proudhon, but also that in *Le Charivari* on February 22, 1849, Daumier had depicted the Fourierist complete with tail attempting to convert (*phalanstériser*) his fellow members of the National Assembly. This plurality of Considerant caricatures encourages the conclusion that Flaubert did not necessarily have a particular example in mind. There is, in fact, no explicit mention of caricature. This forms a contrast with the evocation of the same subject in *Bouvard et Pécuchet*, where a stray caricature from *Le Charivari* on a table at the château is said to represent "un citoyen, dont les basques de la redingote laissaient voir une queue, se terminant par un œil" or "a citizen whose coat-tails parted to reveal a tail ending in an eye" (Flaubert, *Bouvard et Pécuchet* 240–41). The two examples that most readily answer this description are that of Daumier recalled above and, above all, a Cham caricature from *Le Charivari* of 6 December 1848 that depicts a frock-coated and tail-endowed Considerant with large scissors "borrowing" monkey's tails from the Jardin des Plantes. The laughter of the assembled company is dependent on an explanation by the notary Marescot that, judiciously, Flaubert does not reproduce.

It is tempting to attribute still more of the content of *L'Education sentimentale* to Flaubert's familiarity with visual caricature. Takashi Kinouchi has convincingly linked the "marquise d'Amaëgui" in the Alhambra scene to Gavarni's "Andalouse" (*Le Charivari*, January 29, 1842), though he neglects to observe that Gavarni's figure is a cross-dressing male. Cisy's retelling of a claim that at a Tuileries ball the guests were disguised as carnivalesque *chicards* (Flaubert, *L'Education sentimentale* 140) stimulates memories of Gavarni's depictions of such figures. The socialist blue-stocking Mlle Vatnaz recalls series by both Gavarni and Daumier. The novel's full title, *L'Education sentimentale. Histoire d'un jeune homme*, can be related to Gavarni's *Vie de jeune homme*. In addition to more generalized echoes of Gavarni's depictions of *lorettes* and their male companions, Flaubert's evocation of the budding lawyer Martinon's live-in *grisette* darning socks (*L'Education sentimentale* 27) recalls a broadly similar scene in Gavarni's "Il fait son droit" or "He's a law student" (*Le Charivari*, August 5, 1840), while Rosanette's antics with a champagne bottle seemingly derive from "Un déjeuner au petit jour" or "Breakfast at dawn" (*La Caricature*, April 26, 1840). The examples of government repression in 1848 invite memories of Daumier's "Rue Transnonain" (1834), though, as Dussardier's reference to the latter outrage suggests, memories remained sufficiently strong for it not to need to be filtered through this, the most infamous of Daumier's political lithographs.

The same artist's "Le Gamin de Paris" or "The Paris urchin" (*Le Charivari*, March 4, 1848) invites comparison with Flaubert's depiction of the sack of the Tuileries, just as the depiction of Maître Hareng in *Madame Bovary* has been likened to a caricature Daumier published in *Le Charivari* on July 29, 1845. The moneylender Lheureux in *Madame Bovary* has been seen to hark back to visual caricature, while the priest and his catechism class, the blind beggar, and the importunate guide in Rouen cathedral in the same novel are eminent subjects for the same. Yet still more than in the case of Flaubert's explicit allusions to artists or examples of caricature, these figures do not in themselves reveal his writing to constitute a verbal translation of the visual genre; rather, they point to common subject matter, even if the visual corpus may be considered to have provided the writer with at least some of his inspiration.

There are, additionally, in Flaubert's fictions scenes evocative of a generic feature of caricature, namely its recourse to captions. Charles Bovary's confusion regarding the plot of the opera unfolding before him is adroitly rendered with the aid of a naive question that could readily serve as a *légende* to a visual caricature ("pourquoi donc [...] ce seigneur est-il à la persécuter?" "Why is this seigneur persecuting her so?" [Flaubert, *Madame Bovary* 230]). The lack of comprehension betrayed in statements attributed to Félicité in "Un cœur simple" and the all-important prop constituted by her parrot again form examples of the caricaturist's aim to summarize a character, or a life, in a single phrase or image. The incomprehension that greets the harangue delivered in Spanish at the Jacobin Club in *L'Education sentimentale* invites completion in the mind's eye with the aid of familiarity with the art of caricature. Charles's celebrated hat may not have a precise counterpart in a visual source, but its preposterous multi-layered form is the kind of meaningful monstrosity that was the visual caricaturist's stock-in-trade. It is seemingly in recognition of this that the new boy's articulation of his name comes out as a near homonym of *Charivari*: "Charbovari" and leads literally to a hullabaloo. A similar invitation to think of caricature is discernible in the fact that, in *L'Education sentimentale*, it is the fictional caricaturist Sombaz who makes fun of Oudry, calling him Odry after the celebrated comic actor and maintaining that he was descended from the eighteenth-century painter Oudry, characterized dismissively as a painter of dogs. The tell-tale detail is Sombaz's claim to detect the "animal bump" on Oudry's forehead. Both Gavarni and Daumier had demonstrated that Gall's system of phrenological *bosses*, which, needless to say, did not include a "bosse des animaux," was a gift to the caricaturist. The visual nature of Flaubert's scene is enhanced by Sombaz's failed attempt to access Oudry's wig-protected skull.

What is less evident to the naked eye is the way Flaubert, without explicitly evoking caricature, exploits and extends its underlying logic, as may be seen in "Un cœur simple" and *Bouvard et Pécuchet*. At its simplest, this consists of employing mechanisms to thwart the reader's attempts to insert the representation within a perspective of the real as inherently meaningful. An exclusive emphasis on surface appearances and on the external features of the body and its accoutrements is accompanied by distortion. A purely formal exaggeration of similarities and differences has the paradoxical effect of calling into question the very meaningfulness of the distinction.

In "Un cœur simple," Félicité, whose name is purposefully, if not straightforwardly, inappropriate, is not the object of an external portrayal in the manner of caricature, with regard, that is, to physical appearance or costume. In his description of her, Flaubert nonetheless contrives to blur the distinction between human and animal, a procedure that relates to the way contemporary visual caricaturists, especially Daumier and Grandville, the second of whom is recalled in this connection in Flaubert's *Voyage d'Orient*, portrayed human beings in the form of animals. Félicité likewise resembles "une femme de bois fonctionnant d'une manière automatique" or "a female wooden doll with mechanical movements" (Flaubert, "Un cœur" 158). The resemblance to caricature is, nonetheless, not so much visual as revealed through her response to her harsh environment and, still more fundamentally, by her (saintly) absence of a capacity for discrimination. Her deficient understanding is defined by an inability to differentiate between the real and the fictional or symbolic, or between appearance and reality. The "facts" revealed by the Book of Life are, for her, all equally true and equal in their impact (or lack of impact). Her life is characterized by imitation and repetition, to the extent that Loulou the parrot serves as her image. Ironically, she is not merely presented as a live caricature herself: her cast of mind possesses a propensity for distortion that leads to her being productive of caricature, whether in her reception of the visual representations in the stained-glass window and the prints she contemplates or in her confusion of Loulou and the Holy Ghost. Such is the level at which the principles of caricature have been absorbed by Flaubert that the parrot itself is imagined as finding Bourais's face "très drôle" or "highly amusing" (182), while Félicité's eye is drawn to the real-life distortion presented by Père Colmiche, who has a tumour on his arm larger than his head (181), in a scene that looks forward to the afflicted waiting for treatment by the two clerks turned medical practitioners in *Bouvard et Pécuchet* (273).

This internalization of the features of caricature is still more extensive in Flaubert's last, unfinished novel. Starting with the opening encounter of the two protagonists, which centers on the exaggerated significance they attach to the fact that each has inscribed his name in his hat, *Bouvard et Pécuchet* makes abundant use of the props of visual caricature, including that intrinsically absurd object, the umbrella, both the priest's and Bouvard's "canne-parapluie"—"cane-cum-umbrella"—or "parapluie polybranches"— "poly-spoked umbrella" (Flaubert, *Bouvard et Pécuchet* 139)— that accompanies him on the search for fossils. In addition to an array of headgear that includes a handkerchief knotted to resemble a turban and, in the case of the hapless Victor, a dunce's hat, and which sometimes represents the most extraordinary inventions, there is a similarly exaggerated foregrounding of footwear. Dress is highlighted less for itself than for the emphatic awkwardness of its relationship to the human body. Clothing is invariably either too large (Pécuchet "disappears" inside his frock-coat (45), while his torso inside his *houppelande* is said to resemble a bolster [254]) or too small (Mme Bordin is "un peu sanglée dans sa robe" 'slightly strapped inside her dress' [256]). Pécuchet's trousers accentuate the way his legs are out of proportion with the upper part of his body (46). Bouvard initially wears trousers that cling snugly to his paunch (46), but on the geological expedition, he wears a pair hoist to the pit of his stomach by a pair of short braces (139). The body, in general, is an encumbrance, and the former clerks' bodies (especially Pécuchet's) hideous when unclothed (recalling Daumier's various caricatures of male bathers and what Henry James considered that artist's ability to render the human body "with a cynical sense of its possible flabbiness" [141]). Gait and the poses of the two principals when engaged in their various activities, including writing, are comically over-accentuated. Prominent facial features, especially noses, are sometimes given still greater prominence. Pécuchet's stretches a very long way down (46). Zéphyrin Coulin's is exceedingly bony (*très cartilagineux*) at the tip and falls crookedly (*obliquement*) onto his pinched lips (362), though it is an engraving of the duc d'Angoulême that reveals a nose that contributes to an impression of "bonté insignifiante" 'trivial kindness' (183) and a carved version of St. Peter's nose that is likened to a trumpet (155) or a monstrous hunting horn (298). (In one case, an anecdote concerning a nose of record weight takes us out of the realm of caricature into teratology [112]) The relationship with visual caricature is extended through the clerks' passing addiction to the interpretation of cranial bumps and their experiments with magnetization, which recall Daumier's caricatures on the subject, including one of Robert Macaire as magnetizer. Orchestras and their conductors were established subjects of caricature, especially as a metaphor for governments; Pécuchet uses a stick in place of a bow to conduct Victor and Victorine's singing, "comme s'il avait eu un orchestre derrière lui" or "as if he had an orchestra behind him" (380). The visual procedures of caricature are also translated into the naming of François, Denys, Bartholomée Bouvard and Juste, Romain, Cyrille Pécuchet. A specific failure to understand what is said by another, for example a failure to identify the noun to which a pronoun refers or the interrogative "Quoi, donc?" or "Qui?", form part of a lack of comprehension subtending the entire work. The extent of the caricatural portrayal of the eponymous protagonists or the priest is thrown into relief by the unremarkable descriptions of their social superiors or the oil portrait of Bouvard's "uncle," for all the sitter's awkwardness.

The novel is suffused with an emphasis on the mechanical, embracing such details as Vaucanson's invention of an automaton in the shape of a hissing asp and the acquisition of one of Auzoux's puppet-like anatomical mannequins, which the former clerks thought resembled a toy rather than a corpse, and which is indeed dismissed by the doctor as being too far removed from nature. This emphasis is responsible for the clerks' constant surprise (the lexis of which is extensive), which contrasts, in this, the most Voltairean of Flaubert's fictions, with the author's cultivation of a sense of the predictability of an unsatisfactory outcome with regard to each new activity they undertake.

Again deriving from caricature and present in still more exaggerated forms are the numerous examples of disproportion, distortion, deformity, monstrosity, disorder, and anarchy to say nothing of the references to the cataclysmic or the apocalyptic. The new-age country-dwellers' reading of Alexandre Bertrand and Cuvier leads them to imagine a period when the world was populated by giant mammals with misshapen limbs resembling roughly hewn pieces of wood. They see the skeleton in the doctor's volume of anatomical drawings in terms of distortion that may recall Grandville's "Dance of Death." Their kitchen garden produces a monster cabbage (a possible dig at Fourier's exhortation to perfect the humble brassica) and anarchical melons, with gigantism being further present in the form of the dahlia stakes and the contraptions used to support the fruit trees. Disproportion extends to their scientific pastimes, where over-abundant enthusiasm is followed by disenchantment and brutal renunciation.

It is, however, in the play of exaggerated similarities and differences that Flaubert can be seen most significantly to extend one of the most fundamental practices of contemporary French caricature. As Daumier's depiction of the duo formed by Robert Macaire and Bertrand demonstrates, visual caricature gave prominence to exaggerated contrasts between little and large, corpulent and thin. (Earlier nineteenth-century French caricatures had contrasted the slender Frenchman with stout John Bull.) Flaubert duly begins with a contrast between "le plus grand" (Bouvard) and "le plus petit" (Pécuchet), the good-looking (Bouvard) and the ill-favoured (Pécuchet). Bouvard's hat is pushed back on his head, Pécuchet is wearing a cap with a (shiny) peak that is later said to have hypnotized him in the manner of a mirror. Yet, in the absence of explicit contextualization with regard to fashion, class or wealth, which leaves open whether they are types or eccentrics, the opening description of the two clerks is semiologically bland. When later they share a bed, Bouvard is bare-headed, while Pécuchet has recourse to a nightcap. This, together with their opposing reactions to the sight of a prostitute and soldier in the street, might seem to furnish the beginnings of character portrayal, bolstered by further examples of the more timorous Pécuchet's apparent prudishness, but such significance is neutralized by the comic enormity of the contrast itself, which is ultimately of no more consequence than their contrasting laughs or tastes in food. The contrasts lack, or have minimal, pertinence. It seems purely random that Bouvard was inclined to "neptunism" while Pécuchet was a "plutonian." This manifestly relates to the void created by the irreconcilable contradictions the two characters experience in their studies and experiments.

The significance of difference is indeed thwarted by being embedded in a complementary emphasis on sameness that already assumes parodic proportions in the account of the two men's meeting on the boulevard Bourdon. This is highlighted in the statement that their opinions were the same, though Bouvard was *perhaps* more liberal. The initial letters of their surnames represent a phonetic "minimal pair" and in combination with their names in full constitute a brilliant semiological representation of their paradoxical embodiment of sameness and difference. This is carried over into their emotional lives: their petty squabbles and their readiness to make up, together with their momentary hesitation of whether or not to stay with each other, with the subsequent illustration of their mutual dependency, form just one of the ways in which Flaubert's novel looks forward to Beckett's *Waiting for Godot.*

It will be obvious that this internalization by Flaubert of the logic of caricature goes beyond creating the impression of a series of distinct visual examples. His disdain for ekphrasis, which Flaubert scholarship has acknowledged with regard to painting, applies equally to visual caricature. The extent to which memories of caricature saturate his unfinished novel can, however, be measured by the way representative elements are recycled without retention of their caricatural features. This may be illustrated by Flaubert's inclusion in the narrative of turkeys and peacocks. Both birds are prominent among the animals adopted by Daumier and others in caricatures featuring Louis-Philippe and his son Ferdinand. In Daumier's "Conférence de Londres," the turkey is Belgium. As David Kerr has pointed out, the turkey was also associated with the Jesuits, who had introduced it into France. As if in reminiscence of such caricatures, Flaubert has Bouvard and Pécuchet acquire peacocks for ornamental purposes. A coupling between two of the birds later interrupts a sensitive moment in the unfulfilled relationship of Bouvard and Mme Bordin and causes the Parisians' horse to bolt. A neighbouring farmer's wife is observed stuffing a turkey (Flaubert, *Bouvard et Pécuchet* 67). On another farm, the unfortunate turkeys are used in one of their experiments in magnetism (286). After stumbling, Bouvard on all fours is compared to "une tortue avec des ailes" or "a winged tortoise" (143–44).

Caricatural transformations may also be seen to lie behind certain kinds of simile in *Bouvard et Pécuchet*, in which the faint incongruity or the sheer concreteness of the image short-circuits the relational value of the comparison and leaves the new term dominant in its isolation, as for example when rounds of butter are likened to the segments of a copper column (Flaubert, *Bouvard et Pécuchet* 73) or when the home-made paper covering for the dog-roses is said to resemble sugar loaves (79). A more blatant example may be observed in the evocation of Bouvard's tongue overhanging his bottom lip "comme un drapeau," that is, "like a flag" (325). The characteristic short utterances, often in direct speech, which develop a feature of *L'Education sentimentale*, are left similarly exposed and echoing the function of certain types of title or caption in visual caricature, as in the example of Pécuchet's "C'est que, peut-être, nous ne savons pas la chimie" or "Perhaps it's because we don't know any chemistry" (106). "Mais c'est de l'or! c'est de l'or!" "But it's gold, it's gold" (81) and the accompanying account of the liquid manure containing their own urine may be considered to parallel still more closely the way the reality of the visual image in caricature may ironize its verbal accompaniment.

What Flaubert's unfinished novel confirms is that the importance of visual caricature for his literary compositions cannot be calculated solely on the basis of his explicit references to its exponents. Yet if visual caricature was still more fundamental to Flaubert's aesthetics of the novel than these references suggest, it is also the case that the latter are at risk of underplaying the particular importance to his literary art of particular caricaturists, above all Daumier, many of whose most biting caricatures possessed too ephemeral an origin to encourage specific mention. Consideration of the subject in the round makes it clear that Flaubert's unquestionable enjoyment of visual caricature as a medium was subordinated to a focus on its capacity to feed his quest for a new kind of composition that went beyond ironization of inherited fictional norms and conventions. For all the intrinsic allure of the visual image itself, the verbal remained paramount, as was suggested by the prevalence of references to M. Prudhomme. Bourgeois society in both caricature and his writing was implicitly defined by the representative voice of its denizens, in what was, in effect, a vast echo chamber or what Hugh Kenner has termed a feedback loop (22). In short, caricature may be seen as being, for Flaubert, the acceptable face of a contested realism, or what Adrianne Tooke calls the latter's "deviant form" (38).

Works Cited

Chesneau, Ermest. *Les Nations rivales dans l'art.* Paris: Didier, 1868.

Flaubert, Gustave. *Bouvard et Pécuchet.* Paris: Garnier-Flammarion, 1999.

_____. *Correspondance.* Ed. Jean Bruneau. 5 vols. Bibliothèque de la Pléiade. Paris: Gallimard, 1973–2007.

_____. *L'Education sentimentale.* Paris: Garnier, 1984.

_____. *Madame Bovary.* Paris: Garnier, 1971.

_____. *La Première Education sentimentale.* Paris: Seuil, 1963.

_____. "Un cœur simple" *Trois contes.* Paris: Garnier, 1988.

Gombrich, E. H. & E. Kris. *Caricature.* Harmondsworth: Penguin, 1940.

James, Henry. "Honoré Daumier." *Picture and Text.* By Henry James. New York: Harper, 1893: 116–44.

Kenner, Hugh. *The Stoic Comedians: Flaubert, Joyce and Beckett.* Berkeley: U of California P, 1974.

Kerr, David S. *Caricature and French Political Culture 1830–1848: Charles Philipon and the Illustrated Press*. Oxford, England: Clarendon P, 2000.

Kinouchi, Takashi. "La mémoire des images dans *L'Education sentimentale*," *Flaubert:Revue Critique et Génétique* 11 (2014). Web. 25 Sept. 2015. <https://flaubert.revues.org/2256>.

Porter, Laurence M. & Eugene F. Gray. *Gustave Flaubert's 'Madame Bovary.' A Reference Guide*. Santa Barbara, CA: Greenwood, 2002.

Tooke, Adrianne. *Flaubert and the Pictorial Arts: From Image to Text*. Oxford, England: Oxford UP, 2000.

Testament to Disaster: Philosophical Perspectives on *Bouvard et Pécuchet*_____

Elizabeth Rottenberg

I. A Revolutionary Grammar

A. The Legacy of Romanticism

No writer has seen his name more linked to a concept he detested than Gustave Flaubert. From the moment of the publication of *Madame Bovary* in 1857, literary history has hailed Flaubert as the father, "founder, chief practitioner, and high priest" of *realism* (Brombert 3). And yet nothing was more galling to him than theories, systems, schools of thought that made pronouncements about the world: "Peignons, peignons, sans faire de théorie" (CB 2: 209); "je n'aime les doctrinaires d'aucune espèce… Loin de moi ceux qui se prétendent réalistes, naturalistes, impressionnistes… moins de paroles et plus d'œuvres!" (CB 4: 391). He even claimed that *Madame Bovary* was conceived wholly out of a "hatred" of realism (CB 2: 643). Indeed, more than twenty years later, Flaubert is still ranting against realism: "Et notez que j'exècre ce qu'on est convenu d'appeler le *réalisme*, bien qu'on me fasse un de ses pontifes" (GS 521).

And yet, from the outset, Flaubert must concede that *Madame Bovary* no longer conforms to the lyrical, Romantic tradition of French writers. To Sainte-Beuve he insists that he still belongs—in his heart at least—to an earlier generation of writers:

> Ne me jugez pas d'après ce roman. Je ne suis pas de la génération dont vous parlez—par le cœur du moins.—Je tiens à être de la vôtre, j'entends de la bonne, celle de 1830. Tous mes amours sont là. Je suis un vieux romantique enragé, ou encroûté, comme vous voudrez.
>
> Ce livre est pour moi une affaire d'art pur et de parti pris. Rien de plus. D'ici à longtemps je n'en referai de pareils. Il m'a été *physiquement* pénible à écrire. Je veux maintenant vivre (ou plutôt revivre) dans des milieux moins nauséabonds. (CB 2: 710)

"[É]pris de *gueulades*, de lyrisme, de grands vols d'aigle, de toutes les sonorités de la phrase et des sommets de l'idée" (CB 2: 30), Flaubert belongs *in his heart at least* to the generation of Chateaubriand and Victor Hugo. Nothing could be further from Flaubert's heart than the writing of *Madame Bovary*. He is not "*ce* roman," "[*c*]*e* livre"— and, one might add, "*cette* affaire d'art pur et de parti pris"—those things to which he points and which fill him with disgust. *Madame Bovary*, he is telling Sainte-Beuve, ce n'est pas moi, "par le cœur du moins."

For Flaubert, who was born in 1821, Romanticism is not simply a cultural heritage: it is also his immediate and personal past. To refer to the generation of the French Romantics is thus to evoke the generation of writers in whose waning he participates. For what the name "Flaubert" marks in literary history is the place where Romanticism comes to an end. So what would it mean for Flaubert to be an "old Romantic" under these conditions? What would it mean for Romanticism to live on in Flaubert?

This chapter will argue that what Proust calls "le style de Flaubert" allows us to read, on the level of grammar and syntax, a futurity that lies at the "heart" of Romanticism. In the name of Romanticism, precisely against it in its name, Flaubert's style ushers in a new temporality. Paradoxically, in other words, it is by sacrificing his heart, his old romantic heart, that Flaubert conveys what is the non-Romantic essence of Romantic temporality.

B. The Moving Walkway

And perhaps nowhere is the difficulty of reading the revolutionary force of Flaubert's style more obvious than in the famous controversy that takes place in the pages of *La Nouvelle Revue Française* in 1919–1920 between Marcel Proust and Albert Thibaudet. In this debate, the difficulty of reading the "human" in Flaubert emerges precisely as a question of style.

The controversy follows from an article published by Thibaudet, "Le style de Flaubert," in which he argues that Flaubert is not what one might call "un écrivain de race" (156). Were it not for Flaubert's "fiery temperament" and his "Norman obstinacy,"

Thibaudet contends, Flaubert's style might never have overcome its natural indigence (156).

In his article, "À propos du 'style' de Flaubert," Proust takes issue with Thibaudet's characterization of Flaubert's style. Whatever Flaubert's personal history and "breeding," Proust claims, the effects of Flaubert's style on our vision of the world should be compared to the Copernican change of perspective brought about by Kant's radical critique of pure reason:

> J'ai été stupéfait, je l'avoue, de voir traité de peu doué pour écrire, un homme qui par l'usage entièrement nouveau et personnel qu'il a fait du passé défini, du passé indéfini, du participe présent, de certains pronoms et de certaines prépositions, a renouvelé presque autant notre vision des choses que Kant, avec ses Catégories, les théories de la Connaissance et de la Réalité du monde extérieur. (*Écrits sur l'art* 314)

Proust is dumbfounded by Thibaudet's article. How can a writer who has so revolutionized the French language not be "un écrivain de race"? How can a writer whose grammar and syntax have so profoundly modified our vision of the world be lacking in pedigree?

Thibaudet's response to Proust's response begins by reiterating Proust's position in order to reconcile their two positions:

> "J'ai été, dites-vous, stupéfait, je l'avoue, de voir traité de peu doué pour écrire, un homme qui... a renouvelé presque autant notre vision des choses que Kant." J'aurais peut-être droit aussi à quelque stupéfaction devant ce rapprochement... Mettons le style, et comme vous dites, la beauté grammaticale, à leur place, mais sachons aussi les tenir à cette place, et ne cédons pas non plus à la dangereuse mode, si commune aujourd'hui, d'introduire le nom de Kant là où il n'a que faire. (176–77)

Let us not exaggerate, Thibaudet is telling Proust. Style and grammatical beauty have their place, it is true, and this place must be acknowledged. However—and here Thibaudet cautions Proust—let us not give in to so fashionable a name as "Kant," for this kind of name-dropping has dangerous consequences for literature. Literature must not overstep its bounds. It is not philosophy. Style and grammatical beauty cannot literally—let us be serious here!—change our relation to the external world or the way we see things. What astonishes Thibaudet in turn is not only the immodest comparison between literary style and philosophical insight, but the claim that our vision of things has been transformed by anything other than Flaubert's personal or, as Thibaudet will say, "psychological" experience of the world.

In other words, the disagreement between Proust and Thibaudet revolves around a question of grammar. Thibaudet again begins by quoting Proust:

> "Cet imparfait, si nouveau dans la littérature, change entièrement l'aspect des choses et des êtres, comme font une lampe qu'on a déplacée, l'arrivée dans une maison nouvelle, (l'ancienne si elle est presque vide et qu'on est en plein déménagement)." Peut-être est-ce l'aspect des choses et des êtres, tel qu'il s'imposa à Flaubert, qui exigea l'emploi de l'imparfait, puisque l'imparfait exprime le passé dans un rapport soit avec le présent, soit avec une nature habituelle... Ce qui fait que j'entends bien en somme ce que vous voulez dire quand vous proclamez que Flaubert a renouvelé ainsi notre vision des choses autant qu'un philosophe. Et je laisserais passer sans protestations cet ultra-bergsonisme si vous n'affirmiez que cette vision est renouvelée par un instrument non psychologique mais grammatical, non par la vision particulière de Flaubert, mais par son expression verbale. (178–79)

Thibaudet might have let the analogy between literature and philosophy go, he tells us, had it not been for Proust's outrageous claim about grammar. He can agree that our vision of things has been transformed by Flaubert. However, and this is the preposterous claim Thibaudet feels compelled to correct, it is the way in which things and beings imprinted themselves on Flaubert—and not Flaubert's verbal expression—that is responsible for his insight. Flaubert's verbal expression is determined, Thibaudet maintains, by the aspect of things and beings as they appeared to Flaubert.

And yet, in Thibaudet's conciliatory statement, following which he will concede that he does in fact understand and agree with what Proust is saying up to a point, he ends up saying something very different. "Peut-être est-ce l'aspect des choses et des êtres, tel qu'il s'imposa à Flaubert, qui exigea l'emploi de l'imparfait," Thibaudet conjectures. But Proust says exactly the opposite in the sentence Thibaudet has just quoted. Although Thibaudet ignores Proust's metaphors, Proust's statement seems perfectly clear: "Cet imparfait, si nouveau dans la littérature, change entièrement l'aspect des choses et des êtres." And grammatically straightforward. Indeed an "analyse grammaticale" of the sentence would show that the subject of the verb is the one performing the action: "this imperfect... changes." And not only does it change, it utterly changes—"change entièrement"—the aspect of things and beings. How is it, then, that Thibaudet turns a direct object into the subject of his sentence, reverses the direction of the action, and concludes that he and Proust are in agreement: "Peut-être est-ce l'aspect des choses et des êtres... qui exigea l'emploi de l'imparfait"?

Where "the aspect of things and beings" was for Proust the most direct of direct objects, it becomes for Thibaudet not only the subject of two verbs—"s'imposa," "exigea"—but also a formidable subject of coercive action. Where in Proust's description "the aspect of things and beings" was an object that passively experienced the action of the subject, it becomes for Thibaudet a subject (and a matter) so inflexible, so rigid, so unchanging, that it imposes itself on Flaubert and determines his use of the imperfect. Where Proust reads Flaubert's revolutionary imperfect as changing the way we see the world, Thibaudet reads the world's unchanging aspect as imposing the imperfect on Flaubert. It is as if Thibaudet had literally missed Flaubert's revolution by refusing to read Flaubert (and Proust) grammatically.

The paradoxical impact of reducing the grammatical to the psychological is such that Thibaudet loses the very thing that is particular to Flaubert. Indeed, when the imperfect no longer refers to a past in relation to a present, when it absorbs and converts the contingencies of temporal difference into a "défilement continu, monotone, morne, indéfini" (*Écrits sur l'art* 315), it functions very much like a grammar, that is, like a formal, mechanical stucture that streamlines the personal and the psychological. The imperative to read grammatically, as Proust understands it, is thus an imperative to read Flaubert's grammar, but it is also the imperative to read *the grammar that is Flaubert*. Proust will see a machine at work in the "obsessive rhythm" of Flaubert's sentences (*Écrits sur l'art* 323); he will see a juggernaut, but also "a grammatical beauty" (*Écrits sur l'art* 315). Thus, to read the revolution of Flaubert is precisely to read this grammatical beauty: "il n'est pas possible à quiconque est un jour monté sur ce grand *Trottoir roulant* que sont les pages de Flaubert... de méconnaître qu'elles sont sans précédent dans la littérature" (*Écrits sur l'art* 315).

But there is yet a further implication to missing the revolution. By reducing grammar to psychology, Thibaudet loses not only grammar, but also grammar's particular relation to temporality. Indeed the confusion between grammar and psychology returns as the conflation of the literal with the symbolic. Unable to read literally, Thibaudet cannot avoid missing the very thing that Proust finds most beautiful in Flaubert. "À mon avis," writes Proust, "la chose la plus belle de *L'Éducation sentimentale*, ce n'est pas une phrase, mais un blanc" (*Écrits sur l'art* 324). This blank at the end of Chapter 5 marks a pause and a chapter-break: "[E]t Frédéric, béant, reconnut Sénécal" (450). What follows, says Proust, is "a 'blank,' an enormous 'blank'" (*Écrits sur l'art* 324), and without even the hint of a transition, we are thrown into the future on the very next page, not fifteen minutes into the future, but years, decades into the future:

Et Frédéric, béant, reconnut Sénécal.

Il voyagea.
Il connut la mélancholie des paquebots, les froids réveils sous la tente, l'étourdissement des paysages et des ruines, l'amertume des sympathies interrompues.
Il revint.
Il fréquenta le monde...
Vers la fin de l'année 1867... (Flaubert, *L'Éducation* 450)

The raw passage of time, unencumbered by the "scoria of history," is written into an enormous "blank." The future has come and gone in the space of a blank. Hence, the surprise that we register when we begin the next chapter is the surprise of the unexpected; it is the trace left by what has already happened and that the reader can only register as a missing.

Thibaudet will return to Proust's blank in his own article: "Ce que vous admirez le plus, dites-vous, dans *l'Éducation sentimentale*, c'est un blanc" (174). However, he immediately assimilates this "blank" to what he, Thibaudet, finds "most surprising" in Flaubert's literary existence, namely the blank that separates Flaubert's juvenilia from *Madame Bovary*: "Le moment le plus étonnant de l'existence littéraire de Flaubert c'est le blanc qui sépare la première *Éducation* et la première *Tentation* de *Madame Bovary*" (174). Thibaudet has read a syntactical or grammatical marker (a blank, a form of punctuation) as a figure (a blank, a simile that refers to the development of Flaubert's literary talent). But the blank that Proust is talking about cannot simply be assumed as a figure when we read. It is first a blank, a white space on a page. And it is only because it is literally a white space on the page—*and not a figure*—that we can be shocked into consciousness, the consciousness of a future that has already taken place. One might say that figuration comes too late in this case, such that the inevitable shock that we feel when we read the opening lines of Chapter 6 awakens a feeling of pathos before the merciless automatism of time. Pathos arises, in other words, as a result of the reader's lack of preparedness for the intransigence of the "trottoir roulant." Again, Thibaudet misses what is perhaps most affecting (and most personal) in the writing of Flaubert by reducing Flaubert's grammatical, syntactical innovations to the psychology of M. Flaubert.

By refusing to leave the familiar ground of human psychology, by refusing to read the Kant in Flaubert, Thibaudet ends up behaving very much like those benighted thinkers in Kant who fail to grasp the Copernican revolution and entangle themselves to the point of absurdity in cycles and epicycles because they refuse to relinquish the standpoint from which they see the course of human events (Kant 149). Flaubert's moving walkway, the grammatical force that is Flaubert's genius, has proved *affectively* unreadable for Thibaudet. Ironically, thus, it is from the absolute indifference and machine-like neutrality of the "trottoir roulant," from the most formal, mechanical, grammatical disapperance of the personal, that there emerges in Flaubert a surprising temporality that is distinctly and uniquely "human."

II. Reading Grammatically

A. Reading *Bouvard et Pécuchet*

In *Bouvard et Pécuchet*, Flaubert's posthumous novel, the full grammatical force of Flaubert's style enters into the novel in a way that turns out to be far more revealing of its revolutionary temporality than in any of Flaubert's earlier work. In the novel Flaubert calls his "testament" (GS 524), the monotonous, unrelenting force of the "trottoir roulant" becomes the allegorical subject of the novel: whence the absolutely unique nature of *Bouvard et Pécuchet* in the context of Flaubert's corpus. Roland Barthes, who was fascinated by the novel, refers to *Bouvard et Pécuchet* as the pure essence of Flaubert (434). In no other novel, therefore, does the imperative to read grammatically become more pressing than in *Bouvard et Pécuchet*.

The actual story of *Bouvard et Pécuchet* is simple enough: two middle-aged scriveners—the one a ruddy widower, the other an irascible bachelor—meet on a park bench and strike up a friendship. An unexpected inheritance enables them to retire to the Norman countryside where, impelled by their desire to find intelligibility in the world, they study and forsake a huge number of disciplines: gardening, agriculture, arboriculture, chemistry, anatomy, physiology, astronomy, zoology, geology, archeology, history, literature, politics, magnetism, philosophy, religion, pedagogy. Four hundred pages later, discouraged and financially ruined, the two scriveners are galvanized by the same thought and begin copying once again.

But it is hardly the story of the clerks' countless failures that makes *Bouvard et Pécuchet* "one of the most ambitious and one of the

---

strangest books in the history of the French novel" (Gothot-Mersch 13). What makes the novel both unique and perplexing is the entry into the narrative of the force-like movement of Flaubert's grammar and syntax. And yet, when a grammatical movement becomes the story, the reader who continues to read (and not fall asleep, as was Flaubert's fear) cannot help but be disoriented by its strange exigency: a drive that presses onward, indefinitely, relentlessly, leveling everything in its path. As a result, *Bouvard et Pécuchet* is a book that many critics dismiss, beginning with Jean-Paul Sartre who called it a "tentative absurde" (Sartre 3: 656). Roland Barthes, the great defender of *Bouvard et Pécuchet*, declares it to be "un livre fou, au sens propre du terme" (435).

B. Reading Bouvard and Pécuchet Reading

On the one hand, *Bouvard et Pécuchet* tells a story in which the innumerable failures of Bouvard and Pécuchet are endlessly recuperated by the grammatical force of the imperfect, a force that operates like a dialectic. On the other hand, the very movement from sameness to sameness, from imperfect to imperfect, not only repeats the sameness of the past, *it also projects this sameness into the future*. What we will see, in the end, is that this shift in the temporality of "sameness" (from past to future) is no longer simply reducible to a force of indifferentiation.

1. Time as Teleology

For much of the novel, Bouvard and Pécuchet's course of study follows an explicitly dialectical sequence. Gardening, agriculture, arboriculture, canning, distillation, chemistry, anatomy, physiology, astronomy, zoology, geology, archeology, history, literature, politics, magnetism, philosophy, religion, pedagogy: one project leads to the next, and though every project ends in failure, every failure points to a new discipline, and every discipline promises to fill the crucial gap in Bouvard and Pécuchet's education. Failure, in this context, is the determinate negation that sustains the quest. The explosion of the still, which puts an end to Bouvard and Pécuchet's confectionery dream-cream ("la Bouvarine") in Chapter 2, immediately prompts their study of science. If only they had known the basic principles of chemistry, such an accident would not have occurred. The study of science will prove unsatisfactory, as will the study of history, as will the study of literature, etc. However, every new lacuna further stimulates Bouvard and Pécuchet in their totalizing quest.

The dialectical nature of failure emerges in the passé simple. Hence, the passé simple is the tense that attests to each of Bouvard and Pécuchet's countless activities. From their very first day in Chavignolles, the passé simple becomes the simplest expression of their hopes and aspirations: "Bouvard planta une pivoine au milieu du gazon.... Pécuchet fit creuser devant la cuisine, un large trou" (Flaubert, *Bouvard et Pécuchet* 77). The passé simple expects and promises the new, whether in the garden (Pécuchet)—"Il sema les graines de plusieurs variétés dans des assiettes remplies de terreau... Il fit toutes les tailles suivant les préceptes du bon jardinier, respecta les fleurs, laissa se nouer les fruits, en choisit un sur chaque bras, supprima les autres" (86). Or in the fields (Bouvard): "Excité par Pécuchet, il eut le délire de l'engrais... Il employa la liqueur belge, le lizier suisse, la lessive *Da-Olmi*, des harengs saurs, du varech, des chiffons, fit venir du guano, tâcha d'en fabriquer" (89). But direct action, as they soon discover, is a double-edged sword: "Le colza fut chétif, l'avoine médiocre; et le blé vendit fort mal, à cause de son odeur" (89). Where at first the assertiveness of the passé simple expressed real possibility, it quickly comes to signal a call to arms: "Bouvard tâcha de conduire les abricotiers. Ils se révoltèrent. Il abattit leurs troncs à ras du sol; aucun ne repoussa" (96). A battle with nature in the passé simple proves an unwinnable fight.

And the passé simple is not even nature's preferred tense. As if to add insult to injury, the imperfect returns, like a force of nature, laying low what remains of Bouvard and Pécuchet's achievements in the passé simple:

Toutes les meules, çà et là, flambaient... Sous les flammes dévorantes la paille se tordait avec des crépitations, les grains de blé vous cinglaient la figure comme des grains de plomb. Puis, la meule s'écroulait par terre en un large brasier, d'où s'envolaient des étincelles;—et des moires ondulaient sur cette masse rouge, qui offrait dans les alternances de sa couleur, des parties roses comme du vermillon, et d'autres brunes comme du sang caillé. (Flaubert, *Bouvard et Pécuchet* 92–93)

The imperfect emerges as a sheer and simple (even beautiful) force, an absolutely disinterested force of nature. Beyond the battle scenes of the passé simple and the phantasmatic projections of indirect discourse in what may be Flaubert's most abstract use of the "discours indirect libre"—"Le vent s'amusait à jeter bas les rames des haricots" (*Bouvard et Pécuchet* 85)—the eternal imperfect returns.

2. Revolution

It is interesting to note, however, that at the heart of the novel lies an example of an event whose very erasure by the authorities leaves an indelible mark on Bouvard and Pécuchet. It is Flaubert's great irony, I will suggest, to have placed a truly irreversible event in the middle of the historical reversal whose dates punctuate Chapter 6. Chapter 6 begins and ends with a date: "Dans la matinée du 25 février, on apprit à Chavignolles... que Paris était couvert de barricades" (226); "C'était le 3 décembre 1851" (257). The chapter concludes with the terrible massacre that takes place on the boulevard des Capucines in the days following Louis-Napoléon Bonaparte's coup d'état of December 1851, that is, it ends in exactly the same spot (literally) as the shooting that touched off the 1848 revolution with which the chapter begins.

Bouvard and Pécuchet alone note the reversals that are taking place around them. The freedom tree, Bouvard and Pécuchet's gift to Chavignolles, planted and blessed by the curé at the beginning of Chapter 6, is cut down squarely in the middle of the chapter with Bouvard as its only witness. By the end of the chapter, it is as if the revolution had never taken place, as if it had literally been reduced to a "fiction." Finally, when the 1851 massacre meets with the general approval of Chavignolles, Bouvard will throw up his hands in disgust: "Tout me dégoûte. Vendons... notre baraque—et allons au tonnerre de Dieu, chez les sauvages!" (Flaubert, *Bouvard et Pécuchet* 258).

Bouvard and Pécuchet cannot forget Chavignolles's violent erasure of 1848. For them, there can be no return to pre-revolutionary times. The truly revolutionary event thus is not the one that takes place on the boulevard des Capucines, but the one that occurs as a shift in Bouvard and Pécuchet's encyclopedic quest, a shift whose symptom becomes an analytic ability in the face of injustice. In the case of Gorgu, who has been arrested for sedition, Marescot claims they are defending a dangerous man:

—"Vraiment" dit Bouvard, "pour quelques paroles!..."
—"Quand la parole amène des crimes, cher monsieur, permettez!"
—"Cependant" reprit Pécuchet, "quelle démarcation établir entre les phrases innocentes et les coupables? Telle chose défendue maintenant sera par la suite applaudie." Et il blâma la manière féroce dont on traitait les insurgés.

Marescot allégua naturellement la defense de la Société, le Salut Public, loi supreme. (Flaubert, *Bouvard et Pécuchet* 241)

For Marescot, public safety speaks for itself; it is the highest law and that which commands all the rest. But it is not he who introduces the term "naturally" here. "Naturally" stems, rather, from Bouvard and Pécuchet's utter disillusionment with the language of politics, for they expect Marescot to respond exactly as he does. With "naturally," Bouvard and Pécuchet are indicting the (murderous) legacy of charges made in the name of "public safety": "Sa doctrine du salut public les avait indignés. Les conservateurs parlaient maintenant comme Robespierre" (Flaubert, *Bouvard et Pécuchet* 241–42). For the first time in their encyclopedic quest, Bouvard and Pécuchet have encountered a radical negativity, indeed a language of power that resists all dialectical assimilation. For the first time, in other words, the very foundation of progress on which their quest is predicated has been shaken. They have encountered something heterogeneous to the space of knowledge.

3. Present Disruptions: The Intemporal Present

In the midst of their dialectical travails, Bouvard and Pécuchet are further confronted by a tense that squares neither with the activity of the "passé simple" nor with monotony of the "imparfait." This tense, the "intemporal present" of truth and objectivity, is the sign of a specifically textual encounter. From the very beginning, Bouvard and Pécuchet's encyclopedic quest has revolved around the study and absorption of books. Not only must they get hold of the right books for every new project, they must also make sense of these books. But the intemporal present makes possible the coexistence of irreconcilable "truths." The more books they read, the more Bouvard and Pécuchet grow confused by differing, if not blatantly contradictory, factual accounts:

> Ainsi, pour la marne, Puvis la recommande; le manuel Roret la combat... Les jachères, selon Bouvard, étaient un préjugé gothique. Cependant, Leclerc note les cas où elles sont presque indispensables. Gasparin cite un lyonnais qui pendant un demi-siècle a cultivé des céréales sur le même champ; cela renverse la théorie des assolements. Tull exalte les labours au préjudice des engrais; et voilà le major Betson qui supprime les engrais, avec les labours! (Flaubert, *Bouvard et Pécuchet* 88)

Bouvard and Pécuchet not only confuse themselves. Their muddle is also communicated in the text, by the text; it is passed on to the reader. The intemporal present blurs the lines of enunciation such that it becomes impossible to decide who is speaking at any given moment. As Pécuchet later exclaims in exasperation: "Where is the rule, then...?" (*Bouvard and Pécuchet*, Krailsheimer translation 99). Are Bouvard and Pécuchet discussing alternative farming methods? Is this an exchange between them? Is it Bouvard who cites Puvis? Or is it Pécuchet? And is it the same speaker who refutes Puvis with Roret or the other speaker? In Flaubert's use of indirect discourse here—if indeed it is indirect discourse—nothing is certain. Bouvard is the one who mentions "fallows," but can he also be the one to cite Leclerc and refute his own "prejudice"? And who concludes that the theory of crop rotations has been disproved? Is it Bouvard or

Pécuchet? Or is it Gasparin who cites the Lyonnais farmer in order to prove just this point? Or is it Bouvard (Pécuchet?) who recalls Gasparin's reference to the Lyonnais farmer in order to infer from it support for the initial "prejudice"? Or is it the nameless Lyonnais farmer who is being paraphrased here and whose farming practices clearly disprove "the theory of crop rotations"? How indirect is the discourse, in other words? Is it once, twice, or three times removed from the reader? How present is this intemporal present? We cannot know, just as Bouvard and Pécuchet do not know whether to plow or to fertilize their fields.

Moreover, the intemporal present also threatens the foundation of scientific truth:

> Jusqu'alors ils avaient cru à l'insalubrité des endroits humides. Pas du tout! Casper les déclare moins mortels que les autres. On ne se baigne pas dans la mer sans avoir rafraîchi sa peau. Béguin veut qu'on s'y jette en pleine transpiration. Le vin pur après la soupe passe pour excellent à l'estomac. Lévy l'accuse d'altérer les dents...
>
> Qu'est-ce donc que l'hygiène?
>
> —"Vérité en deça des Pyrénées, erreur au delà" affirme M. Lévy; et Becquerel ajoute qu'elle n'est pas une science. (Flaubert, *Bouvard et Pécuchet* 136)

If the same things can be both healthy and unhealthy at the same time, then hygiene can have no scientific value. The cultural irony, set forth by M. Lévy, absolutely confirms Bouvard and Pécuchet's thinking about hygiene. But how is it that we have gotten from "damp places" to saltwater? Who has made this transition and, therefore, this argument, possible? Is it Casper who merely asserts that "damp places" are less dangerous—less "fatal"—than other places? Is it Béguin who has something to say about the virtues of saltwater? Or is it Bouvard and Pécuchet who make the transition between dampness and total immersion, between Casper and Béguin? Because the passage from "damp places" (Casper) to saltwater (Béguin) escapes all personal assignation, it seems to have posed a problem for one of the English translators of *Bouvard and Pécuchet* whose chosen translation brings out the treacherousness of this passage. The translator does this by changing the meaning of the transitional phrase:

> Up till then they had believed that damp places are unhealthy. Not at all! Casper asserts that they are less dangerous than others. *One should not bathe in the sea without first cooling down one's skin.* Béguin thinks it better to plunge in actually sweating. (*Bouvard and Pécuchet*, Krailsheimer translation 83, my emphasis)

Instead of positive refreshment (one cannot not be refreshed), we have an actual, negative prescription (do not bathe in the sea without first cooling down). Can we or can we not bathe without being refreshed? Like Bouvard and Pécuchet, we are left hanging at the end of this paragraph, without any consensus about the hygiene of saltwater bathing. In other words, the intemporal present leads to a dilemma that is not resolved but rather conveyed by the dialectic. Although Bouvard and Pécuchet have moved on to astronomy within a page, the intemporal present has introduced a moment or space of impossible passage.

4. Present Disruptions: The Testimonial Present

Though Bouvard and Pécuchet will spend the post-revolutionary chapters in search of a bottom line with which they might rest secure in their knowledge, a terrible desperation has taken hold of their quest. Nothing, it would seem—not love, or gymnastics, or magnetism, or spiritism, or philosophy, or religion—can quite reverse the trend. Their occupations of the past no longer sustain them. Their happy days, their age of innocence, seem so distant from them now:

> Pourquoi ne suivaient-ils plus les moissonneurs? Où étaient les jours qu'ils entraient dans les fermes cherchant partout des antiquités? Rien maintenant n'occasionnerait ces heures si douces qu'emplissaient la distillerie ou la Littérature. Un abîme les en séparait. Quelque chose d'irrévocable était venu. (Flaubert, *Bouvard et Pécuchet* 320–21)

Something irreversible has occurred. And yet, syntactically, nothing but a lone and mawkish conditional separates the imperfect of the past ("suivaient," "entraient," "emplissaient") from the imperfect of the present ("séparait," "était [venu]"). There remains only the future, but soon the future, too, will meet with a similar fate. In search of an antidote to their depression, Bouvard and Pécuchet resolve to take a walk in the fields. What they meet up with, however, is not simply the sumptuous display of nature's imperfects:

> —De petits nuages moutonnaient dans le ciel, le vent balançait les clochettes des avoines, le long d'un pré un ruisseau murmurait, quand tout coup une odeur infecte les arrêta; et ils virent sur des cailloux, entre des joncs, la charogne d'un chien.
>
> Les quatres membres étaient désséchés. Le rictus de la gueule découvrait sous des babines bleuâtres des crocs d'ivoire; à la place du ventre, c'était un amas de couleur terreuse, et qui semblait palpiter tant grouillait dessus la vermine. Elle s'agitait, frappée par le soleil, sous le bourdonnement des mouches, dans cette intolérable odeur, une odeur féroce et comme dévorante. (Flaubert, *Bouvard et Pécuchet* 321)

What they meet up with is also their future: "Nous serons un jour comme ça" (Flaubert, *Bouvard et Pécuchet* 321)—grinning, as it were, in the imperfect. Past, present, and future: time as such has fallen prey to the all-consuming force of the imperfect. Not only can all of life be represented by the imperfect, but life itself has also become identified with its intolerable movement to which death alone promises to put an end: "N'importe quoi valait mieux que cette existence monotone, absurde, et sans espoir" (321). Having examined the question of suicide, Bouvard and Pécuchet briefly deliberate on the best method of death; they decide to hang themselves. Their suicide will of course fail like all their other projects. What disrupts this particular project, however, takes a familiar and ironic form:

> La chandelle était par terre—et Pécuchet debout sur une des chaises avec le câble dans sa main.

> L'esprit d'imitation emporta Bouvard: —"Attends-moi!" Et il
> montait sur l'autre chaise quand s'arrêtant tout à coup:
> —"Mais… nous n'avons pas fait notre testament?"
> —"Tiens! c'est juste!" (Flaubert, *Bouvard et Pécuchet* 323–24)

Bouvard and Pécuchet cannot die intestate. They have forgotten to write their wills. For the second time, in other words, there occurs in Flaubert's text a *testamentary disruption* whose (untimely) timeliness will drive life forward. Once again, the arrival of salvation in testamentary form occurs in response to the inexorable movement of (life in) the imparfait.

Similarly, in Chapter 1, at a moment when the hopeless monotony of the imperfect threatens to overwhelm them, Bouvard and Pécuchet are saved by an untimely missive:

> La monotonie du bureau leur devenait odieuse. Continuellement le
> grattoir et la sandaraque, le même encrier, les mêmes plumes et les
> mêmes compagnons!…
>
> Quelle situation abominable! Et nul moyen d'en sortir! Pas même
> d'espérance!
>
> Un après-midi (c'était le 20 janvier 1839) Bouvard étant à son
> comptoir reçut une lettre, apportée par le facteur. (Flaubert, *Bouvard
> et Pécuchet* 62)

The letter, we learn, is an official letter from a lawyer informing Bouvard of his inheritance. The shock is twofold, for not only does salvation come unexpectedly, but it also comes in the form of a present tense that asserts a truth wholly incompatible with the past. "Je vous prie," reads the letter, "de vous rendre en mon étude, pour y prendre connaissance du testament de votre père naturel" (Flaubert, *Bouvard et Pécuchet* 63). In this legal summons, Bouvard comes into his inheritance by discovering his identity. The shock of this present, which transforms an uncle into a father, is what opens the future to new possibility.

Bouvard's father returns in the scene that precedes Bouvard and Pécuchet's suicide attempt:

Et chacun tirant à soi la boîte, le plateau tomba; une des tasses fut brisée, la dernière du beau service en porcelaine.

Bouvard pâlit. —"Continue! saccage! ne te gêne pas!"

—"Grand malheur, vraiment!"

—"Oui! un malheur! Je la tenais de mon père!"

—"Naturel" ajouta Pécuchet, en ricanant."

—"Ah! tu m'insultes!" (Flaubert, *Bouvard et Pécuchet* 323)

The spirit of Bouvard's father returns in a broken teacup. And it is perhaps this spirit that calls for a testament at this point of no return. What emerges from Bouvard and Pécuchet's botched suicide is thus not only the intolerable monotony of the imperfect tense, but also, simultaneously, the driving force of what is called a "testament."

III. Futurity

In the final pages of the novel, or in what would have been its transition to Bouvard and Pécuchet's Copy had Flaubert lived to write it, we find the traces of a shift from one notion of time to another. The move from time as teleology (Bouvard and Pécuchet's encyclopedic quest) to time as tautology (Bouvard and Pécuchet's Copy) was to have absorbed time itself into the endless stutter of the walkway and to have marked the final languishing of difference. Like a thermodynamic force, the Copy of Bouvard and Pécuchet would have "absorb[ed] all sorts of texts, and cruelly level[led] out the most heterogeneous of references, the most disparate of 'authors'" (Neefs 39). In the last known scenario for the end of the novel, it is understood that Bouvard and Pécuchet will copy everything indiscriminately: "Ils copient au hasard... cornets de tabac, vieux journaux, lettres perdues, affiches" (Flaubert, *Bouvard et Pécuchet* 442).

But a question remains: would Bouvard and Pécuchet, precisely by leveling out all textual accounts in their Copy, not have become, in some sense, the best, most faithful readers of Flaubert? Would their Copy not have taken Flaubert's style to its most literal (and perhaps modern) extreme by stringing heterogeneous things together and thereby arriving at a terribly ironic understanding of Flaubert's style, a style in which "toutes les parties de la réalité sont converties en une même substance, aux vastes surfaces, d'un miroitement monotone... Tout ce qui était différent a été converti et absorbé" (Proust, *Contre Sainte-Beuve* 201)?

But before the particular story of Bouvard and Pécuchet can come to an end, indeed before the Copy can be given its final and quasi-narrative form, Flaubert himself will come to an untimely end. *Bouvard et Pécuchet* remains suspended in a state of literal incompletion. Guy de Maupassant, Flaubert's disciple and protégé who will tend both to the body of Flaubert and to the eight-inch pile of notes left behind for the second volume of *Bouvard et Pécuchet*, sees an intimate connection between the writing of the book and the death of the man:

> [L]'œuvre... était de celles qu'on n'achève point. Un livre pareil mange un homme, car nos forces sont limitées et notre effort ne peut être infini. Flaubert écrivit deux or trois fois à ses amis: "J'ai peur que la terminaison de l'homme n'arrive avant celle du livre—ce serait une belle fin de chapitre."
>
> Ainsi qu'il l'avait écrit, il est tombé, un matin, *foudroyé* par le travail, comme un Titan trop audacieux qui aurait voulu monter trop haut. (GM 286, my emphasis)

But the last word of *Bouvard et Pécuchet*, Maupassant concedes, is missing —

> Ce surprenant édifice de science... devait avoir un couronnement, une conclusion, une justification éclatante. Après ce réquisitoire formidable, l'auteur avait entassé une *foudroyante* provision de preuves, le dossier des sottises cueillies chez les grands hommes. (GM 298, my emphasis)

The last word is missing, unless, that is to say, "foudroyant" is the last word, for it is Maupassant's chosen word to describe Flaubert's end: "Puis, j'ai vu, au dernier jour, étendu sur un large divan, un grand mort au cou gonflé, à la gorge rouge, terrifiant comme un colosse *foudroyé*" (GM 329, my emphasis).

"Foudroyé" as one is struck down by lightning, but also "ébahi," dumbfounded, as one is dumbfounded by a work of art according to Flaubert. Although Flaubert's notes and scenarios may indicate that the Copy's lists and enumerations were to be the final result of Bouvard and Pécuchet's encyclopedic quest, it would be wrong to read this projected finality as closure. For a bit of material irony slips in to the novel to ensure that this striving remains *permanently* heterogeneous to the recuperative force of the "trottoir roulant." Flaubert's death, one might say, imposes itself as the decisive textual excess in terms of which his "trottoir roulant" delivers up a terribly ironic and non-figurative blank. Although this blank is immediately recuperated by the editor—"Ici s'arrête le manuscrit de Gustave Flaubert" (Flaubert, *Bouvard et Pécuchet* 409)—one thing is clear: the shift from a teleological to a tautological model of time in *Bouvard et Pécuchet*, from the impersonal narrative of the first ten chapters to the eight-inch pile of notes, lists, citations of the virtual second volume literally, comes to us as a testamentary disruption, as a narrative blank monumentalized by an editorial present: "Ici s'arrête."

This performative utterance registers an event: "Ici" marks the spot, the blank, the space in Chapter 10 where the "trottoir roulant" literally encounters a ghostly present, namely the "posthumous present" of Flaubert's final notes for *Bouvard et Pécuchet*:

> Bonne idée nourrie en secret par chacun d'eux. Ils se la dissimulent—De temps à autre, ils sourient, quand elle leur vient;—puis se la communiquent simultanément: copier.
> Confection du bureau à double pupitre...
> Achat de registres—et d'ustensiles, sandaraque, grattoirs, etc.
> Ils s'y mettent. (414)

The book that is Flaubert's testament ends in a present tense whose power lies in the very unexpectedness of its occurrence. Let me suggest here that this posthumous present, the power of death as it imposes itself on every reader of *Bouvard et Pécuchet*, constitutes a terribly ironic event of difference in the midst of a story of indifferentiation. A difference (the space and time of a death) emerges here from the shock of the present tense. The relentless force of indifferentiation of Flaubert's "trottoir roulant" leaves us not with a body, in the end, but with the event of a death; it leaves us not with a death described in realistic terms, but with the living force of a testament. And one cannot help but wonder whether the event of this posthumous present is not already the language of futurity— what Mallarmé will call "la disparition élocutoire du poète, qui cède l'initiative aux mots" (Mallarmé 211).

Works Cited

Barthes, Roland. *Œuvres complètes III*. Paris: Éditions du Seuil, 1995.

Brombert, Victor. *The Novels of Flaubert*. Princeton: Princeton UP, 1966.

Flaubert, Gustave. *Bouvard et Pécuchet*. Ed. Claudine Gothot-Mersch. Paris: Gallimard, 1979.

_____. *Bouvard and Pécuchet*. Trans. A. J. Krailsheimer. New York: Penguin Books, 1976.

_____. *Correspondance*. Eds. René Dumesnil, Jean Pommier & Claude Digeon. 9 vols. Paris: Conard, 1926–1933. [CC]

_____. *Correspondance*. Eds. René Dumesnil, Jean Pommier & Claude Digeon. 4 vols. supplement. Paris: Conard, 1954. [S]

_____. *Correspondance*. Ed. Jean Bruneau. 4 vols. Paris: Gallimard, 1973–1998. [CB]

_____. *Correspondance Gustave Flaubert-George Sand*. Ed. Alphonse Jacobs. Paris: Flammarion, 1981. [GS]

_____. *Correspondance Gustave Flaubert-Ivan Tourguéniev*. Ed. Alexandre Zviguilsky. Paris: Flammarion, 1989. [IT]

_____. *Correspondance Gustave Flaubert-Guy de Maupassant*. Ed.Yvan Leclerc. Paris: Flammarion, 1993. [GM]

_____. *L'Éducation sentimentale*. Ed. Claudine Gothot-Mersch. Paris: Flammarion, 1985.

Gothot-Mersch, Claudine. "Introduction." *Bouvard et Pécuchet.* By Gustave Flaubert. Paris: Gallimard, 1979.

Kant, Immanuel. *The Conflict of the Faculties*. Trans. Mary J. Gregor. Lincoln: U of Nebraska P, 1979.

Mallarmé, Stéphane. *Œuvres complètes II*. Ed. Bertrand Marchal. Paris: Gallimard, 2003.

Neefs, Jacques. "De Flaubert à Pérec." *Théorie - Littérature - Enseignement* 5 (1987): 35–47.

Proust, Marcel. *Écrits sur l'art*. Ed. Jérôme Picon. Paris: Flammarion, 1999.

_____. *Contre Sainte-Beuve*. Paris: Gallimard, 1954.

Sartre, Jean-Paul. *L'Idiot de la famille*. 3 vols. Paris: Gallimard, 1971–1972.

Thibaudet, Albert. *Sur Baudelaire, Flaubert et Morand*. Ed. Antoine Compagnon. Paris: Éditions Complexe, 1987.

Flaubert and Modernism: The Meaning of a Book about Nothing

Anthony J. Cascardi

Among the most vexing questions of literary criticism, and indeed of aesthetics more generally, is periodization. In times past, one could construct the concept of a "period" in literature or art on the basis of a temporal delimitation (often by reference to a specific century or even a generation) or by reference to shared stylistic and formal markers. The late music critic Charles Rosen, for example, wrote books both about the "Classical Style" and the "Romantic Generation." One could understand "classical" (more accurately, "neoclassical") as referring both to a period that invoked ancient Greek and Rome and to a set of aesthetic preferences that manifested themselves in Augustan literature in English, in the plays of Corneille and Racine in French drama, and the "Directoire" or "Empire" style in architecture and the decorative arts. In a similar fashion, the term "baroque" could be regarded as having a significance that reached across a particular historical era, but that also referenced a set of aesthetic features marking a recognizable style (including particular kinds of ornamentation, a predilection for elaborate tropes, for Latinate syntax, and the like). And yet all these associations beg the question of the specific connection between a period as *historical* and a period as *aesthetic*. Additionally, they say nothing about the status of any individual work and the "period" to which it may belong, or vice-versa, about the notion of a "period" and the set of works from which its features are presumably imputed. The largely discredited notion of a *Zeitgeist* was once invoked as a way to address these questions, yet it grew discredited precisely because it was recognized as a question-begging term, i.e., one that had no grounding except in the very things it was supposed to explain. Indeed, it was only with the turn toward various forms of "deep structure" accounts in historical approaches to literature and the arts (e.g., Marxism, psychoanalysis) that critics became interested in grappling with these questions in a systematic way.

Of all the "periods" that one might contend with, modernism is especially complex, and perhaps unique. At its root stands a notion—the "modern"—which, as a term, has a history that reaches back as far as the fifth century CE. Needless to say, perhaps, identifying the "modern" with something this broad and diffuse may also render it useless, at least as a critical historical category. To hinge any account of "modern*ism*" on it would be to introduce more confusion into an already confused landscape of terms. If we wish to think of "modernism" as an intensification of the historical reality of whatever is modern or, as I would argue, as the modern brought to aesthetic self-consciousness, then we need a much clearer lens by which to view that history. And yet this is easier said than done. Even while cordoning off "ancient" motions of modernity, the kind of historical delimitation that would identify modernism with an understanding of modernity as it was expressed, e.g., by the writers and artists of the early twentieth century avant-gardes, is itself subject to a kind of historical "creep," one that inevitably discovers some earlier antecedent for whatever beginning moment is posited for it, and that consequently ends up moving the beginnings of modernity back from the early twentieth century to the nineteenth, and from there to the Enlightenment in eighteenth century, and then still farther back, to the "early modern" period (the sixteenth and seventeenth centuries). This historical regression has no clear end, except perhaps at a line of demarcation drawn at some other fathomless historical divide, such as the one that distinguishes the Renaissance from the Middle Ages. I signal these risks because it would be all too easy to think that the conjuncture announced in the title of this essay—the nexus of Flaubert and modernism—is meant to claim some kind of historical priority for Flaubert, i.e., to argue that he *anticipated* modernism, that he "got there" before many of the canonically recognized modernists or "high modernists" (e.g., Joyce and Woolf) did, or that his works contain the germ (or more) of things that were later to find much fuller expression in what remains a vexing conjuncture.

Whatever Flaubert's position and role, the "modernity" on which modernism relies was different from other historical periods not just by virtue of any "objective" set of factors, but by the way in which it was constituted. Specifically, modernity was distinctive among historical periods in establishing itself on the basis of its self-conception. A period like the Renaissance did not describe itself in order to validate itself as a distinctively new moment in time. The same is true of whatever we call "classical," "baroque," etc. Modernity was, by contrast, constructed in large measure on the basis of its own claims, claims to be *new*. This is the process that Hans Blumenberg described as "historical self-assertion." This is to say that neither "modernity" nor "modernism" was fashioned descriptively and *post hoc*. Rather, the force of these crucial terms—"modernity" and "modernism"—derives in substantial measure from two related sources: first, from the self-declared interest in making a break with the historical past, and second from a revolutionary ideology that had its deepest roots, in France at least, in the social and political changes precipitated by the revolutions of 1789 and 1848. Rather than locate the "roots" of literary modernism in Flaubert and rather than attempt an argument that would make a historical claim about the beginnings of modernism in relation to a relatively long view of what modernity was, attending to the conjuncture of historical self-assertion and the hopes that were planted by these revolutions can deepen a set of insights into the relationship between aesthetics and history, i.e., between a particular set of works and the historical world to which they relate.

My argument is that Flaubert presents an especially complex—some would say "modern" or "modernist"—version of that relationship. On the one hand, Flaubert's work can be understood by reference to a set of concrete historical developments, ones recognizable "objectively" as modern: the emergence of the bourgeoisie, the transformation of daily urban life (e.g., in Paris through the efforts of Haussmann) along increasingly rational lines, the gradual secularization of culture, and a set of changes in what could broadly be described as the "moral" domain. These changes could be characterized both as providing increased opportunities for freedom and as a weakening of the moral compass. Yet on the other hand, Flaubert's work refuses to be placed in any position that would relativize it to the historical "world" that provides its context. Indeed, there are ways in which his work is emphatically opposed to the very historical conditions in which it found itself situated. But neither did Flaubert imagine a return to the past, which in his writing is clearly gone for good. By virtue of this complex position vis-à-vis history, his work stakes out a peculiar role for art, one that shifts the ground of questions about the temporal boundaries and stylistic markers of any given period and, by way of asking about the relationship *between* individual works and their social and historical contexts, goes on to valorize those elements that are not wholly reducible to contextual factors. While Flaubert's work is, of course, thoroughly "historical" in the sense that it is inconceivable without the broad developments mentioned above, it is also committed to its independence, i.e., to the "autonomy" of art. And yet there is another turn of the screw to me made: "autonomous" art is only ever just ideologically autonomous; it requires a history to be refused, and that history is always particular.

The phrase in which Flaubert himself best and most famously captures his commitment to the autonomy of art is in a letter to Louise Colet from 1852. This is the letter where Flaubert expresses the often-cited desire to write a book "sur rien," or as he says more specifically, to write a book "sans attache extérieure." As he explains in this letter, the writing of *La Tentation de Saint Antoine* had allowed him to go remarkably far in that direction, though obviously not far enough toward his ultimate desire: its subject afforded considerable freedom and allowed him to pursue his stylistic ambitions with nearly complete abandon: "[Dans *Saint Antoine*] prenant un sujet où j'étais entièrement libre comme lyrisme, mouvements, désordonnements, je me trouvais alors bien dans ma nature et je n'avais qu'à aller. Jamais je ne retrouverai des éperdûments de style comme je m'en suis donné là pendant dix-huit grands mois" (January 16, 1852; Flaubert had completed a first version of *La Tentation* in 1849, but continued working on it for years; it was first published in its final form in 1874). Yet the extraordinary length of time Flaubert spent working on the *Tentation* is one indication of the difficulties that such a degree of freedom presented. Indeed, Flaubert himself famously commented on *les affres du style* (letter to Louise Colet, January 14, 1852). Flaubert's frustrations notwithstanding, the wider context in which he explains his desire is worth quoting at greater length, since it helps flesh out what a "subject-less" work might imply for the way we think about the status and the value of literature—historically, stylistically, formally, and materially:

> Ce qui me semble beau, ce que je voudrais faire, c'est un livre sur rien, un livre sans attache extérieure, qui se tiendrait de lui-même par la force interne de son style, comme la terre sans être soutenue se tient en l'air, un livre qui n'aurait presque pas de sujet ou du moins où le sujet serait presque invisible, si cela se peut. Les oeuvres les plus belles sont celles où il y a le moins de matière; plus l'expression se rapproche de la pensée, plus le mot colle dessus et disparaît, plus c'est beau. Je crois que l'avenir de l'Art est dans ces voies... La forme, en devenant habile, s'atténue; elle quitte toute liturgie, toute règle, toute mesure; elle abandonne l'épique pour le roman, le vers pour la prose; elle ne se connaît plus d'orthodoxie et est libre comme chaque volonté qui la produit. Cet affranchissement de la matérialité se retrouve en tout et les gouvernements l'ont suivi, depuis les despotismes orientaux jusqu'aux socialismes futurs. (January 16, 1852).

The concluding words of this passage are a telling indication of Flaubert's will to aesthetic self-creation, but also have implications for the relationship between Flaubert's work and history. The ideal of a "freedom of form" that would respond only to the will of its creator would stand apart from or beyond history: verse yields to prose, epic to novel, and indeed form eventually leaves behind everything that is associated with the past (e.g., liturgy, rule, measure), such that it is responsive only to the will of the creative spirit (Flaubert). At the same time, the ideal, "subject-less" work would also try to shed all material traces (so as to contain *le moins de matière*), such that not even language, no matter how immaterial, would intervene between thought and expression.

The latter claim and the accompanying observations that Flaubert makes about prose and verse, epic and novel, are uncannily reminiscent of Hegel's *Ästhetik* (*Lectures on Aesthetics*). On the one hand, Hegel valued art as the "sensuous" manifestation of the highest form of truth (the "Idea"). And yet in Hegel's view, it was art's very materiality that impeded it from becoming the highest of all possible manifestations of that Idea. Not surprisingly, then, Hegel's scheme of the arts accorded the highest place to poetry because it is the least bound to physical materials:

> Poetry... has as its general principle spirituality and therefore it no longer turns to heavy matter as such in order, like architecture, to form it symbolically into an analogous environment for the inner life, or, like sculpture, to shape into real matter the natural form, as a spatial external object, belonging to the spirit; on the contrary, it expresses directly for spirit's apprehension the spirit itself with all its imaginative and artistic conceptions... Poetry, to a still ampler extent than painting and music, can comprise in the form of the inner life not only the inner consciousness but also the special and particular details of what exists externally. (960–1)

These remarks about poetry are worth bearing in mind for two reasons. First, they provide a useful way of calibrating what Flaubert did and did not mean to say in writing about the ideal of a work without subject or matter (materiality). And second, they provide a strong point of contrast with some of the most influential theses about modernism in the arts, views most often associated with the criticism of Clement Greenberg. Greenberg wrote principally about the visual arts (and especially about painting), but his views were broadly influential, as witnessed, for example, in Stanley Cavell's approach to the techniques of film in *The World Viewed* (see especially Greenberg, "Modernist Painting" 85, and Greenberg, "Newer Laocoön" 23–41). Greenberg posited that modernism in the arts developed not so much in relation to historical factors, but rather through its own process of self-reflection, extending the work that Kant's project of critique had begun in philosophy to the aesthetic domain. In the visual arts, "self-reflection" meant coming to grips with the basic conditions of painting, conditions that had been obscured by convention—attending to the flatness of the painted canvas, for example, rather than to the illusion of depth and figure that could be created by the techniques of artificial perspective. What modernism showed, Greenberg argued, was not anything that was unique and irreducible about art in general, but "that which was unique and irreducible in each particular art" ("Modernist Painting" 86). Flatness was one of painting's most basic conditions, yet it had gone unacknowledged for as long as painting was committed to using the canvas to create the illusion of three-dimensional, sculpture-like images. In "Towards a Newer Laocoön," Greenberg had argued that lurking behind painting's ambition to be like sculpture, and limiting its ability to come to terms with its own essential conditions, was the desire to be like literature, which was, relatively speaking, medium-light (23–41). To be sure, Greenberg's objections to the literary model for painting has a number of antecedents within modernism, including Cézanne, who explicitly voiced his dislike for literary painting (Kendall 304). He also saw literature as having fewer conventions to eliminate than painting: "The process of self-purification appears to have come to a halt in literature simply because the latter has fewer conventions to eliminate before having arrived at those essential to it. In music, the same process, if not halted, seems to have slowed down because it is already so far advanced, most of the expendable conventions of music having proved relatively easy to isolate" (Greenberg, "American-type Painting" 208). While these last claims may be disputed—not least by the example of Flaubert, who was keenly aware of all the conventions that literature involves—the notion that modernism strives to suppress those elements in art that are fundamentally literary in nature is important, since it would imply a movement of literature against itself. This is indeed a process that one sees across Flaubert's work: an effort to write literature that is fundamentally opposed to the conventions that literature would seem to presuppose—formally, stylistically, and also historically. Indeed, it is this very opposition to its own conventions, conventions that were transmitted from the past and that had re-rooted themselves in the nineteenth century, which marks Flaubert's work as "modernist."

In a chapter entitled "The Destruction of the Subject" in his book on Manet, Georges Bataille offered one of the most memorable statements of the exhaustion of the aesthetic conventions inherited from the past, a statement about the need for an aesthetic revolution that could also be taken as illuminating a basic condition of Flaubert's work:

> There came a day... when this vast didactic structure—erected and renewed time and again in the form of castles, churches, palaces and works of art calculated to awe the masses and bend them beneath the yoke of authority—lost its power to sway. It fell to pieces, its message was shown up as mere grandiloquence, and the once obedient masses turned away in search of something else... Reaction against the stale and conventional, which lies at the source of this disorder, is a recurrent phenomenon in the history of art (and in history in general). But we are prone to overlook the fact for the simple reason that, until recently, art history had been the history of the *fine* arts, of *beautiful* works of art, rarely if ever dealing with that fundamental divergence of outlook which opposes present-day art to that of the past. (38, 42)

And yet in extending this argument to Flaubert, one crucially important fact needs to be added: that Flaubert had witnessed the re-establishment of new social structures following the collapse of the order of the past—a new structure revolving around the bourgeoisie—and found it to be equally distasteful, if not even more objectionable than anything that had preceded it. Since this new social reality was very much Flaubert's world, his task involved a resistance to it and not just a resistance to the conventions of the past. The suppression of the "subject" that is expressed in his desire to write a book about nothing, which goes beyond the "destruction" of the subject that Bataille described in Manet, is bound up with a resistance to the fact that the bourgeoisie had in fact become the "subject" of history.

Flaubert builds his version of modernism out of a reaction to the particular social forms in which the promise of the "new" had been realized, or rather, breached—namely, in such a way as to pre-empt the possibility of there being anything truly new at all. No wonder, then, that he is suspicious of any effort to rekindle a revolutionary spirit, if the best that might emerge from it would be slavish adherence to ideology. A representative passage from *L'Education Sentimentale* (*Sentimental Education*) captures this point:

> [Sénécal] connaissait Mably, Morelly, Fourier, Saint-Simon, Comte, Cabet, Louis Blanc, la lourde charretée des écrivains socialistes, ceux qui réclament pour l'humanité le niveau des casernes, ceux qui voudraient la diverter dans un lupanar ou la plier sur un comptoir; et, du mélange de tout cela, il s'était fait un idéal de démocratie vertueuse, ayant lae double aspect d'une métaire et d'une filature, une sorte de Lacédémone américain où l'individu n'existerait que pour server la Société, plus omnipotente, absolue, infaillible et divine que les Grands Lamas et les Nabuchodonosors. Il n'avait pas un doute sur l'éventualité prochaine de cette conception; et tout ce qu'il jugeait lui être hostile, Sénécal s'acharnait dessus, avec des raisonnements de géomètre et une bonne foi d'inquisiteur. (57)

Flaubert's anti-bourgeois pronouncements are legendary, in part because he expressed them so shamelessly (e.g., in a letter of 1846, where he wrote to Louise Colet: "Quelle atroce invention que celle du bourgeois, n'est-ce pas? Pourquoi est-il sur la terre, et qu'y fait-il, le misérable? Pour moi, je ne sais pas à quoi peuvent passer leur temps ici les gens qui ne s'occupent pas d'art. La manière dont ils vivent est un problème," September 22, 1846). It is a sentiment Flaubert repeated throughout his career (e.g., in a letter to George Sand: "Axiome: la haine du Bourgeois est le commencement de la vertu. Moi, je comprends dans ce mot de «bourgeois» les bourgeois en blouse comme les bourgeois en redingote," May 10, 1867).

These views remain shocking despite the fact that they have become a typical stance of high art. The more interesting question is how Flaubert incorporated this antipathy into the project to write a book "about nothing." The answer, as witnessed by *Madame Bovary*, involved the writing of a book whose "subject" was not *literally* null, but which was otherwise vacant, banal, and uninteresting, and whose emptiness was all the more striking because of the easy appeal of "romantic" fantasies to the novel's heroine, as in the famous passage where she marvels at having a lover, and where the narrator describes her as a kind of female Quixote:

> Elle se répétait: "J'ai un amant! un amant!" se délectant à cette idée comme à celle d'une autre puberté qui lui serait survenue. Elle allait donc posséder enfin ces joies de l'amour, cette fièvre du bonheur dont elle avait désespéré. Elle entrait dans quelque chose de merveilleux où tout serait passion, extase, délire; une immensité bleuâtre l'entourait, les sommets du sentiment étincelaient sous sa pensée, et l'existence ordinaire n'apparaissait qu'au loin, tout en bas, dans l'ombre, entre les intervalles de ces hauteurs.
>
> Alors elle se rappela les héroïnes des livres qu'elle avait lus, et la légion lyrique de ces femmes adultères se mit à chanter dans sa mémoire avec des voix de sœurs qui la charmaient. Elle devenait elle-même comme une partie véritable de ces imaginations et réalisait la longue rêverie de sa jeunesse. (Flaubert, *Madame Bovary* 225)

Emma Bovary's state of mind as reflected in this passage might be called "absorptive" in the sense in which Michael Fried used that term (see Fried, *Absorption and Theatricality*). Absorption is part and parcel of her love affairs and involves a kind of reading she shares with the most "literary" of her lovers, Léon:

> "On ne songe à rien, continuait-il, les heures passent. On se promène immobile dans des pays que l'on croit voir, et votre pensée, s'enlaçant à la fiction, se joue dans les détails ou poursuit le contour des aventures. Elle se mêle aux personnages; il semble que c'est vous qui palpitez sous leurs costumes."
>
> "C'est vrai! c'est vrai! disait-elle." (Flaubert, *Madame Bovary* 114–15)

Flaubert nonetheless remains very much on the outside of these states, which he would associate with the desires cultivated by market-driven literary tastes that encouraged mindless reading. As he wrote to Colet in 1853 about Alexandre Dumas, the popular author of works including *Les Trois Mousquetaires (The Three Musketeers)* and *Le Comte de Monte-Cristo (The Count of Monte Cristo)*:

> "D'où vient le prodigieux succès des romans de Dumas? C'est qu'il ne faut pour les lire aucune initiation, l'action en est amusante. On se distrait donc pendant qu'on les lit. Puis, le livre fermé, comme aucune impression ne vous reste et que tout cela a passé comme de l'eau claire, *on retourne à ses affaires.* Charmant!" (June 20, 1853; italics in the original).

The taste is one that Emma Bovary shares: "'J'adore les histoires qui se suivent tout d'une haleine, où l'on a peur. Je déteste les héros communs et les sentiments tempérés, comme il y en a dans la nature'" (Flaubert, *Madame Bovary* 57). However, she is married to the epitome of the commonplace:

> La conversation de Charles était plate comme un trottoir de rue, et les idées de tout le monde y défilaient dans leur costume ordinaire, sans exciter d'émotion, de rire ou de rêverie. Il n'avait jamais été curieux, disait-il, pendant qu'il habitait Rouen, d'aller voir au théâtre les acteurs de Paris. Il ne savait ni nager, ni faire des armes, ni tirer le pistolet, et il ne put, un jour, lui expliquer un terme d'équitation qu'elle avait rencontré dans un roman. (57)

Though she struggles to find an escape from banality, she does not recognize that she is herself one of the commonplace figures she professes to detest.

It was similarly Flaubert's resistance to this "bourgeois" aesthetic that drove him to create various impediments to reading, to muddy the water and halt the flow of the plot, sometimes by long phrases that function as extended close-ups and that concomitantly generate a sense of distortion. According to Pierre Bourdieu in *The Rules of Art*, Flaubert's many notable stylistic innovations—including the development of "impersonal" narration and the invention of free indirect discourse—can be attributed to his ongoing efforts to find his place with respect to the antagonistic relations between art and money, bourgeois pragmatism and romantic idealism. Absent any other foundation for values, the desire to resist bourgeois existence leads Flaubert to a modernist aesthetic that distances itself from the energy of life and that, in the detachment of art from life, finds its principal basis for value in art itself. Yet the disaffection of modern life leads many of Flaubert's characters in a different direction, either impelling them to romantic ideals (some of which, as the episode of the ball at La Vaubyessard in *Madame Bovary* shows, lead them toward dreams of aristocratic indulgence), or disinclining them toward any excitement or originality at all, like Bouvard and Pécuchet, who live as prisoners of the *idée reçue*, content in their status as (mere) copyists. Roland Barthes called them "copiers of codes" (Barthes 98). Objections to Bourdieu's strictly sociological approach to literature notwithstanding, the fact remains that these relations were deeply problematic for Flaubert, who could envy the financial success of a writer of bourgeois taste like Dumas and yet adhere to aesthetic principles designed to resist it. This was a typical predicament of the bourgeoisie. As Eugene Goodheart wrote of Flaubert in *The Failure of Criticism*, "though liberty, fraternity, and equality belong to the heroic past of the bourgeoisie, the ideal is moneymaking, the cash nexus. The poverty of idealization in bourgeois life makes the sensitive bourgeois vulnerable to self-hatred" (Goodheart 138–9).

Nonetheless, the project of resistance to the bourgeoisie and its literary tastes poses serious challenges. Some critics would argue that this was why Flaubert's writing *must have* and *can only have* an aesthetic basis. To push as far as might be necessary in the direction of aesthetic autonomy, however, puts pressure not just on bourgeois ideals, but on the core principles of intelligibility that have conventionally supported signification in fiction. All Flaubert's strictly *narrative* inventions move in this direction, but his work with visual scenes, ones that resemble painting, or directly invoke paintings, is equally remarkable in this regard. Here the Greenbergian notion that modernist painting had to revoke literature needs to be re-thought, for literature had long adhered to principles that had, in fact, set painting as its ideal (as Horace put it in his so-called *Ars Poetica*: "ut pictura poiesis"). The reveries of Emma

Bovary conjure moments from fiction that she "enters" in her imagination because they are painterly. And yet there are scenes that Flaubert himself "paints" as if to demonstrate just how difficult it is for his bourgeois characters to overcome their own ordinariness—so difficult, in fact, that anything "extraordinary" seems to appear without anticipation or causal precedent. The following passage from *Madame Bovary* is representative of the way in which the ordinariness of an already ordinary scene is further flattened in the light of something extraordinary (the invitation to visit La Vaubyessard) that is disconnected from it and comes nearly "out of nowhere" (see Sayeau, *Against the Event*). Furthermore, that event is presaged by a purely emotional response to a scene that makes a painterly collage of colors and light appear as if it has no sense:

> Dans l'avenue, un jour vert rabattu par le feuillage éclairait la mousse rase qui craquait doucement sous ses pieds. Le soleil se couchait; le ciel était rouge entre les branches, et les troncs pareils des arbres plantés en ligne droite semblaient une colonnade brune se détachant sur un fond d'or; une peur la prenait, elle appelait Djali, s'en retournait vite à Tostes par la grande route, s'affaissait dans un fauteuil, et de toute la soirée ne parlait pas. Mais, vers la fin de septembre, quelque chose d'extraordinaire tomba dans sa vie: elle fut invitée à la Vaubyessard, chez le marquis d'Andervilliers. (Flaubert, *Madame Bovary* 63)

What can a writer do to resist the same temptations that lure his characters? One answer, which is crucial to an understanding of Flaubert as a modernist, is to confront his characters with illegible objects and, in particular, with paintings that are not manifestly "about" anything except the materiality of their own colored surfaces. There are passages in Flaubert where paintings appear simply as material things, as part of the furnishings of a room, and where the images on their surfaces are nothing more than a meaningless blur, as in *L'Education Sentimentale* when Frédéric Moreau enters Pellerin's studio: "On remarquait en entrant chez lui deux grands tableaux, où les premiers tons, posés çà et la, faisaient sur la toile blanche des taches de brun, de rouge et de bleu. Un réseau de lignes à la craie s'étendait pardessus, comme les mailles vingt fois reprises d'un filet; il était même impossible d'y rien comprendre" (21). (Reed discusses this passage and one other like it; see Reed 66. He goes on to argue that the *tache* or "stain" epitomizes what Flaubert came to understand about the "book about nothing," 71). An example like this could be taken as an instance of what a "painting about nothing" might be, and that in turn can serve as a surrogate for Flaubert's ideal of a subject-less book. In spite of the fact that Flaubert dreamed of a book *sur rien*, his work demonstrates the difficulty of resisting the obligation to "make sense" in a legible way. This is a task that painting found easier to accomplish, as it moved to become one with its own materiality. And yet painting—painting described—enables Flaubert to introduce an opacity that impedes the customary procedures of reading and interpretation on which his bourgeois readers were (and are) apt to rely.

Works Cited

Barthes, Roland. *S/Z*. Trans. Richard Miller. New York: Hill & Wang, 1974.

Bataille, Georges. *Manet*. New York: Skira, 1983.

Blumenberg, Hans. *The Legitimacy of the Modern Age*. Trans. Robert M. Wallace. Cambridge, MA: MIT Press, 1985.

Bourdieu, Pierre. *The Rules of Art*. Trans. Susan Emanuel. Stanford: Stanford UP, 1996.

Cascardi, Anthony J. "The Value of Criticism and the Project of Modernism." Ed. Rónán McDonald. *The Values of Literary Studies*. Cambridge: Cambridge UP, 2015. 13–26.

Cavell, Stanley. *The World Viewed: Reflections on the Ontology of Film*. Cambridge, MA: Harvard UP, 1979.

Fried, Michael. *Absorption and Theatricality*. Berkeley: U of California P, 1980.

Flaubert, Gustave. *Correspondance, Anneé 1846 (*Édition Louis Conard*)*. Ed. Danielle Girard and Yvan Leclerc. University of Rouen, 2003. Web. August 2015. <http://flaubert.univ-rouen.fr/correspondance/conard/outils/1846.htm>.

_____. *Correspondance*: *Anneé 1852* (Édition Louis Conard). Ed. Danielle Girard and Yvan Leclerc. University of Rouen, 2003. Web.

August 2015. <http://flaubert.univ-rouen.fr/correspondance/conard/outils/1852.htm>.

_____. *Correspondance*: *Anneé 1867 (*Édition Louis Conard*)*. Ed. Danielle Girard and Yvan Leclerc. University of Rouen, 2003. Web. August 2015.<http://flaubert.univ- rouen.fr/correspondance/conard/outils/1867.htm>

_____. *L'Education Sentimentale. Œuvres complètes*, II. Paris: Seuil, 1964.

_____. *Madame Bovary. Œuvres complètes*. Paris: Louis Conard, 1921.

Goodheart, Eugene. *The Failure of Criticism*. Cambridge, MA: Harvard UP, 1978.

Greenberg, Clement. "American-type Painting." *Art and Culture: Critical Essays*. Boston: Beacon Press, 1961. 208–229.

_____. "Modernist Painting." *The Collected Essays and Criticism, IV: Modernism with a Vengeance, 1957–1969*. Ed. John O' Brian. Chicago: U of Chicago P, 1993. 85–93.

_____. "Towards a Newer Laocoön." *The Collected Essays and Criticism, I: Perceptions and Judgments, 1939–1944*. Ed. John O'Brian. Chicago: U of Chicago P, 1986. 23–41.

Hegel, Georg Wilhelm Friedrich. *Lectures on Aesthetics*. Trans. T. M. Knox. Oxford: Clarendon Press, 1975.

Kendall, Richard, ed. *Cézanne by Himself*. New Boston: Little, Brown, 1988.

Reed, Arden. *Manet, Flaubert, and the Emergence of Modernism*. Cambridge: Cambridge UP, 2003.

Rosen, Charles. *The Classical Style*. New York: Viking, 1971.

_____. *The Romantic Generation*. Cambridge MA: Harvard UP, 1995.

Sayeau, Michael. *Against the Event: The Everyday and the Evolution of Modernist Narrative*. Oxford: Oxford UP, 2013.

RESOURCES

Chronology of Gustave Flaubert's Life_____

1821	Gustave Flaubert is born on December 12 in Rouen, to Achille-Cléophas Flaubert, head surgeon at the Hôtel-Dieu in Rouen, and Anne-Justine-Caroline Flaubert, *née* Fleuriot. Gustave's elder brother, Achille, will follow their father into the medical profession.
1825	The servant Julie begins her work for the Flaubert family and becomes Gustave's nurse. She remains with the family until Gustave's death in 1880.
1830	Flaubert meets Ernest Chevalier, forming the first of many close friendships.
1832	Flaubert enrolls as a boarder at the Collège de Rouen. He is good at the subjects of literature and history.
1834	Flaubert finds a classmate in Louis Bouilhet, a future writer, and their close friendship flourishes from the mid-1840s to Bouilhet's death in 1869.
1835	Family holidays at Trouville, a seaside resort.
1836	Flaubert is attracted to Mme Élise Schlésinger at Trouville. Two years later, he will draw on this in his autobiographical story *Mémoires d'un fou*. This is also possibly the year in which he has sex with one of his mother's maidservants.
1837	*Le Colibri*, a magazine based in Rouen, brings out Flaubert's first published work.
1839	Flaubert writes *Smarh*, a mysterious work that looks forward to *La Tentation de saint Antoine*.

1840	Flaubert receives his *baccalauréat*. He travels in the Pyrenees and in Corsica. He has a liaison at Marseille with Eulalie Foucauld.
1841	Flaubert enrolls in the Paris Law Faculty during the fall, but continues to live at home.
1842	July: Flaubert moves to Paris. Autumn: he completes *Novembre,* another autobiographical story, and therefore something of a companion piece to *Mémoires d'un fou.* December: Flaubert passes his first-year law exams.
1843	Over 1842/43, Flaubert befriends the writer Maxime Du Camp; he also, in 1843, befriends the Schlésingers, and meets Victor Hugo. He commences the writing of the first novel bearing the title of *L'Éducation sentimentale.* The second novel of that name, published in 1869, is a different work, and NOT a "second version." August: Flaubert fails the second-year law exams.
1844	January: Flaubert suffers his first bout of epilepsy, which has also been described as his "recurring nervous illness." He abandons his law studies. June: his family move to Croisset, near Rouen.
1845	Travels in Italy and Switzerland. In Genoa, at the picture gallery of The Palazzo Balbi, Flaubert becomes fascinated by Brueghel's *The Temptation of Saint Anthony*, with implications for a future novel.
1846	Death of Flaubert's father and of his sister Caroline. Flaubert will raise her daughter, who is also called Caroline. He meets Louise Colet, his future lover and the recipient of many of his important letters, in which he discusses his artistic ideals. Flaubert is unhappy at the news that his friend Alfred Le Poittevin is getting married.

1847	Flaubert visits Brittany in the company of Du Camp, and writes about the trip in his *Par les champs et par les grèves*.
1848	February: Flaubert witnesses the Revolution in Paris. First rupture with Louise Colet. April: Flaubert is devastated by the death of his friend Alfred Le Poittevin.
1849	September: Flaubert reads the first version of *La Tentation de saint Antoine* to Du Camp and Bouilhet, who tell him to destroy it. November: Flaubert arrives in Alexandria with Du Camp via Marseille and Malta.
1850	With Du Camp, he travels in the Near- and Mid-East: Egypt (where he contracts syphilis), the Red Sea, the Holy Land, Beirut, Rhodes, Constantinople, Athens. This is the year of his notorious sexual encounter with the courtesan Kuchuk Hanem. He is also becoming increasingly bald and stout.
1851	Flaubert is in Sparta, the Peloponnese, Brindisi, Naples, Rome, Florence. By March, he is back in Croisset and begins writing *Madame Bovary*. He resumes his relationship with Louise Colet. December 2: Coup d'état of Louis-Napoléon Bonaparte, soon to become the Emperor Napoléon III.
1854	Final rupture with Louise Colet.
1855	Flaubert takes rooms in Paris.
1856	October: *Madame Bovary* is serialized in the *Revue de aris*. Flaubert starts to re-write *La Tentation de saint Antoine*.

1857	January: Prosecution of *Madame Bovary*; acquittal on February 7. The book appears in volume form. The priest of a parish neighboring Croisset bans his flock from reading the book. Autumn: Flaubert works on *Salammbô*. Winter: He visits Carthage.
1858	Flaubert continues his trip to Tunisia and Carthage in preparation for *Salammbô*; he is also in Algeria.
1862	November: publication of *Salammbô*.
1863	Flaubert begins his friendships with George Sand and the Russian novelist Ivan Turgenev; he meets the latter at the "dîners Magny." He also begins to attend the salon of Princess Mathilde Bonaparte, The niece of Napoléon I.
1864	Flaubert is presented to Napoléon III. Between this year and 1869, he works on *L'Éducation sentimentale*, the second and more celebrated novel with that title. During these years, he is residing most often in Paris and is out and about at Princess Mathilde's salon and at the "dîners Magny" in the company of other writers, such as the Goncourt brothers, Théophile Gautier, and Charles Sainte-Beuve.
1865	Flaubert travels in Germany.
1866	Flaubert is awarded the *Légion d'Honneur.*
1869	Publication of *L'Éducation sentimentale*. Flaubert mourns the deaths of Louis Bouilhet and Charles Sainte-Beuve.
1870	Flaubert mourns the death of Jules de Goncourt. Franco-Prussian War: Croisset is occupied by the Prussians; Flaubert moves to Rouen.

1871	Flaubert encounters Mme Schlésinger. Travels to Brussels and to England.
1872	April 6: death of Flaubert's mother. He completes the third version of *La Tentation de saint Antoine*.
1873	Flaubert feels increasingly lonely, despite his warm friendships with George Sand and Turgenev. He writes a play, *Le Candidat*.
1874	*Le Candidat* is a flop. Publication of the final version of *La Tentation de saint Antoine*. Flaubert is preparing his last novel, *Bouvard et Pécuchet*. Travels to Switzerland.
1875	Flaubert mentors the young Guy de Maupassant. Financial ruin of Ernest Commanville, the husband of his niece Caroline: this places Flaubert himself in serious financial difficulty. He starts writing "La Légende de saint Julien l'Hospitalier."
1876	March 8: Death of Louise Colet. June 8: Death of George Sand. Flaubert completes "La Légende de saint Julien l'Hospitalier," writes "Un cœur simple" and begins "Hérodias."
1877	Publication of *Trois contes*. Flaubert resumes work on *Bouvard et Pécuchet*, which he will never finish. During his last years, Flaubert's work is much celebrated, and he is not a total recluse. Nevertheless, he still feels lonely.
1879	Flaubert slips on ice and sustains an injury. Victor Hugo and other friends try to arrange a pension for him. He becomes supernumerary librarian at the Bibliothèque Mazarine.

1880	May 8: Flaubert dies suddenly at Croisset, reputedly of a cerebral hemorrhage, though this cause of death has been disputed; epilepsy has also been cited.
1880-81	Posthumous publication of *Bouvard et Pécuchet*.
1884-92	Publication of Flaubert's correspondence, though much censored by his niece.

Works by Gustave Flaubert

Un parfum à sentir (1836)

Rêve d'enfer (1836)

Mémoires d'un fou (1838)

Smarh (1839)

Novembre (1842)

Madame Bovary (1856)

Salammbô (1862)

L'Éducation sentimentale (1869)

Le Candidat (1874), play

La Tentation de saint Antoine (1874)

Trois contes: Un Cœur simple, La Légende de saint Julien l'Hospitalier, Hérodias (1877)

Bouvard et Pécuchet (1881), unfinished

Par les champs et par les grèves (1886), (also, *Voyage en Bretagne*)

Mémoires d'un fou (1901), written in 1838

Œuvres de jeunesse inédites (1910)

Dictionnaire des idées reçues (1913)

Premières œuvres (1914–1920), 4 vol.

Novembre (1928), written in 1842

Bibliomanie et autres textes 1836–1839 (1982)

Collected Editions

Œuvres complètes (1964), 2 vols. Paris: Scuil

Œuvres complètes (1971–76), 16 vols. Paris: Club de l'Honnête Homme

Œuvres complètes (2001), Vol. 1: *Œuvres de jeunesse*. Paris: Gallimard

Œuvres complètes (2013), Vol. 2. *1845–1851*. Paris: Gallimard

Œuvres complètes (2013), Vol. 3. *1851–1862*. Paris: Gallimard

Œuvres complètes (in preparation), Vol. 4. & Vol. 5. Paris: Gallimard

Correspondence

Correspondance (1973–2007), Vol. 5. Paris: Gallimard

Editor's note: Details of other editions can be found in the Works Cited section of each chapter in this volume.

Bibliography_____

The secondary literature on Flaubert is vast, and the following bibliography lists only book-length works that either have the name Flaubert in their titles or study his work at some length. Readers should be aware that there is also much excellent work on the writer in journals and in composite works, as well as in books on nineteenth-century French literature generally. The following bibliography should be used together with the works cited sections following each essay in the present work.

Readers are also recommended to consult the excellent select bibliographies in *A Gustave Flaubert Encyclopedia*, edited by Laurence M. Porter (Greenwood, 2001) and *The Cambridge Companion to Gustave Flaubert*, edited by Timothy Unwin (Cambridge University Press, 2004). See also David J. Colwell's *Bibliographic des études sur Gustave Flaubert*. 4 vols. (Egham: Runnymede: 1988–90).

Online resources for Flaubert studies are cited at the end of the following bibliography.

Addison, Claire. *Where Flaubert Lies: Chronology, Mythology, History.* Cambridge, England: Cambridge UP, 1996.

Amann, Elizabeth. *Importing* Madame Bovary: *The Politics of Adultery.* New York: Palgrave Macmillan, 2006.

Bancquart, Marie-Claire, ed. *Flaubert, la femme, la ville: Journee d'etudes.* Paris: Presses Universitaires de France, 1983.

Barnes, Hazel B. *Sartre and Flaubert.* Chicago: U of Chicago P, 1981.

Barnes, Julian. *Flaubert's Parrot.* London: Cape, 1984.

Baron, Scarlett. *"Strandentwining Cable": Joyce, Flaubert and Intertextuality.* Oxford: Oxford UP, 2011.

Bart, Benjamin F. *Flaubert.* Syracuse: Syracuse UP, 1967.

_____. ed. Madame Bovary *and the Critics.* New York: New York UP, 1966.

Berg, William J. & Laurey K. Martin. *Gustave Flaubert.* New York: Twayne, 1997.

Bernheimer, Charles. *Flaubert and Kafka: Studies in Psychopoetic Structure*. New Haven: Yale UP, 1982.

Bloom, Harold, ed. *Gustave Flaubert*. New York & Philadelphia: Chelsea House, 1988.

_____. *Emma Bovary*. New York & Philadelphia: Chelsea House, 1994.

Bourdieu, Pierre. *Les Règles de l'art: genèse et structure du champ littéraire*. Paris: Seuil, 1992.

Brombert, Victor. *The Novels of Flaubert*. Princeton: Princeton UP, 1966.

Brown, Frederick. *Flaubert: A Biography*. New York: Little, Brown & Company, 2006.

Bruneau, Jean. *Les Débuts littéraires de Gustave Flaubert, 1831–1845*. Paris: Armand Colin, 1962.

Butor, Michel. *Improvisations sur Flaubert*. Paris: La Différence, 1984.

Carlut, Charles. *La Correspondance de Flaubert: étude et répertoire critique*. Columbus: Ohio State UP, 1968.

Cascardi, Anthony J. *The Bounds of Reason: Cervantes, Dostoevsky, Flaubert*. New York: Columbia UP, 1986.

Collas, Ion K. *A Psychoanalytic Reading of* Madame Bovary. Geneva: Droz, 1985.

Conroy, Mark. *Modernism and Authority: Strategies of Legitimation in Flaubert and Conrad*. Baltimore: Johns Hopkins UP, 1985.

Culler, Jonathan. *Flaubert: The Uses of Uncertainty*. Ithaca: Cornell UP, 1974.

De Biasi, Pierre-Marc. *Flaubert: les secrets de "l'homme-plume."* Paris: Hachette, 1995.

_____. *Gustave Flaubert: l'homme-plume*. Paris: Découvertes Gallimard, 2002. [With color illustrations.]

Debray-Genette, Raymonde & Jacques Neefs, eds. *L'Œuvre de l'œuvre: études sur la correspondance de Flaubert*. Saint-Denis: Presses Universitaires de Vincennes, 1993.

Diamond, Marie J. *Flaubert: The Problem of Aesthetic Discontinuity*. London & New York: National University Publications, 1975.

Donaldson-Evans, Mary. *Madame Bovary at the Movies: Adaptation, Ideology, Context*. Amsterdam: Rodopi, 1994.

Donatio, Eugenio. *The Script of Decadence: Essays on the Fictions of Flaubert and the Poetics of Romanticism.* Oxford & New York: Oxford UP, 1993.

Douchin, Jacques-Louis. *La Vie érotique de Flaubert.* Paris: Carrère, 1984.

Dufour, Philippe. *Flaubert et le pignouf: essai sur la représentation romanesque du langage.* Saint-Denis: Presses Universitaires de Vincennes, 1993.

Durr, Volker. *Flaubert's "Salammbô": The Ancient Orient as a Political Allegory of Nineteenth-Century France.* New York: Peter Lang, 2002.

Fairlie, Alison. *Flaubert:* Madame Bovary. London: Arnold, 1962.

_____. *Imagination and Language: Collected Essays on Constant, Baudelaire, Nerval and Flaubert.* Cambridge: Cambridge UP, 1981.

Fauvel, Daniel & Yvan Leclerc, eds. Salammbô *de Flaubert: histoire, fiction.* Paris: Champion, 1999.

Fried, Michael. *Flaubert's "Gueuloir":* On Madame Bovary *and* Salammbô. New Haven: Yale UP, 2012.

Gans, Eric. *The Discovery of Illusion: Flaubert's Early Works, 1835–1837.* Berkeley: U of California P, 1971.

_____. Madame Bovary: *The End of Romance.* Boston: G. K. Hall, 1989.

Ginsburg, Michal Peled. *Flaubert Writing: A Study in Narrative Strategies.* Stanford: Stanford UP, 1986.

Giraud, Raymond, ed. *Flaubert: A Collection of Critical Essays.* Englewood Cliffs: Prentice Hall, 1964.

Gothot-Mersch, Claudine. *La Genèse de* Madame Bovary. Genève: Slatkine, 1980.

Green, Anne. *Flaubert and the Historical Novel:* Salammbô *Reassessed.* Cambridge: Cambridge UP, 1982.

Haig, Stirling. *Flaubert and the Gift of Speech: Dialogue and Discourse in Four Modern Novels.* Cambridge: Cambridge UP, 1986.

_____. *The Madame Bovary Blues: The Pursuit of Illusion in Nineteenth-Century French Fiction.* Baton Rouge: Louisiana State UP, 1987.

Heath, Stephen. *Flaubert:* Madame Bovary. Cambridge: Cambridge UP, 1992.

Ippolito, Christophe. *Narrative Memory in Flaubert's Works.* New York: Peter Lang, 2001.

Israel-Pelletier, Aimée. *Flaubert's Straight and Suspect Saints: The Unity of* Trois Contes Amsterdam and Philadelphia: Benjamins, 1991.

Kaplan, Louise J. *Female Perversions: The Temptations of Emma Bovary.* New York: Doubleday, 1991.

Kempf, Roger. *Bouvard, Flaubert et Pécuchet.* Paris: Grasset et Fasquelle, 1990.

Kenner, Hugh. *Flaubert, Joyce and Beckett: The Stoic Comedians.* London: W. H. Allen, 1964.

Knight, Diana. *Flaubert's Characters: The Language of Illusion.* Cambridge: Cambridge UP, 1985.

LaCapra, Dominick. Madame Bovary *on Trial.* Ithaca, New York & London: Cornell UP, 1982.

Lambros, Anna V. *Culture and the Literary Text: the Case of Flaubert's* Madame Bovary. New York: Peter Lang, 1996.

Le Calvez, Éric. Bouvard et Pécuchet*: Gustave Flaubert.* Paris: Nathan, 1994.

_____. *Flaubert topographe:* L'Education sentimentale: *essai de poétique génétique.* Amsterdam: Rodopi, 1997.

_____. *Genèses flaubertiennes.* Amsterdam & New York: Rodopi, 2009.

_____. ed. *Gustave Flaubert: A Documentary Volume.* Detroit: Thomson Gale, 2004.

_____. *Gustave Flaubert: un monde de livres.* Paris: Textuel, 2006.

_____. *La Production du descriptif: exogenèse et endogenèse de* L'Éducation sentimentale. Amsterdam: Rodopi, 2002.

_____. *Salammbô sous la tente (génétique, poétique, autotextualité).* Paris: Bibliothèque Nationale, 2000.

Leclerc, Yvan. *La Spirale et le monument: essai sur* Bouvard et Pécuchet. Paris: SEDES, 1988.

Lloyd, Rosemary. *Flaubert:* Madame Bovary. London: Unwin Hyman, 1989.

Lottman, Herbert R. *Flaubert: A Biography.* Boston: Little, Brown & Company, 1989.

Lowe, Margaret. *Towards the Real Flaubert. A Study of* Madame Bovary. Oxford: Clarendon, 1984.

Maraini, Dacia. *Searching for Emma: Gustave Flaubert and* Madame Bovary. Chicago: U of Chicago P, 1998.

Marder, Elissa. *Dead Time: Temporal Disorders in the Wake of Modernity* [On Baudelaire and Flaubert]. Stanford, CA: Stanford UP, 2001.

Meyer, Priscilla. *How the Russians Read the French: Lermontov, Dostoevsky, Tolstoy* [On Tolstoy and Flaubert]. Madison: U of Wisconsin P, 2008.

Mills, Kathryn Oliver. *Formal Revolution in the Work of Baudelaire and Flaubert.* Newark: U of Delaware P, 2012.

Nadeau, Maurice, *The Greatness of Flaubert.* Trans. Barbara Bray. London: Alcove Press, 1972.

Neiland, Mary. Les Tentations de saint Antoine *and Flaubert's Fiction: A Creative Dynamic.* Amsterdam: Rodopi, 2001.

Olds, Marshall C. *Au pays des perroquets: féerie théâtrale et narration chez Flaubert.* Amsterdam: Rodopi, 2001.

Orr, Mary. *Flaubert: Writing the Masculine.* Oxford: Oxford UP, 2000.

_____. *Flaubert's* Tentation: *Remapping Nineteenth-Century French Histories of Religion and Science.* Oxford: Oxford UP, 2008.

_____. Madame Bovary: *Representations of the Masculine.* Bern: Peter Lang, 1999.

Paulson, William. *Sentimental Education: The Complexity of Disenchantment.* New York: Twayne, 1992.

Porter, Laurence M., ed. *Critical Essays on Gustave Flaubert.* Boston: G. K. Hall, 1986.

_____. *A Gustave Flaubert Encyclopedia.* Westport, CT: Greenwood, 2001.

Porter, Laurence M. & Eugene F. Gray, eds. *Approaches to Teaching Flaubert's* Madame Bovary. New York: MLA, 1995.

_____. *Gustave Flaubert's* Madame Bovary: *A Reference Guide.* Westport, CT: Greenwood, 2002.

Poyet, Thierry. *Pour une esthétique de Flaubert d'après sa correspondance.* Saint-Pierre-du- Mont: Eurédit, 2000.

Prendergast, Christopher. *The Order of Mimesis: Balzac, Stendhal, Nerval, Flaubert.* Cambridge: Cambridge UP, 1986.

Privat, Jean-Marie. *Bovary, Charivari: Essai d'ethno-critique.* Paris: CNRS, 1994.

Raitt, Alan. *Flaubert:* Trois contes. London: Grant and Cutler, 1991.

_____. *Flaubert et le théâtre*. Bern: Peter Lang, 1998.

_____. *The Originality of* Madame Bovary. Bern: Peter Lang, 2002.

Ramazani, Vaheed K. *The Free Indirect Mode: Flaubert and the Poetics of Irony.* Charlottesville: UP of Virginia, 1988.

Reed, Arden. *Manet, Flaubert and the Emergence of Modernism: Blurring Genre Boundaries.* Cambridge: Cambridge UP, 2003.

Rees, Kate. *Flaubert: Transportation, Progression, Progress.* New York: Peter Lang, 2010.

Robert, Marthe. *En haine du roman: Étude sur Flaubert.* Paris: Balland, 1982.

Roe, David. *Gustave Flaubert.* Basingstoke: Macmillan, 1989.

Rottenberg, Elizabeth. *Inheriting the Future: Legacies of Kant, Freud and Flaubert.* Stanford: Stanford UP, 2005.

Sarraute, Nathalie. *Paul Valéry et l'enfant de l'éléphant: Flaubert le précurseur.* Paris: Gallimard, 1986.

Sartre, Jean-Paul. *L'Idiot de la famille: Gustave Flaubert de 1821 à 1857.* 3 vols. Paris: Gallimard, 1971–1972, 1988.

Sayeau, Michael. *Against the Event: The Everyday and the Evolution of Modernist Narrative* [on Flaubert, Wells, Conrad and Joyce]. Oxford: Oxford UP, 2013.

Schehr, Lawrence R. *Flaubert and Sons: Readings of Flaubert, Zola and Proust.* New York: Peter Lang, 1986.

Schlossman, Beryl F. *Objects of Desire: The Madonnas of Modernism* [on Joyce, Flaubert, Baudelaire, Stevens]. Ithaca & London: Cornell UP, 1999.

_____. *The Orient of Style: Modernist Allegories of Conversion* [on Flaubert, Proust and Baudelaire]. Durham, NC: Duke UP, 1991.

Schmid, Marion. *Processes of Literary Creation: Flaubert and Proust.* Oxford: Legenda, 1998.

Schor, Naomi & Henry F. Majewski, eds. *Flaubert and Postmodernism.* Lincoln: U of Nebraska P, 1984.

Sherrington, R. J. *Three Novels by Flaubert: A Study of Techniques.* Oxford: Clarendon, 1970.

Spencer, Philip. *Flaubert: A Biography.* London: Faber, 1952.

Starkie, Enid. *Flaubert: The Making of the Master*. London: Weidenfeld, 1967.

_____. *Flaubert the Master*. London: Weidenfeld, 1971.

Steele, H. Meili. *Realism and the Drama of Reference: Strategies of Representation in Balzac, Flaubert, and James*. University Park: Pennsylvania State UP, 1988.

Strauss, Alexandra, ed. *Baudelaire, Poe, Mallarmé, Flaubert: interpretations par Odilon Redon: textes et illustrations réunis et présentés*. Paris: RMN Grandpalais, 2011.

Thorlby, Anthony. *Gustave Flaubert and the Art of Realism*. New Haven, CT: Yale UP, 1956.

Tillett, Margaret G. *On Reading Flaubert*. London: Oxford UP, 1961.

Tooke, Adrianne. *Flaubert and the Pictorial Arts: From Image to Text*. Oxford: Oxford UP, 2000.

Toulet, Suzanne. *Le Sentiment religieux chez Flaubert d'après sa correspondance*. Montréal: Éditions Cosmos, 1970.

Traire, Sylvie. *Une esthétique de la deliaison: Flaubert (1870–1880)*. Paris: Champion, 2002.

Troyat, Henri. *Flaubert*. New York: Viking, 1992.

Unwin, Timothy. *Art et infini: l'œuvre de jeunesse de Gustave Flaubert*. Amsterdam: Rodopi, 1992.

_____. ed. *The Cambridge Companion to Gustave Flaubert*. Cambridge, England: Cambridge UP, 2004.

VanderWolk, William. *Flaubert Remembers: Memory and the Creative Experience*. New York: Peter Lang, 1990.

Wall, Geoffrey. *Flaubert: A Life*. London: Faber, 2000.

Williams, D. A. *Psychological Determinism in* Madame Bovary. Hull: University of Hull Publications, 1973.

_____. *"The Hidden Life at its Source": A Study of Flaubert's* L'Éducation Sentimentale. Hull: Hull UP, 1987.

Williams, D. A. & Mary Orr, eds. *New Approaches in Flaubert Studies*. Lewiston: Edwin Mellen, 1999.

Online Resources

Amis de Flaubert et de Maupassant: www.amis-flaubert-maupassant.fr

Site Flaubert (University of Rouen): http://www.univ-rouen.fr/flaubert/

About the Editor

Tom Hubbard is a Scottish novelist, poet, and itinerant scholar who has worked in many countries. He has been a visiting professor at the University of Budapest (ELTE), the University of Connecticut (where he was Lynn Wood Neag Distinguished Visiting Professor of Scottish Literature in 2011), and the University of Grenoble (as professeur invité) as well as a writer in residence at the Château de Lavigny in Switzerland. His short book *The Integrative Vision: Poetry and the Visual Arts in Baudelaire, Rilke and MacDiarmid* (1997) is based on lectures to design students at Glasgow School of Art. He was the first librarian of the Scottish Poetry Library, from 1984 to 1992. His first novel *Marie B.* (Ravenscraig Press, 2008), based on the life of the Ukrainian-born painter Marie Bashkirtseff, was longlisted for a Saltire Society book award.

His recent book-length poetry collections are *The Chagall Winnocks* (2011) and *Parapets and Labyrinths* (2013), both from Grace Note Publications, as well as a pamphlet collection, *The Nyaff and Other Poems* (2012), from Windfall Books. An essay on the Scottish poet Harvey Holton (1949–2010) was published as a pamphlet by Fras Publications as *Harvey Holton: Bard, Makar, Shaman* (2013). His second novel, *The Lucky Charm of Major Bessop*, subtitled "A Grotesque Mystery of Fife," appeared from Grace Note in 2014; reviewers have described it as a "dark, slightly unsettling yet strangely gripping tale" and as "interspersed with philosophical musings, literary references, humour and passages of poetic description [...] [it] draws you in and keeps you guessing right to the end." He has made English and Scots versions of poems by the nineteenth-century Russian poet Lermontov for the anthology *After Lermontov*, edited by Peter France and Robyn Marsack (Carcanet, 2014).

Hubbard is also the volume editor of *Charles Baudelaire* in the Critical Insights series (Grey House Publishing, 2014), as well as the forthcoming *Henry James* volume in the series. His more recent Baudelaire project is as coeditor of, and contributor to, a pamphlet of translations—by various Scottish poets and into English and Scots—of Baudelaire's prose poems: *Scottish Spleen* (Tapsalteerie, 2015). Another current project is the three-volume *Selected Writings of Andrew Lang* for Pickering & Chatto/Taylor & Francis.

He is on the editorial board of the journal *Scottish Affairs* and an honorary visiting fellow at the University of Edinburgh Institute of Governance, where he is working on a "Scotland and Europe" project with Dr. Eberhard Bort.

Between 2000 and 2010, he was research fellow and editor of two major bibliographical projects: first, BOSLIT (the Bibliography of Scottish Literature, based at the University of Edinburgh and the National Library of Scotland and located online at http://boslit.nls.uk [2000–2005]) and then BILC (the Bibliography of Irish Literary Criticism, based at the National University of Ireland Maynooth and available online at http://bilc.nuim.ie [2006–2010]).

Contributors

Leah Anderst is assistant professor of English at Queensborough Community College, CUNY. She earned her PhD in comparative literature from the CUNY Graduate Center, and her research interests include film studies, narrative theory, French novels, autobiography, and writing pedagogy. Her articles have been previously published in *Narrative, a/b: Auto/Biography Studies, Senses of Cinema, Bright Lights Film Journal,* and *Orbis Litterarum.* Her edited volume of essays, *The Films of Eric Rohmer: French New Wave to Old Master,* was published by Palgrave Macmillan in 2014.

Anthony J. Cascardi is dean of arts and humanities at UC Berkeley, where he is also Sidney and Margaret Ancker Distinguished Professor in Comparative Literature. He has written widely on the relationship between literature and philosophy, on aesthetic theory, and on the literature and arts of the early modern and modern periods. His books include *Consequences of Enlightenment: Aesthetics as Critique*; *Cervantes, Literature, and the Discourse of Politics*; and *The Cambridge Introduction to Literature and Philosophy.*

Mark Conroy is professor of English at Ohio State University, teaching the modern novel, film, and criticism. He is the author of *Modernism and Authority: Strategies of Legitimation in Flaubert and Conrad, Muse in the Machine: American Fiction and Mass Publicity,* and various articles and reviews. Currently, he is writing a study whose working title is *Public Lettering: Portraits from the New York Moment in Criticism,* focusing on Van Wyck Brooks, H. L. Mencken, Edmund Wilson, Lionel Trilling, Dwight Macdonald, and Susan Sontag.

Germaine Greer was born in Melbourne and educated in Australia and at Cambridge University. Her first book, *The Female Eunuch* (1969), took the world by storm and remains one of the most influential texts of the feminist movement. Germaine Greer has had a distinguished academic career in Britain and the USA. She makes regular appearances in print and other media as a broadcaster, journalist, columnist, and reviewer.

Since 1988, she has been director (and financier) of Stump Cross Books, a publishing house specializing in lesser-known works by early women writers.

Élodie Laügt is a lecturer at the University of St. Andrews (Scotland). She works on twentieth-century and contemporary literature, poetry, critical theory, and adaptation. She has published on Flaubert, Rancière, and Chabrol and the question of adaptation (*Forum for Modern Language Studies*, 2013); is the author of *L'Orient du signe: Rêves et derives chez V. Segalen, H. Michaux et E. Cioran* (Peter Lang, 2008); and has coedited issues on 'Littérature et Architecture' (*Etudes Littéraires*, 42.1 2011) with Élise Hugueny-Léger and 'Nouvelles lectures de l'exotisme' (Nottingham, 2005) with Jean-Xavier Ridon. Her current research focuses on the notion of 'partage' at the intersection of literature and philosophy.

Éric Le Calvez is professor of French at Georgia State University (Atlanta, USA) and member of the research group on Flaubert at the Institut des textes et manuscrits modernes (Centre National de la Recherche Scientifique, Paris). A specialist in nineteenth-century narratives, he focuses mostly on Flaubert (and has also worked on Balzac and Zola). His methodology combines narratology, poetics, and genetic criticism and examines, within a theoretical framework, the transformations of Flaubert's writing in his rough drafts. He has published seven books—the latest to date is *Genèses flaubertiennes* (Amsterdam-New York, "Faux Titre," 2009)—and over forty articles. He is currently directing a voluminous *Dictionnaire Flaubert*, to be published by the Classiques Garnier in Paris.

Priscilla Meyer is professor of Russian at Wesleyan University in Middletown, CT. She earned her PhD from Princeton University. She has written a book on Nabokov's *Pale Fire* (*Find What the Sailor Has Hidden*, 1998, Russian translation, 2007). Her next book, *How the Russians Read the French: Lermontov, Dostoevsky and Tolstoy* (Russian translation, 2011) won the ASEEES award for the best book of 2008 in literary and cultural studies. Meyer published the first collection of Andrey Bitov's stories in English; edited collections of essays on Dostoevsky, Gogol, Nabokov, and Yuz Aleshkovsky; and translated stories by Zoshchenko, Gogol, Bitov, Aleshkovsky, and Zinovy Zinik. She is currently writing a book about indeterminacy in Nabokov's *The Real Life of Sebastian Knight*. For her publications, see http://works.bepress.com/pmeyer/.

Kathryn Oliver Mills is currently chair of the French and French Studies Department at Sewanee, the University of the South, where she has been since 1997. She has published a number of articles on various aspects of Baudelaire, and her book, *Formal Revolution in the Work of Baudelaire and Flaubert*, was published by the University of Delaware Press in 2012. Mills has also extended her purview beyond nineteenth-century French literature by editing the *Selected Poems of Wilmer Mills*, her late husband (University of Evansville Press, 2013), and she has just edited for publication two more full-length manuscripts of his work. She is now writing critically about the roles that both faith and doubt play in his view of language and of poetry, and she is developing her interest in the *roman policier* in the classroom.

Vaheed Ramazani is professor of French at Tulane University, where he holds the Kathryn B. Gore Chair in French Studies. His areas of specialization include nineteenth-century French literature and culture; critical theory; gender studies; war and media; trauma and cultural memory; and international humanitarian law and ethics. His articles appear in *Nineteenth-Century French Studies*, *PMLA*, *Boundary 2*, *Cultural Critique*, and various other journals. He is the author of two books: *The Free Indirect Mode: Flaubert and the Poetics of Irony* (University Press of Virginia) and *Writing in Pain: Literature, History, and the Culture of Denial* (Palgrave Macmillan).

Elizabeth Rottenberg teaches philosophy at DePaul University and is a practicing psychoanalyst in Chicago. She is one of six founding members of the Derrida Seminars Translation Project and the translator, most recently, of Jacques Derrida's *The Death Penalty, Volume II*. She is the author of *Inheriting the Future: Legacies of Kant, Freud, and Flaubert* (Stanford, 2005) and the translator of many books by Blanchot, Derrida, Lyotard. She is the editor of *Negotiations: Interventions and Interviews* (1971–2001) by Jacques Derrida (Stanford, 2001) as well as the coeditor (with Peggy Kamuf) of the two volume edition of Jacques Derrida's *Psyche: Inventions* *of the Other* (Stanford, 2007/2008). Her forthcoming book is titled *For the Love of Psychoanalysis*.

Michael Sayeau is a lecturer in English at University College London. His monograph, *Against the Event: The Everyday and the Evolution of Modernist Narrative*, was published by Oxford University Press in 2013. He is currently working on a project on contemporary fiction.

Beryl F. Schlossman has published widely on modern literature and the arts. Her books include *Joyce's Catholic Comedy of Language* (on the sacred and the comic in Joyce's major works); *The Orient of Style: Modernist Allegories of Conversion* (on style and the role of the writer in Flaubert, Proust, and Baudelaire); and *Objects of Desire: The Madonnas of Modernism* (on love, poetics, and the visual image in classical, Anglo-Irish, and French literature). Her poetry and prose fiction have been published on both sides of the Atlantic. *Angelus Novus* (Editions Virgile, Fontaine-lès-Dijon) and several artists' books have been published in France. New projects include a volume of poetry, a study of Baudelaire, essays on travel writing, and short fiction. She is professor of comparative literature at the University of California, Irvine, where she teaches literature, film, and writing, and she can be reached at bschloss@uci.edu. In 2014, she published *Left Bank Dream*, a novel, with punctum books.

Michael Tilby has been fellow in French at Selwyn College, Cambridge, since 1977. He is the author of a chapter in the *Cambridge Companion to Flaubert* (2004) and has published extensively on Balzac, as well as on a range of other nineteenth- and twentieth-century French authors. He has also written about the relationship between French literature and the visual arts in the nineteenth century, and he is the author of a chapter on Balzac's early works for the forthcoming *Cambridge Companion to Balzac*. Recently, he completed a book-length study of the early Parisian *flâneur*. His current projects include a short biography of Balzac (Reaktion Books), a comprehensive study of Balzac's early novels, and a book provisionally entitled *Playing with Words: Language, Fiction and Text in Balzac's 'Comédie humaine.'*

Index
